320.96

Globalization,
Human Security, and the
African Experience

Globalization, Human Security, and the African Experience

EDITED BY
Caroline Thomas
& Peter Wilkin

LYNNE
RIENNER
PUBLISHERS

BOULDER
LONDON

Published in the United States of America in 1999 by
Lynne Rienner Publishers, Inc.
1800 30th Street, Boulder, Colorado 80301

and in the United Kingdom by
Lynne Rienner Publishers, Inc.
3 Henrietta Street, Covent Garden, London WC2E 8LU

Library of Congress Cataloging-in-Publication Data
Globalization, human security, and the African experience /
    edited by Caroline Thomas and Peter Wilkin.
        p.   cm. — (Critical security studies)
    Includes bibliographical references and index.
    ISBN 1-55587-699-4 (alk. paper)
    1. Africa—Economic policy. 2. Economic security—
Africa. 3. International economic relations. 4. Competition,
International. I. Thomas, Caroline, 1959– . II. Wilkin, Peter,
1963– . III. Series.
HC800.G548   1999
338.96—dc21   98-35595
                                                                    CIP

British Cataloguing in Publication Data
A Cataloguing in Publication record for this book
is available from the British Library.

Printed and bound in the United States of America

The paper used in this publication meets the requirements
of the American National Standard for Permanence of
Paper for Printed Library Materials Z39.48-1984.

5 4 3 2 1

Contents

Part 3 Conclusion

Acknowledgments

We would like to acknowledge the superb administrative support provided by Anita Catney of the Department of Politics, Southampton University, who worked on the manuscript over a period of months and coordinated between us at Lancaster and Southampton with exemplary efficiency. We would also like to acknowledge the technical support offered by our friend and colleague John Glenn, who gave freely of his time to help get the manuscript into house style at the eleventh hour. The cheerful involvement of these two individuals helped to turn a potential nightmare into a memorable experience of teamwork.

The Editors

Acknowledgments

1

Introduction

Caroline Thomas

The immediate aims of this volume are twofold: to explore security from a human perspective and to illustrate this perspective by drawing on case material from sub-Saharan Africa. The underlying objective is to help generate an alternative debate and understanding of security in a global economy.

The approach adopted here, the human security approach, involves a fundamental departure from an orthodox security analysis, in which the state is the primary referent object. Instead, human beings and their complex social and economic relations are given primacy. This change in the primary referent object of security has implications both for understanding the sources of threats to security and for elucidating strategies to increase security. A key argument is that the security discourse must be embedded within the global capitalist economy and associated global social structures. Thus, the main focus and starting point is understanding security in terms of the real-life, everyday experience of humanity embedded within global social and economic structures, rather than the experiences of territorially discrete sovereign states operating in an international system composed of similar units. This is not to argue that states are unimportant—they certainly are important—but rather that it is helpful to understand their significance in terms of their contribution to human security and not simply for their own sake. In the current context of globalization, the interconnections between the evolving global economy, the state as intermediary, and the human experience of security are important. The relationship between development and human security is central.

Development, security, and globalization are all contested concepts. We have entered these debates in a previous collection, *Globalization and the South* (Thomas and Wilkin, 1997). Our task here is explicit: to offer an alternative to the realist, state-centric, militaristic, male-dominated terrain of orthodox security and strategic studies. We have consciously chosen to privilege human beings (not the individual in the neoliberal sense being promoted during the 1980s and 1990s) as the primary referents, along with the related key social groups—such as household—to which they belong. We explore the links between globalization and the human (rather than state) experience of security.

A few words on the editors' interpretation of globalization are in order. We argue that globalization, interpreted most importantly but not solely as the latest stage of capitalism, is directly affecting human security by compounding inequalities of power and resources already in place and creating new ones. The process is supported by a liberal ideology that places a premium on individual choice in the marketplace. Globalization as used here refers broadly to the processes whereby power is located in global social formations and expressed through global networks rather than through territorially based states. The contributions in this volume mostly see globalization as being driven by capitalism, which has entered a stage where accumulation is taking place on a global rather than a national scale. This process of globalization has been accelerating with the restructuring of the global capitalist economy since the demise of the Bretton Woods system in the early 1970s. Deepening inequalities resulted from this process during the 1970s and 1980s. Although current developments in global capitalism are affording untold wealth and luxury for a significant stratum of the world's population, this affluence is being achieved at the expense of others. This global tendency of redistribution of resources from South to North and from poor to rich is especially acute in Africa. This is considered in more detail later.

In addition to the accumulation of capital as classically understood, there is the accumulation of power in other forms—for example, knowledge—that have often been ignored in political economy. The priority accorded to Western rational scientific knowledge has been at the expense of local knowledge. Global accumulation in all its aspects undermines the value of local diversity and offers legitimacy to the dominant liberal agenda. We take these effects to be incompatible with the attainment of general human security. (This is not to claim that local diversity has in every instance through time and space attended to general human security; obviously it has not.)

Globalization is transforming the authority and capacity of states differentially to set the social, political, and economic agenda within their respective territorial boundaries. Decisionmaking authority is being ceded to actors such as the International Monetary Fund (IMF), the World Bank, transnational corporations, the World Trade Organization (WTO), and so forth. (Those institutions are not autonomous actors, of course; rather they represent the interests of the leading states, particularly the United States, and such states represent other interests, notably those of global capital.) For the majority of states in the world, this reallocation of authority to external actors is nothing new but merely a continuation and intensification of the loss of control over matters technically falling within the domestic domain. If the authority of state governments is further eroded as a result of globalization, the fostering of state-society relations will become less relevant, and in its place will be increased scope for forging civil society through nongovernmental channels. The private sphere will extend in scope. For sub-Saharan Africa, the changing context for the fostering of community will be significant. Whether this is desirable is another matter.

The rest of this introduction is divided into three sections. The first section explores the contours of human security. Building on this, the second investigates key factors affecting human security in sub-Saharan Africa. The third section offers a brief outline of the remaining chapters of the book.

Human Security

The human security endeavor represents a conscious attempt to relocate the security discourse, to move it from the terrain of an international system composed of discrete territorial units called sovereign states and to embed it in a global social structure composed of humanity in a capitalist world economy that has been developing since the sixteenth century. The emphasis shifts from the pursuit of the national interest to the fulfillment of human security.

Importantly, we wish to differentiate clearly between security of the individual as conceived in the currently fashionable neoliberal sense (i.e., the extension of private power and activity based around property rights and choice in the marketplace; Wilkin, 1997: 25) and human security. Human security describes a condition of existence in which basic material needs are met and in which human dignity, including meaningful participation in the life of the community, can be realized. Such human security is indivisible—it cannot be pursued for or by one group at the expense of another. Human security is pursued for the majority of humankind as part of a collective, most commonly the household, sometimes the village or the community defined along other criteria such as religion or caste. At the most basic level, food, shelter, education, and health care are essential for the survival of human beings. But human security entails more than physical survival. Emancipation from oppressive power structures—be they global, national, or local in origin and scope—is necessary for human security.

Human security has both qualitative and quantitative aspects. At one level it is about the fulfillment of basic material needs, and at another it is about the achievement of human dignity, which incorporates personal autonomy, control over one's life, and unhindered participation in the life of the community. Human security is therefore engaged directly with discussions of democracy at all levels, from the local to the global. (See Wilkin and Ray, both in this volume.) Under study is the search by human beings to make daily life more stable, predictable, and autonomous. The immediate medium through which that search is conducted will vary; for example, it may be the household, a grassroots organization, an ethnic network, or a combination of these. The state will also play a role that can vary along the spectrum from facilitating to obstructive. Human security therefore requires a starting point and a cognitive map that are different from those of orthodox security.

Human insecurity is understood not as some inevitable occurrence but as a direct result of existing structures of power that determine who enjoys the entitlement to security and who does not. Such structures can be identified at several levels ranging from the global through the regional, the state, and finally the local level. For a growing number of people, the failure of the state and of the global market to facilitate human security has resulted in the expansion of the so-called informal sector, beyond the reach of the formal institutions of state.

The level of entitlement to human security seems to relate directly to the propensity for conflict (defined not in orthodox interstate terms but in the wider sense to include the most frequent form of warfare, intrastate). Over the period 1990–1995, 57 percent of countries experiencing war were ranked low on the United Nations Development Program's (UNDP) Human Development Index, whereas only 14 percent were ranked high and 34 percent were ranked medium. There seems to be a causal relationship between a lack of entitlement—to material goods, health, and education—and war (figures from D. Smith, 1997: 48).

Some authors have argued that human security is delivered best by strong states. This suggestion is flawed on two main counts. First, it ignores the nonmaterial dimension of human security, which is part of the essence of the concept; second, it is simplistic, overlooking the fact that strong states remain strong at the expense of weaker states and that such relationships, which promote social contradictions at national, regional, and global levels, are too fragile as a basis for human security.

In 1994, in the run-up to the World Social Summit at Copenhagen, the UNDP's *Human Development Report* focused on human security and thereby tried to push the associated concerns onto the center stage of global politics. The report argued:

> For too long, the concept of security has been shaped by the potential for conflict between states. For too long, security has been equated with threats to a country's borders. For too long, nations have sought arms to protect their security. For most people today, a feeling of insecurity arises more from worries about daily life than from the dread of a cataclysmic world event. Job security, income security, health security, environmental

security, security from crime, these are the emerging concerns of human security all over the world. (UNDP, 1994: 3)

Two main aspects of human security are identified in the UNDP report: safety from chronic threats such as hunger, disease, and repression, and protection from sudden disruptions in the pattern of daily life, whether in homes, jobs, or communities (UNDP, 1994: 23). Threats to human security broadly fall within seven categories: economic, food, health, environmental, personal, community, and political (UNDP, 1994: 25).

For the majority of the inhabitants of the planet, such concerns are far from new. Indeed, they are the ancient concerns of humanity. It is not the case that human security has suddenly developed out of nowhere and that the need for it did not exist before; rather, the ontological and epistemological assumptions that have served to underpin orthodox security and policy formation did not recognize, include, or value it. There were, of course, both practitioners and academics outside the mainstream discourse who advocated an alternative conception of security long before it became fashionable (Falk, 1971 and 1975; Mendlovitz, 1975; Thomas, 1985 and 1987).

In the post–Cold War era, there was a great surge of hope that the peace dividend would be channeled into improving human security for the many millions who exist without any control over their social, political, economic, or physical environment. Unfortunately this has not happened. As the report notes, global military spending declined over the period 1987–1994 at about 3.6 per year, yielding a cumulative dividend of $935 billion. Yet "there has been no clear link between reduced military spending and enhanced spending on human development" (UNDP, 1994: 8). Moreover, wars continue. The majority are internal and fought with low technology. In contrast to the turn of the century, now most of the casualties—75 percent—are civilian (D. Smith, 1997: 14). Even if the peace dividend had been channeled into human development, it would not have led to a transformation of the fundamental economic and social structures by which a privileged elite globally and within states controls a large share of available resources. In the words of Smith:

> When a privileged elite defends its too large share of too few resources, the link is created between poverty, inequality and the abuse of human rights. The denial of basic freedoms—to organize, to express yourself, to vote, to disagree—forces people to choose between accepting gross injustice and securing a fairer share by violent means. As conflict unfolds, the political leaders that emerge often find that the easiest way of mobilizing support is on an ethnic basis. Thus do the various causes of conflict weave in and out. War will only end if, and when, and where its causes are removed. (Smith, 1997: 15)

Over the past few years the UNDP *Human Development Report* has been developing and refining the notion of human security, reflecting both the qualitative and quantitative aspects mentioned hitherto. In 1997, the focus was on human development, which refers not simply to the income aspects of poverty but to poverty as a denial of choices and opportunities for living a tolerable life (UNDP, 1997: 2). Importantly, a distinction was made between income poverty ($1 a day and below) and human poverty (illiteracy, short life expectancy, etc.). Broadly, these refer to aspects of the quantitative/qualitative distinction drawn above. Income poverty and human poverty are often, but not always, linked; for example, in the Gulf states, people may suffer human poverty without being income poor.

Let us consider quantitative material indicators first. One-quarter of the global population lives in severe poverty. However, the picture is uneven between and within countries. It is informative to present this uneven picture at a state and a nonstate level.

At the state level, the majority of poor people are still located in the developing, or "southern," countries, though the countries of Eastern Europe and the Commonwealth of Independent States have experienced the greatest deterioration since the mid-1980s. Income poverty in the latter has spread from a small part to a third of the combined population, with 120 million people living below a poverty line of $4 a day. One-third of people in developing countries—1.3 billion—have incomes of less than $1 a day. South Asia has the greatest number of people affected by human poverty (515 million). Sub-Saharan Africa, by contrast, has the highest proportion of people in, and the fastest growth in, human poverty. Also it is estimated that half its inhabitants will be income-poor by 2000. It is important to recognize that even in the so-called developed countries, the proportion of the population living below the poverty line (assessed there as enjoying below half of the individual median income) is increasing; the number now stands at 100 million.

This situation is being affected by the processes of globalization that impact directly on human security. Although the 1997 UNDP *Human Development Report* (1997: 9–10) argues that "the great unanswered question is whether the winds of globalization will be viewed as a great opportunity or a great threat, as a fresh breeze or a violent hurricane," the direct experience of millions of the world's people has already provided an answer.

Globalization at the broadest level is resulting in polarization between rich and poor throughout the world. Whereas human security for some is being enhanced, for many it is being eroded. The UNDP *Human Development Report* for 1997 indicates that the world's poorest people—20 percent of the population—received 1.1 percent of global income compared with 1.4 percent in 1991 and 2.3 percent in 1960. The ratio of income of the top 20 percent to the poorest 20 percent now stands at 78:1, having risen from 30:1 in 1960 and 61:1 in 1991. In the 1990s, therefore, income inequalities are increasing very sharply. Neoclassical liberal economics does not assume any negative correlation between growing inequality and the achievement of human security; quite the opposite. Two-thirds of the global population seem to have gained little or nothing from the economic growth that has occurred as a result of globalization to date. Moreover, even in the developed world, "the lowest quartile seems to have witnessed a trickle up rather than a trickle down" (*Financial Times*, December 24, 1994).

Globalization is creating winners and losers. We are concerned here particularly with those for whom human security is being eroded rather than enhanced. The easiest way to determine who these are is to fall back on the statist analyses of the World Bank and similar institutions. However, if we look at the condition (both quantitative and qualitative) of human beings in a global economy rather than measuring the output or resources of states, a different picture is presented.

James Gustave Speth of the UNDP has spoken of ways in which "an emerging global elite, mostly urban-based and inter-connected in a variety of ways, is amassing great wealth and power, while more than half of humanity is left out" (reported in the *New York Times*, July 15, 1996: 55). The urban/rural divide has been a key feature of postindependence African states. Increasingly, the connection of a small urban elite in African states to the global urban elite is becoming more pronounced, and the distance between it and the rest of African society more marked. Within Africa, the disparity between the very few who have plenty and the majority who have very little is enormous and is made more stark by the absence of a sizable middle class.

Perhaps more important still is the qualitative aspect of the emerging global human condition. Let us consider human dignity in the African context. Having some control over one's destiny, playing a full part in the community, exercising choices, and experiencing personal autonomy are rights that many of Africa's citizens have not enjoyed. Although underlying global economic structures militate against such enjoyment, it is the legitimacy crisis of the state that has posed the most immediate constraint. Almost all sub-Saharan African states, and therefore many of their citizens, have experienced armed conflict in the 1990s. Perhaps 40 percent of refugees globally in the mid-1990s are in Africa, and of them over half are internally displaced people rather than refugees that have fled across borders. In such circumstances, attention to the expressions of human dignity aforementioned is difficult. There has been a push from within Africa for democratization. In contrast to previous decades, when Western states were comfortable with their friendships with rulers such as Mobutu, there has been a tendency in the 1980s and 1990s for external powers to promote Western-style democracy as an important element of human dignity.

The style of democracy being advocated, often by outsiders, may not necessarily be the most appropriate to the African cultural context; nor may Western-style political liberalization in Africa be compatible with economic liberalization there. (See below, this chapter; and Wilkin, this volume.)

The development of human security for Africans (as for all global citizens, for that matter) requires knowledge based on nonstate criteria. Alternative statistical surveys to the orthodox state-centric ones might usefully be conducted along the lines of gender, urban/rural differentiation, class, race, age, and so forth. Such analyses are scarce. However, there are indications that this style of counting, which would suit a human perspective, may be developing, and it needs to be extended. What is clear already is that there is no simple outcome; the results to date suggest complexity and diversity.

Various UN agencies are beginning to undertake more of such disaggregated studies. The World Bank has just begun to examine differential impacts on groups within states and in some cases has disaggregated by gender, ethnic group, or region. The UNDP has been engaged in this sort of disaggregation for a few years with human development reports disaggregating the human development index along racial, gender, regional, and ethnic groups for various countries, including Nigeria and South Africa. The 1994 *Human Development Report* revealed that South Africa's human development index was 0.650; the index for whites was 0.878 and for blacks, 0.462. (UNDP, 1994: 132–133). The 1996 *Human Development Report* showed the importance of specificity even more clearly. It revealed that in India, even to disaggregate by gender is insufficient, for there may be disparities in female opportunities among regions, ethnic groups, or urban and rural areas (UNDP, 1996: 34). Because of specific government policy interventions or cultural practices, such disaggregation, even class or gender groupings, may well highlight diversity as much as uniformity. Generating such figures is crucial because they show in a very stark manner the complexity of human security and the inappropriateness of bland, universalistic assumptions and solutions that pay no respect to local specificity.

Human Security in Sub-Saharan Africa

The shortcomings of the dominant approach to security are perhaps seen more starkly in sub-Saharan Africa than in any other region of the world. All of the case studies in this collection demonstrate to differing degrees the significance of historical and internal factors centering around state legitimacy, and the important impact of the global economy.

Colonial-inspired territorial boundaries accepted by the international community and by the Organization of African Unity (OAU) in 1963 bear no relation to social reality on the continent. Thus, the seeds were sown for tremendous strife. The dominant state-centric security orthodoxy provided at best a very partial representation of reality and at worst completely misunderstood, misrepresented, or ignored other important security concerns of the continent. Attention was deflected from the predominant intrastate nature of armed conflict, which reflected the legitimacy crisis of the state, and from the relationship between developments in the global economy and insecurity in the continent. The dominant approach to security overlooked the failure to establish effective state-society relations as a key security concern. The state was assumed to be the provider of security rather than the source of citizen insecurity that it actually was (see Salih, this volume). The security crisis in Africa is not and never has been simply or even predominantly an interstate affair. A human security approach is necessary both to understand the nature of persisting conflict in the region and to posit solutions.

In the best of circumstances, the security challenge would have been enormous. But the circumstances have not been the best, for a number of reasons: the appalling legacy of slavery and colonialism; the nature of the African leadership; the external environment, which was dominated by Cold War politics; the workings of the global economy, which have rendered development planning all but impossible; and most recently the neoliberal drive emanating from the international financial institutions and behind them key governments serving the interests of global capital. All have served to undermine the possibility of legitimate states developing around an inclusive politics. All contribute to the violence and instability on the continent. The words of Michel Chossudovsky, although written with respect to the Rwandan tragedy, apply to many other African tragedies: "The combined impact of the historical legacy of colonialism and the divisions it imposed on Rwandan society, when coupled with the vulnerability of such a weak economy forced to confront global market forces, proved to be the central factors in the unraveling of Rwandan state-society relations" (this volume).

History is essential to understanding the causes of human insecurity in Africa. Europe underdeveloped Africa, just as global capital now continues to do. In the words of one commentator: "If the Europeans had traded with the Africans on an equal basis, they would have brought them, in exchange for African products, carts and wheels, materials which could increase production. If they had also provided some education and training, the simple art of harnessing oxen, for example, instead of searching for slaves and easy money, the situation in Africa today would certainly be very different" (Dumont, 1988: 36).

European powers, motivated by strategic or economic interests and missionary zeal, dispossessed Africans of their home, land, way of life, and wealth. More significant even than this, they attempted to take away their humanity by reconstructing the native as subhuman. The human toll was indescribable. The direct and indirect toll of the slave trade has been estimated at 60–150 million (Dumont, 1988: 36). In the first thirty years of colonial rule of the Belgian Congo (then Zaire), 50 percent of the indigenous population was eradicated, either killed by colonists or dying as a result of forced labor (D. Smith, 1997: 52).

Independence has been more imaginary than real, and the political achievement has not been matched by economic achievement. Locked into the extraction or production and export of raw materials and basic commodities, the continent has always been at the whim of unstable commodity markets and the development fashions of various international institutions. Often the wealth that has been generated has been used by elites to feather their own nests and to sustain themselves in power rather than to promote sustainable economic development to meet general human security needs of citizens.

Africa now stands as the most marginalized continent in the global economy. In the process of globalization, the continent has quite literally been left behind in terms of the distribution of the spoils of the process. The promised advantages of economic restructuring, as hailed by the IMF, World Bank, and individual developed countries, have not been borne out. Foreign investment fails to flow in; debt burdens continue; commodity prices fluctuate; environmental degradation proceeds, albeit in a patchy fashion; and industrialization fails to occur. Globally, official overseas development aid is falling and foreign direct investment, increasing; yet over 66 percent of the latter went to just eight countries in 1995, none of which were in Africa. Over half of developing countries received little or none (Brown, 1996: 158). "Private capital has not been pouring into sub-Sahara Africa where a child today is still more likely to go hungry than to go to school" (Brown, 1996: 159). Social and economic polarization is deepening within the continent, urban unemployment has swelled and includes the small middle classes as well as the unskilled workforce, and education and health services have been eroded. Literally millions of people are on the move, either internally displaced or political refugees or economic migrants. The economic and social conditions of the continent exemplify wider global trends of social and economic polarization.

If we remove territorial boundaries from our cognitive map, we are left with the picture of people across the continent attempting to pursue security within the hostile and unpredictable environment of a global capitalist economy that has been developing over several centuries. Households are attempting to secure their basic needs in conditions of extreme adversity, as governments and state managers either fail to or are unable to pursue policies that will increase the human security of their citizens. The ability of governments to play a mediatory role between global capitalism and the domestic, intrastate arena is being transformed in an uneven manner because states exhibit different capacities and different resources as well as different levels of social and political motivation. Guest (this volume) shows how "a clever government can still be effective as a gatekeeper between its own people and the external pressures." There is some evidence that African governments may be consciously trying to promote human security more now given the growth in civil society and the democratic imperative. How effective this effort can be, however, given the power of external institutions and global capital relative to African states, is open to debate. There are instances of governments negotiating changes in IMF and World Bank prescriptions, but these tend to be modifications of the neoliberal economic package rather than a rejection of it.

Although it is true that most African states are responding to the external pressures of the international financial institutions, their governments still bear responsibility for promoting an approach to development that in its adulation of all things modern sometimes fails to understand and value African socioeconomic systems that have evolved over generations. Some such systems have evolved to manage the risks inherent in pursuing self-sufficiency in harsh climatic conditions. The simple but important point is that just as all things modern are not necessarily helpful in human security terms, all things traditional are not necessarily unhelpful. Attention to specifics is important.

The international financial institutions have been instrumental in promoting the idea that it is commonsense or natural that we are reaching the end of history, where the free market gains universal acceptance as the legitimate form of economic organization with its attendant social and political relations. Wealth created by the rich will trickle down to the poor. These institutions have also developed an interest in good governance, so we see the pursuit of political liberalization at the same time as economic liberalization (Gillies, 1996: 101–102; Leftwich, 1994). In Africa this has created many problems, and it cannot be assumed that economic liberalization is supportive of political liberalization; indeed, the opposite may be true in some cases. The adverse consequences of economic liberalization can undermine the consolidation of democracy (Shaw and Quadir, 1997). There are plenty of examples of economic liberalization contributing directly to anarchy and civil wars, such as in Rwanda (Chossudovsky, this volume), Sierra Leone (Sesay, this volume), Angola and Sudan (Hoogevelt, 1997: 176), or simply to political unrest and instability. Riley and Parfitt argue that the deprivations experienced by certain groups who "have been deprived of their stake in society by some aspect of an austerity programme that has moved them towards or below the poverty line" (1994: 140) result in violence. For example, state employees who have been laid off become more critical of the regime and become actively opposed to the economic policies they see as disadvantaging them. Thus, they argue that the overall result of such economic policies is often "to destabilize the recipient states as key groups in the populace rebel against the combination of rising prices and declining real wages and public services" (1994: 140).

Structural adjustment programs (SAPs) have done little to foster the social, political, and economic conditions in Africa that could contribute to the development of stable state-society relations and a stable social order so vital to the enjoyment of human security. The promotion of exports for debt repayment and the cutting of public expenditure on welfare in a region where 240 million people (i.e., 30 percent of the total) are undernourished (UNDP, 1994: 27), where there is 1 doctor for 36,000 people compared with 1 for 400 people in industrial countries, and where 9 million out the 15 million HIV-infected people worldwide reside (UNDP, 1994: 28) is a scandal. One author has even referred to SAPs as a form of economic genocide. When compared to genocide in various periods of colonial history, its impact is devastating. Structural adjustment programs directly affect the livelihood of more than 4 billion people (Chossudovsky, cited in *Third World Resurgence,* no. 74, October 1996: 17).

Although the voluminous assessments of SAPs fall into two broad camps, those who believe the programs can be reformed and those who think they must be transformed, there is at least broad agreement that SAPs often put the poor at risk. However, the poor are not an undifferentiated group. For example, in some cases there may be greater negative consequences for the urban rather than rural poor. The former rely more on subsidies and government services, employment, and so forth than the latter.

Aware of criticism of SAPs, the World Bank in 1987 introduced the Social Dimensions of Adjustment Program (Bird and Killick, 1995: 34). Ghana's SAP was the first in Africa to formally integrate the Program of Actions to Mitigate the Social Costs of Adjustment, or PAMSCAD, on the joint initiative of the government, the World Bank, and the UN Children's Fund (UNICEF). A recent World Bank study (World Bank, 1996b: 110) notes that PAMSCAD, "with resources of more than $80 million, only reached about fifty thousand beneficiaries (0.3 percent of the population), of which just three thousand benefitted from direct job creation. Too large a portfolio of projects made it difficult to co-ordinate financing and implementation, while complex bureaucratic procedures and limited transparency and participatory processes reduced support for the programme. PAMSCAD was terminated in 1993." The same report also notes the limited impact of Uganda's Program for the Alleviation of Poverty and the Social Costs of Adjustment (PAPSCA; World Bank, 1996b: 110).

The international financial institutions are creating a more enabling environment for direct foreign investment in Africa and elsewhere. As mentioned earlier, foreign investment has not materialized to the extent expected. The history of foreign investment in Africa raises questions about its contribution to human security. Many operations have come under critical scrutiny. The activities of Shell Oil in Nigeria came under the media spotlight in November 1995 when Ken Saro-Wiwa, the leader of the Ogoni people in Nigeria, was executed by the government. Saro-Wiwa, a human rights activist, was campaigning for recognition of the rights of the Ogoni. Ogoniland provides 80 percent of Nigeria's oil income, but its people do not see any benefit. Moreover, the activities of Shell, which over the period 1958–1993 earned US$30 billion, have caused serious environmental damage (D. Smith, 1997: 55). The government, in an effort to facilitate the oil extraction by Shell, has dispossessed and terrorized villagers in much the same way that the government of Colombia has done to facilitate the activities of British Petroleum (BP). If foreign investment in Africa increases, it is important that it occurs in a manner consistent with human security requirements.

Human security in Africa is under threat both from illegitimate states and from the impact of developments in the global economy. The balance of factors will vary across time and space, but the underlying problems are similar. The human security approach opens up the possibility of analyses that acknowledge complexity and try to posit solutions more appropriate to the problem than the traditional buildup of military arsenals.

Structure of the Book

The first part of this volume explores the relationship between the processes of globalization and the experience of human security. The authors consider the effects of globalization on various social groups, in particular addressing class, gender, and community. In the second part of the book, the authors examine particular case studies to better understand the challenges to human security in Africa. The two parts are directly interconnected. For example, we see gendered outcomes of globalization affecting human security in Tickner's chapter in Part 1, and Tickner's observations are reinforced by some of Guest's detailed findings in her case study on security in the Senegal River basin in Part 2.

Let us turn to a brief outline of chapter contents. In Chapter 2, Peter Wilkin considers two key questions: first, the role that class might play in an account of human security and second, what processes of globalization might mean for the way class is to be understood both generally and within the concrete setting of Africa.

Wilkin argues that class plays a central role in understanding and promoting the human security endeavor, which in part depends on reconnecting state and society in our understanding of international relations. Globalization can be detrimental to human security because of its antidemocratic and anti–needs satisfaction aspects. The new global liberal economic norms of liberalization, privatization, and deregulation undermine and exacerbate existing tensions in state-society relations by polarizing more starkly than ever the class inequalities of social power that are a central concern of human security. Such global economic norms have been introduced in Africa largely through state institutions applying various forms of IMF and World Bank restructuring programs. The latter have the practical effect of threatening services (such as subsidized food and medicines) essential to the human security of sectors of the population and to a secure society. Of course, there will be variations across countries, reflecting the particular circumstances of peoples, histories, institutions, and so on. However, the general tendency holds true. Moreover, the democratic character of national, regional, and international political institutions is diminished by placing key decisions over policymaking in the hands of ever further removed officials and institutions. Such globalization from above prompts globalization from below, in other words diverse and fragmented resistance to and support for expanding private social power at the expense of the satisfaction of basic needs. Both state and market provide a focus for resistance.

Feminist perspectives on security in a global economy are the focus of Chapter 3. Having offered some feminist perspectives on the contending assessments of globalization, J. Ann Tickner turns to an examination of the importance of gender as an analytical category for understanding why women's security is so often adversely affected by forces of globalization. Feminists define security in multidimensional and multilevel terms as the diminution of all forms of insecurity including physical, economic, and ideological. They focus on social relations rather than interstate relations and are concerned to uncover how gender hierarchies and their intersection with race and class exacerbate women's insecurities.

The chapter concentrates on the economic dimensions of women's security resulting from the processes of globalization. Tickner contends that neoliberalism's metanarratives about the end of history and the triumph of rationality are a disguise for a form of knowledge that tells only a partial story, one that excludes the experiences of marginalized groups including many women. Feminists call for locally specific knowledge that takes account of various forms of oppression including gender, race, and class. Some feminists, such as April Gordon writing on African women, argue that patriarchy, rather than the global capitalist economy, is the real source of women's oppression. The increase in global inequality, the feminization of poverty, and the discriminations women often face when they attempt to compete in the global marketplace are matters of concern, but again acknowledgment of a general tendency must not blind us to the incidence of important differences and even contrary examples.

Some evidence is offered of how women resist globalizing forces when they perceive such forces as detrimental to their human security. Tickner argues that for feminists, such resistances are important not simply for the practical achievements produced but because they generate new knowledge from the margins with which to counter the hegemonic liberal consensus and contend with the role of the state in a globalizing economy. This new knowledge is in part about asserting the need for women's human security, something neither the market nor the state has yet addressed.

The relationship between security and community in a global economy is discussed by Jan Aarte Scholte (Chapter 4). Scholte argues that whereas community was often precarious in the territorialized past, it is perhaps even weaker in the globalizing world of the present. He is interested in whether globalization has tended to undermine previous prevailing structures of social solidarity to the point where any form of community is rendered unviable or whether, more positively, globalization has opened up possibilities for novel constructions of community. If the latter, then could these arrangements contribute to wider and deeper conditions of security in both local and world politics? Scholte identifies the expanded or holistic conception of security that has been gaining more attention post–Cold War as touching on the problem of community. Increasingly, it is recognized that security in the deeper sense than merely the absence of armed conflict entails, inter alia, that people enjoy an experience of social cohesion.

Scholte identifies two principal approaches to community in the modern world system: cosmopolitanism and communitarianism. He describes each approach, highlighting associated shortcomings. Scholte argues that globalization has created both a requirement and an opportunity to develop alternatives, and he calls for a third way, a nonuniversalist, nonculturalist, nonviolent model of community that might yield greater opportunities to build substantive social solidarity and enhance human security. The emphasis would shift to the microlevel, where bonds of social solidarity that neither state nor market have so far provided would be sealed in grassroots, voluntary, community-based organizations.

In Africa, security in relation to community has been fragile, and the politics of community have produced considerable violence. In the 1990s, various voluntary development organizations and some governments have attempted to forge community in new ways. Scholte suggests that experiences in South Africa and Uganda are encouraging.

In Chapter 5, Aswini Ray discusses the relationship between security and justice. Stressing the historical context, he identifies the current phase of globalization as simply the latest stage of a process that has been ongoing for centuries. He argues that the guiding principles of international relations and security on both the scholarly and diplomatic planes have been stability, predictability, and order at the expense of justice. He explores some of the reasons for the abiding continuity of these guiding principles and argues that the situation is really no different today despite the superficial changes of the post–Cold War global order. The universal is still being defined by the powerful, and at the cost of justice for the majority of humankind. Whereas there may be a new opportunity for academics and practitioners to rethink and rework the guiding principles of international relations, Ray argues that history teaches that we must be cautious. A new global consensus on the relationship between security and justice may emerge through a network of nongovernmental organizations (NGOs), but even these actors have considerable operational inadequacies. Central to this new relationship will be democratization of the UN system, enforcement of the Universal Declaration of Human Rights, and development with the Human Development Index being used as an operational measure of entitlement as justice. Interestingly, Ray points to the inadequacies of the "statist fetishism" of international relations scholarship and associated state-inspired and state-based official data. He calls for the inclusion of previously marginalized knowledge, such as that in the fields of creative and visual arts, to help us develop our understanding of justice and human security.

The second half of this collection is dedicated to an exploration of human security in sub-Saharan Africa. The various contributions reveal important specificities and diversity but also powerful commonalities that are pivotal to understanding human security in the region. The causes of human insecurity are complex, but two factors stand out: the illegitimate state and the global capitalist economy, which through polarization acts to undermine already fragile social orders, albeit differentially.

In Chapter 6, Anne Guest explores the nature of security in the Senegal River basin. Guest argues that until recently, the middle basin of the Senegal River, though divided between Senegal and Mauritania, contained a cohesive and functioning society. The chapter explores and explains how events initiated at national and global levels affected the security of this society to the extent that from 1989 to 1992 Senegal and Mauritania broke off diplomatic relations over disputes originating in the valley. The security of the peoples of the Senegal River basin reflects the struggles among local people, national governments, and state managers and the pressures exerted by various international organizations.

The evidence presented by Guest suggests that in this particular example, state managers and national governments retained a significant degree of autonomy to pursue policies that could have been more in line with the human security needs of the local populations. State-society relations are thus highlighted as central to human security. Guest argues that the governments of Senegal and Mauritania could have chosen to listen to their citizens and modify their development schemes accordingly and, moreover, that the economic needs of the states were not incompatible with the needs of the valley farmers. Although the forces of globalization undoubtedly reduced the choices of those governments, they and not globalization clearly presented the greatest immediate challenge to the human security of the people of the Senegal River basin.

The contribution by Michel Chossudovsky (Chapter 7), while acknowledging the mix of internal and external factors contributing to human insecurity, suggests that in the case of Rwanda developments in the global economy played a crucial role in undermining an already fragile situation. The combined impact of the historical legacy of colonialism and the divisions it imposed on Rwandan society, and the vulnerability of a very weak economy forced to confront global market forces, were too powerful for Rwandan state-society relations to withstand.

Chossudovsky rejects the commonplace assumption of the inevitability of domestic strife in Rwanda and other countries in transition to democracy and the free market. Instead, he highlights the underlying economic factors that generated the conditions for the ensuing social conflict, conditions that both the international media and academia have failed to explain. The Rwandan civil war was preceded by the flare-up of a deep-seated economic crisis. Chossudovsky argues that it was the restructuring of the agricultural system that precipitated widespread abject poverty and destitution. By the early 1990s, neither cash crops nor food crops were economically viable in Rwanda. The 50 percent decline in the price of coffee in 1989 and the global neoliberal restructuring through the Bretton Woods institutions wreaked havoc. The consequent deterioration of the economic environment exacerbated simmering ethnic tensions and accelerated the process of political collapse. Responsibility for the ensuing human tragedy therefore lies not simply with state managers but with external actors. The impact of currency devaluations—50 percent in November 1990 and a further devaluation in June 1992 at the height of the civil war—on an already critical situation was devastating. The World Bank showed no concern or sensitivity as to the likely social or political repercussions of economic shock therapy applied to a country on the verge of civil war. In Rwanda, untrammeled market forces undermined the possibility—limited though it was—of stable social orders.

In Chapter 8 on the Horn of Africa, Mohamed Salih questions the appropriateness of the orthodox approach to understanding security by focusing on the limitations of nation-states as maintainers of regional peace via multilateral institutions dependent on military coercion. He argues that a concept of security grounded on interstate relations often overlooks the fact that the state itself can be a source of citizen insecurity. Moreover, citizen security is often sacrificed in order to maintain an element of security based on militarism. There is a need for the state to act as a provider of citizen security rather than being a source of citizen insecurity. The shift in focus from the state to human beings or citizens opens the state up for critical scrutiny. It also flags the importance of scrutinizing global processes that jeopardize citizen security.

In the Horn of Africa, states have been made to fail. Thus the region is characterized by both state insecurity and human insecurity, which compound each other. States have neither control over the direction of their domestic affairs nor the necessary powers to influence the structure of international relations into which they have been locked. Artificial borders, superpower rivalry, heightened expectations post–Cold War, the workings of the global economy, and multilateral interventions have conspired to deepen political instability in the region. The post–Cold War transition from bipolar to unipolar politics has resulted neither in reduced expenditure on arms nor in the reorientation of the region's national economies away from militarization and toward human security. New forms of hegemonic instability prevail. The regional context is conducive neither to traditional state-centric security nor to human security. Citizen insecurity results from states' actions, such as human rights abuses, from the absence of democratic institutions, and from the experience of general political discontent. It results also from the incompatibility between market liberalism and democracy. Civil wars have continued in the region, as the end of bipolarity has produced new forms of polarization—ethnic, religious, and economic—that have engulfed civil society, threatening both the state and citizens. The nature of multilateral military-humanitarian interventions has been inappropriate.

In Chapter 9 on Liberia and Sierra Leone, Max Sesay focuses on the balance between internal and external factors affecting the human insecurity experienced by the majority of citizens. He suggests that the collapse of the state in Sierra Leone and in Liberia has come about not as the result of any obvious external military threat but is rather due to a complex interaction of political and social forces at the national and subnational levels and insecurity in the global economic system. To understand this process, Sesay examines the dynamics and unravels the levels, extent, and consequences of the polarization that has occurred and continues to occur in both states. The significance of class, race, gender, and community, as well as justice, is illuminated and understood against the backdrop of the social, political, and economic crises that have afflicted Sierra Leone and Liberia both in the past and in recent times.

The case study demonstrates the severe shortcomings of traditional approaches to security in explaining how states function in the international system. In both Sierra Leone and Liberia, there is no obvious external military threat, and yet both states belong to a group of collapsed states in contemporary Africa. Both historically and contemporaneously, the sources of threat to the state in Sierra Leone and Liberia can be identified both within and outside these societies. The major internal threat was the inability of political functionaries to establish valid, representative, inclusive, and accountable political systems. Weak and incompetent political elites employed exploitative, suppressive, and highly divisive methods of governance that heightened tensions in disparate communities. In addition, both states suffered severe vulnerability to fluctuating external markets and price shocks for their exports. Uncertainty of income from exports resulted in increased external borrowing and indebtedness and undermined political leaders with weak political bases.

Ali Mazrui's contribution (Chapter 10) identifies two streams of global change that have great significance for security globally and within Africa. The first is the rise and decline of the state; the second is the rise and decline of race as a basis for human relations. These two processes have helped construct orthodox ideas of security, but the current demise of the nation-state and race as a basis for discrimination are forcing us to revise these views. Mazrui speculates as to whether we are indeed witnessing a decline in racial prejudice and a rise in religious prejudice or whether indeed both race and religion are giving way to two entirely different confrontations—class and gender struggles. Looking for the connecting link between the erosion of the state and the decline of race prejudice, Mazrui points to the continuing expansion and globalization of capitalism. Capitalism has been eroding the exclusivity of state sovereignty, and political apartheid in South Africa was killed as much by the logic of capitalism as by the forces of African nationalism and struggle. Racism restrained the pursuit of profit; therefore the decline of racism was in part a response to the logic of global capitalism.

The conclusion to the collection highlights a few signposts that may contribute to furthering the debate on human security. The people of Africa are pursuing human security through their own efforts, and these efforts are stressed. An alternative agenda for research is put forward that will promote a better understanding of the impact of the global economy on human security. From this improved understanding will grow the opportunity for international financial institutions to develop more sensitive policies. Ultimately, human security requires different developmental strategies.

Notes

The author would like to thank many friends and colleagues for helpful discussions concerning this chapter, particularly Ken Booth, Peter Clegg, Tony Evans, Anne Guest, James Mayall, Nana Poku, Heloise Weber, Martin Weber, and Peter Wilkin.

PART 1
Concepts

2

Human Security and Class in a Global Economy

Peter Wilkin

Some recent work in security studies has sought to connect international relations (IR) theory with a range of ideas and themes that have their roots in established debates in both development studies and social theory. Triggered in part by the "end of the Cold War,"[1] these developments in security studies have sought to challenge central premises of what we might usefully call orthodox security. Key criticisms include the argument that orthodox security studies either overlook the wider meaning of security (the satisfaction of human needs, for example) or are in part instrumental in generating the very problems that they aspire to deal with (as critical theorists might charge) (Lipschutz, 1995; Krause, 1996; Ashley, 1986).

As will become clear, there is no consensus within the evolving critical security studies as to what constitutes the parameters of the field of inquiry; this is not altogether surprising given that it is an emerging area within international relations. In this chapter and in this volume more generally, the concern is with identifying the important implications of globalization both for orthodox ideas of security and for more recent notions of human security. Africa is chosen as a general site of entry into these debates because it stands as the most marginalized continent in geopolitical terms in orthodox international relations and represents perhaps the most dramatic area of concern for those focusing on human security. A continent in which 300 million out of 500 million people live in absolute poverty is a major global concern for both international relations as a discipline and the practice of politics (Bygrave, 1997: 26; Elliott, 1997b; Watkins, 1997; Barratt Brown, 1995).

In particular this chapter considers the role that class might play in an account of human security and what processes of globalization might mean for the way in which class is to be understood both generally and within the concrete setting of Africa itself. If human security is in part concerned with reconnecting state and society in our understanding of international relations, then class has a central part to play. However, before we turn to the interplay of class and human security, it is important to set out a coherent overview of the central parameters of orthodox security in order to understand what those who advocate human security are reacting against.

The Orthodox Security Approach

What is described as the orthodox account of security has its roots in the rise of the modern nation-state in seventeenth-century Europe. It rests on a reasonably clear and coherent account of what constitutes the legitimate realm of concern both for international relations and for those political actors concerned with exercising and managing state power. Without wishing to give an unduly extended account of these premises underpinning orthodox security, I will recall the major assumptions established over centuries, about the relationship between security and the state. The first and perhaps the most significant factor shaping the behavior of states is the idea that the international system is fundamentally anarchic with no overall governing authority to enforce rules, norms, laws, or, more widely, some conception of international justice. This factor constitutes what Waltz has described as the organizing principle for state behavior and security concerns in international relations, with anarchy acting as a constant force to encourage and coerce states into pursuing certain policies rather than others (Waltz, 1979: 118).

In such a self-help system no state can be sure that its security will be guaranteed by any other body no matter how firm an alliance might appear at any given time. The supposed universal rationality of state actors means that they will, by and large, converge around similar international policies and aspire to similar goals in order to render themselves as secure as possible in what is a perpetually insecure system. Most important to this assumption is a military-defense framework that serves to act as a minimum deterrent to external aggressors who might threaten the sovereignty of the state, embodied in its territory, boundaries, political institutions, and the general population's right to self-determination (Buzan, 1983, 1991a; Lee, 1969; Booth, 1994; Gerberding, 1966). A key factor here that has been firmly entrenched in orthodox security is the idea that international politics is a separate realm of study and activity from the domestic. As is commonly expressed in the literature, the international is the realm of survival whereas the domestic is the realm of the good life; there, the pursuit of something like the common good and a just society is both practicable and meaningful. However, in order to secure the good life for its citizens, the state itself must be rendered secure; security therefore entails a concern with the military might needed to make this possible (Wight, in Butterfield and Wight, 1966). As Pasha (1996) and Lee (1969) have pointed out, the impact of colonialism on the Third World in general and Africa in particular has been in part to embed these ideas of security in the postcolonial state system, frequently with disastrous consequences. Indeed, it is this fact that has brought tremendous problems for the possibility of constructing and maintaining secure state-society relationships in Africa.

What is important for orthodox security on the basis of these assumptions is that in the international realm states pursue policies that are above the demands of any *single* group in society. The state-society relationship, therefore, is separated from international relations, and this separation is necessary for security in the domestic realm. The interests of national security are said to be above and beyond those of any single group in domestic politics simply because if a state is not externally secure, there can be little hope of the goals of domestic politics (the good life, for example) ever being realized (Kennan, 1966). Thus, the state is the neutral arena within which the complexities of domestic political and social life can be played out.

. . . And Its Problems

Given the core features of the orthodox case, there are three major criticisms of such an understanding of security that help to fuel the human security debate. The first of these concerns is the ahistoric and abstract quality of the orthodox account of states and security. The model of the international system and its constituent units embodied in orthodox approaches to security portrays an international system in which essential characteristics and interests recur regardless of time and space. The often drawn analogy between the Cold War and the Peloponnesian War is a familiar example of this tendency (Viotti and Kauppi, 1992; Dunne, 1997). As critics have noted, such an account of the international system and security is based on an abstraction that is so violently divorced from the concrete processes of history that it appears to imply that nothing ever *substantively* changes in the international system in its essential characteristics. Rationality, anarchy, power, and the state itself remain universal and constant factors in a world of timeless essences. The importance of this weakness in orthodox security and international relations has been recognized by a range of writers both within and outside the tradition who have sought to modify the framework so as to make it more amenable to questions of history, change, and diversity or who have rejected it as a plausible approach to understanding international relations and security altogether (Buzan, Jones, and Little, 1993; Griffiths, 1992).

The issue of essentialism in social theory needs to be clarified a little here, as it is crucial to this particular problem of orthodox security. Simply expressed, essentialism is the doctrine that things have properties that (a) distinguish them from others and (b) constitute what they can actually do. Orthodox security and international relations theory tend to posit strong forms of essentialism, which suggests that there is little substantive difference in the essential properties of natural and social phenomena within the "thing" called international relations (Griffiths, 1992). They are of the same kind. Hence, as Rosenau has observed, "as a focus of study, the nation-state is no different from the atom or the single cell organism. Its pattern of behaviour, idiosyncratic traits, and internal structure are as amenable to the process of formulating and testing hypotheses as are the characteristics of the electron or molecule. . . . In terms of science-as-method, [physics and foreign policy analysis] are essentially the same." (Rosenau, 1980: 32). This is a problematic basis for a social ontology because it leads to the kind of reductionism and determinist accounts of the behavior of states in international relations that both neoliberalism and neorealism have been accused of. Such approaches rest on the assumption that the international system is a closed one; that is, these essential properties (power, states, anarchy, balance of power) can be isolated and understood as largely determining the outcomes of behavior in this system in regular and recurring patterns that are not affected by history, culture, ideology, or any of a host of other factors. As such it is a model of the international system that aspires to the parsimony and elegance of the natural sciences, such as physics. However, its failure to generate any substantive predictions (the definition of science, according to Rosenau's approach) illustrates the ultimate failure of the model and the inappropriateness of the social ontology. A prominent recent alternative to this strong essentialism of neoliberalism and neorealism has been social constructivism, the view that there are no essential properties to social phenomena and that all meanings and interpretations are contingent on history, culture, and language. It is argued here that this view also needs to be rejected in favor of a moderate essentialism that accepts the following ontological premises for international relations theory (Bhaskar, 1979):

1. Some social phenomena have essential properties (states), but not all do (gender).
2. The essential properties of natural phenomena are *not of the same kind* as those of social phenomena. Social phenomena can have essential properties, but these properties can and do change over time; for example, the rules of a sport can be seen as part of its essential property, but they can and do change over time.
3. The essential properties of social phenomena are generative powers and potentials, not deterministic powers. They act in conjunction

with an array of concrete and contingent factors such as beliefs, knowledge, culture, and ideology to generate particular events.

4. Social systems are open and not closed phenomena. Social systems are complex; it is the historical structures within them that endure over time and place and serve to enable and constrain particular outcomes in conjunction with an array of other contingent factors. Although there are tendencies for certain outcomes to occur (e.g., under capitalism, firms tend to pursue profit), there is no simple linear and deterministic relationship between essential properties and events. It is the complex interplay of necessary and contingent factors that generates specific outcomes.

5. Needs are natural features of human nature but in practice they are socially and historically mediated. The need for food, for example, is universal, but what I want to eat will reflect my upbringing, culture, history, religion, and so on.

The second and related criticism of the orthodox approach has been the lack of theorizing of the state itself as the constituent unit or agent of the international system. The idea, for example, of the functional equivalence of the tasks that all states must perform overlooks the fact that states have varied both over time and within particular epochs. As Robert Cox has argued, it is important to typologize states into different kinds that reflect the way they have come into the international system, the relationship between their internal characteristics and their external actions, and the fact that particular states change over time in terms of their structure and institutions (Cox, 1987). The need to theorize the state adequately has again proven to be an area of growing concern in international relations theory and is of particular importance to those concerned with the construction and durability of states within Africa. The European roots of the modern nation-state should not be mistaken for an apparently universal political structure.

Finally, the assumption of the neutrality of the state raises substantial problems for orthodox accounts of security. In this view, states are discrete and separate rational actors pursuing their national self-interest in an unchanging self-help system (Baldwin, 1993a; Linklater, 1995; Buzan, Jones, and Little, 1993). They inhabit a neutral space between domestic and international relations—which are posited as distinctly different spheres—and they are, further, above and beyond the conflicts of domestic political and social life. This orthodox analysis of security and the international system denies the integrated nature of a global system in which, as Jarvis has argued, we are concerned with drawing out the historical and structural relations among states, societies (social forces), and geopolitics (Jarvis, 1989).

Within Africa, the assumption that states are neutral frameworks in which social and political conflicts can be played out among interested citizens, parties, and so on, is simply false (see Salih and Chossudovsky, this volume). States do not provide a neutral arena within which social and political matters can be resolved. Rather, states are interested parties acting to structure society and its social and political organization, usually in relationship with dominant social forces.[2] Rather than providing security for their citizens, states are frequently the instruments that destroy the security of their populations, as illustrated by Ethiopia in the mid-1980s and more recently Rwanda (Prunier, 1995; Chossudovsky, 1994a, 1994b, 1997, and this volume).

In practice such assumptions about the neutral state do little more than legitimize any state actions on the pretext that there is a concern with a transcendent "national security." In addition, and this is a point that has been much discussed elsewhere, there is no necessary separation of domestic and international politics in a modern world order that has been developing since the expansion of Europe in the sixteenth century into the Americas. The ensuing development of this world order has been one in which all states and societies have been integrated into a global system, bound together through the complex interplay of institutions, ideas, and social forces, in Cox's terms.

There are, then, many reasons to at least question the grounds upon which orthodox security has been established. Having set out some of these reasons, this chapter now turns to a discussion of the critical security studies approach to human security.

The Critical Security Studies Approach

The evolving critical security studies embrace diverse themes and trends within social theory, but there are perhaps two main strands that tend to recur in the literature. The older and more established approach to critical security has emerged from writers concerned with the relationship between development and international relations, usually focusing on an account of human security and human needs as the crucial link between state and society (Thomas, 1987; Acharya, in Krause, 1997). Although this approach has tended to concern itself with the security of societies in developing countries, it increasingly recognizes such security as being a matter that, to differing degrees, affects *all* states-societies in global and local terms. Thus critical security studies increasingly focus on the failure of states and international institutions, both private and public, to evenly satisfy human needs at even the most basic level when seen on a global scale. The emphasis here is on the satisfaction of needs as not simply a domestic political issue but within the context of a world order that connects states, societies, and geopolitics globally (Jarvis, 1989). This world order is shaped by forms of social power that help to enable and constrain the distribution and control of resources globally between states and social forces. For example, as writers such as Sen and Saurin have emphasized in the case of the African continent, famine is a human-made disaster and its causes have to be understood within the context of the institutions, public and private, that shape the production, distribution, and control of food in a capitalist world economy (Sen, 1981; Saurin, 1996; Watts, 1991). It is, then, this approach to security that largely informs the direction of this chapter in its concern with class and globalization.

More recently critical security studies have increasingly come to be informed by analyses that draw on ideas taken from social theory in general. Thus various writers have sought to utilize the insights of critical theory, feminist theory, postmodernism, and poststructuralism in order to question the foundations on which orthodox security rests (Lipschutz, 1995; Booth, 1991; Krause, 1996; Sjolander and Cox, 1994). (Interestingly, class is largely absent as a concern for security in these texts.) To different degrees such approaches have proven to be fruitful in raising important questions about the way in which the tradition of orthodox security has been constructed over time and in relation to prevailing forms of social power embedded in various institutions and practices.

There is no rigid separation between these two strands of critical security studies, and many writers move between both camps. Thus critical security studies arose in response to a number of weaknesses that were seen to afflict orthodox security in particular and orthodox international relations in general, weaknesses that have led some to conclude that the orthodox view needs to be either rejected or substantially modified as a basis for understanding international relations.

There are, then, a number of strands within the evolving critical security studies, but what I would take to be central to them in general and of particular significance for this chapter is the emphasis on the need to recognize and understand the relationship between states and societies in international relations and the way they *co-determine each other* (Lovering, 1987: 296). Given this emphasis, three related issues arise that are important to human security and social change. First, the satisfaction of human needs is fundamental to the possibility of establishing anything like a secure social order. As noted, the satisfaction of human needs is not simply a matter of national political economy but has to be understood within the context of a global economy structured by capitalist relations of production and social organization. Consequently, the co-determination approach argues that the primacy of the idea of the national interest, so central to orthodox security, frequently poses a major obstacle to the satisfaction of needs in general.

In practice, nationalism as an ideology and the national interest as an objective of state policy are often opposed to the satisfaction of *general* human needs. Various writers and organizations have noted, for example, that needs-based programs for the general provision of water, sanitation, vaccination, and so on suffer chronic underfunding when compared to the money spent on arms sales and purchases (Thomas, 1987: Chapters 5 and 6; Bradshaw and Wallace, 1996; R. Smith, 1997: 26–28). Given the priorities of orthodox security, this is not altogether surprising. It prioritizes the national interest, whereas these underfunded programs target general human needs. Thus the powerful relationship among nationalism, the national interest, sovereignty, and the state in orthodox security, long embedded in the practices of modern nation-states, is a major obstacle to the goal of satisfying human needs both globally *and* locally. Orthodox security rests on a picture of the world order wherein needs and interests are particular, not general, and the priorities of state managers tend to reflect this view (Chomsky, 1994). The question of class intrudes here, as we will see shortly, because it impinges on the autonomy of state managers with regard to setting these national policy goals and objectives.

The second related issue has to do with the exercise of social power in international relations. What are the primary mechanisms and institutions that act to constrain and enable the outcomes regarding politics, the economy, and society that might make the satisfaction of human needs an attainable goal? Social power is a complex phenomenon and is hardly dealt with at all in orthodox security (Griffiths, 1992: Chapter 6). Questions of social power focus on not only political-military power but also economic and cultural-ideological factors. In understanding the way in which such mechanisms and institutions act in international relations, we might be able to construct viable programs for the satisfaction of human needs in general.

The final issue concerns the conflict between global interests and so-called national interests. As we have seen, critical security studies represent an attempt to move the focus of political concern away from simply the level of the nation-state toward the recognition that securing a stable and just state-society is both a global and a local issue (Falk, 1995). In prioritizing the national interest as the foundation of security, we are often in practice constructing the very conditions that help to generate instability and conflict in the world order. History illustrates that struggles over poverty, needs, inequality, and justice have proven to be as central to social change as the geopolitical concerns of nation-states (Moore, 1978; Mann, 1995; Lovering, 1987).

In practice, both class conflict *and* geopolitics have been intimately connected in social change. Many African states have found that it is quite possible for a well-funded and -equipped military and defense structure to oversee either a society polarized into different and conflicting groups or a society that is largely impoverished (Chossudovsky, this volume). And excessive military spending is often a cause of domestic poverty. The implication is that the promotion of human security involves the recognition and promotion of global *and* local interests and needs. Having considered how critical security studies have developed and the approach that is of particular significance for this chapter—human security—we now turn to the ways in which class informs this analysis and what it tells us about developments in social power.

Class and Human Security

Class is of great importance to understanding the dynamics of the contemporary world order for many reasons. As a concept that is central to social and political thought, class hardly registers in the concerns of orthodox security and international relations theory. Only in the concerns of writers outside the mainstream have questions of class tended to take on any prominence (Kolko, 1969). Nonetheless, it is difficult to understand the emergence of the modern world order, the spread of capitalism, and the construction of nation-states without paying due attention to the role that classes and class conflict have played in these processes (Wood, 1995). Class remains of great significance for critical security studies, especially human security, because inequality of social power between classes manifests itself in the myriad forms of exploitation, subordination, and unequal access to resources that help to generate conflict within and between states and societies (Shaw and Heard, 1979: Part 1; Kasfir, 1984; Leys, 1996: Chapter 8).

The meaning of class remains a central debate in social theory with much recent work offering various syntheses of the structural and relational accounts of class as a social and economic category established by Marx and Weber (Scott, 1997; Leys, 1996: Chapter 8; Charney, 1987; Block, 1987; Edgell, 1993; Onimode, 1988: Chapter 5; Gill and Law, 1990). If the global increase in both absolute poverty and the concentration of ownership of wealth would seem to offer support to structural accounts of class, then equally it has long been noted that the transformation of working practices in many of the core sectors of the world order have served to fragment class as a form of social and political identity. Fundamentally I take it that class is a factor determined by the relationship of people to the means of production, as it is this relationship that is crucial in determining the questions of social power with which critical security, and more particluarly human security, are concerned. More practically we can see that class manifests itself on four levels in social and political life:

1. Class is shaped by the economic structure of society.
2. Class is a pattern of life, for example, work and health.

3. Class is a disposition that shapes how we think about and act in social and political life.
4. Class is collective or social action (Katznelson, 1981; Katznelson and Zoldberg, 1986).

All of these factors are important in understanding class, as we need to avoid what Polanyi called the "economistic fallacy," the idea that class is simply determined by the economy as opposed to it being an economic and social category of structural position and lived experience.

Although class has fallen out of focus in many areas of social and political thought, it is argued here that it is more transparently important to an understanding of the contemporary world order than it ever has been. For example, the global increase in both absolute poverty and the concentration of the ownership of wealth offer a great deal of support to the explanatory purchase that such an understanding of class can bring to current developments in the world order (UNDP, 1997; Bradshaw and Wallace, 1996; Brittain and Elliott, 1997; Hayter, 1992; Thomas, 1997). The interests of classes give a powerful explanation, for example, of the ideological underpinnings and motivations behind the establishment of a global neoliberal orthodoxy that has seen a flow of resources in the past twenty years not only from periphery to core but also more generally from the poor to the rich.[3] It is difficult to ignore the explanation that class and class interests provide for these developments.

Human security is concerned with state-society relations in all their complexity instead of treating social and political life as simple categories outside the concern of international politics (as orthodox security is prone to do). Class is a central dynamic in state-society relations and is therefore a major concern for ongoing debates around human security. In particular class raises questions of social power that cut across state-society relations. Two particular aspects of the relation of class to human security are drawn out here; the interplay of class and the exercise of state power and democracy and the way in which class manifests itself in social life generally.

Class, State Power, and Democracy

As is commonly acknowledged in most areas of social and political thought, class is a major factor in understanding the directions of any modern state's policy. The inequalities of social power that exist between different classes within a nation-state enable the dominant social forces at any given time to assert the primacy of their interests over those of subordinate groups (Anderson, 1992: Chapter 4). A key debate here is the extent to which state managers are able to act independently of the interests of such dominant social forces. Irrespective of where we draw the line with regard to state autonomy, class and its relationship to the exercise and management of state power is a crucial factor that human security needs to focus on, emphasizing as it does the link between what orthodox security would refer to as domestic and international politics.

The issue of democracy arises here because satisfying human needs depends in part on the political and economic institutions that serve as mechanisms for attaining such a goal. Simply put, democracy has different meanings and it remains an open question as to which model of democracy is most appropriate for satisfying needs and constructing secure societies. As this chapter suggests, there are powerful reasons for arguing that economic *and* political democracy are necessary for the attainment of such objectives. The current trend in the world order is toward the opposite—increasing the private power that acts to undermine and curtail such possibilities. This is a particularly pertinent problem in Africa, where a transition away from military and authoritarian rule toward forms of democratic political organization is seen by many as an increasing tendency (Wiseman, 1990; *Economist,* 1997; Clapham, 1993, 1996; 'Nyong'o, 1992).

In practice, state managers are both constrained and enabled by and susceptible to the pressures and influence of dominant social forces in the establishment of their policy objectives, and this susceptibility is a major obstacle to the construction of substantively democratic and secure societies (Block, 1987). State managers pursue policies that reflect the broad interests of dominant social forces. This is not to argue that state managers simply adhere to the interests of powerful domestic or transnational class groupings, but the interests of both the state and the dominant classes, in terms of their need to preserve their own social power, frequently tend to dovetail in practice. They are mutually supportive rather than simply having the same goals. For example, powerful social forces tend to utilize state power wherever possible to defend their own particular interests (Edgley, 1995). Equally, state institutions are dependent on a successful and productive economy for their own power and legitimacy. The two structures of capitalism and the interstate system are in crucial areas co-determining each other (Lovering, 1987: 296).

If human security is concerned with human emancipation, as Booth (1991) has persuasively argued, then the possibility of attaining such a goal depends on the nature of the institutions and procedures constructed to realize it. The reason that class is so important for human security is that conflict between classes remains a central feature of modern state-society relations. Various writers have observed that dominant classes have tended to constrain, limit, or even oppose the extension and deepening of democracy whenever it is perceived to threaten their particular interests (Chomsky, 1992). The history of many African states illustrates this tendency (Harris, 1986: Chapter 4). Following on from this point, Robert Dahl has noted that historically state-societies split by huge inequalities of social power tend toward authoritarian forms of political rule as the powerful seek to protect themselves against the claims of those excluded from substantive political participation. Dahl noted that rather than too much democracy presenting a threat to individual liberty, history suggests that the greatest threat to democratic order (a precondition for attaining secure societies) is societies split with widening inequalities of social power.

Simply expressed, a threat to democracy arises as those with the necessary social power and wealth are able to dominate political processes and institutions, excluding those who have little substantive influence in the realm of formal political practice. The consequence of this exclusion, Dahl suggests, is illustrated throughout history by social conflict that can ultimately lead to civil war and perhaps the disintegration of the state itself (Dahl, 1985: Chapter 1; Bayart, 1993b: 153). Recent events in the former Zaire are one contemporary illustration of this tendency. The relationship between states and classes in Africa, as elsewhere, is crucial in understanding the behavior of a state as an international actor and the state-society relations that persist within its territory. If dominant classes are able to constrain and enable state power to reflect and maintain *wherever possible their own particular ends*, both domestically and internationally, then the idea of a secure state-society relationship that is concerned with general and particular needs of the kind that critical security focuses on breaks down (Bayart, 1993b: 26).

Thus class raises two particular issues for human security. First, considerations of class forces us to analyze and understand the way in which state managers are susceptible to the pressure of dominant (and subordinate) social forces in the formulation of national and international policies. Second, they bring to light a central obstacle to securing a democratic political order: state-society relations split by social forces exercising radically unequal forms of power. *Again, dominant social forces throughout the world have an interest in limiting the extension of democracy lest it undermine their own power. This is not simply a problem facing Africa* (Chomsky, 1992; Seabrook, 1996). Let us now turn to the ways in which class as a social and economic category is realized and its implications for the goal of human security.

Class and Economic Power

The social power of conflicting classes rests in determining ways on their economic position in the wider state-society nexus. This is a long-established understanding of class in social theory and it is of particular importance for human security with its emphasis on the satisfaction of human needs. If the material position of conflicting classes is directly related to their social power and the subsequent uneven satisfaction of human needs, then it is reasonably clear that state-societies split by class inequalities can never hope to reconcile this dichotomy. Class conflict remains a central division in such state-society relations. There are many ways in which the economic basis of class serves to polarize and reinforce unequal social relations and power between classes and these all act to undermine the possibility of secure societies. The particular issue to be drawn out here, though, is that of needs satisfaction.

The "shaping of lives" refers to a concern with the ways people's lives and experiences are shaped by their differential access to the resources they need. Recent UN human development reports, for example, provide stark data to illustrate the colossal scale of the ways in which these inequalities of wealth manifest themselves in a range of categories including health, poverty, mortality, and education (Hayter, 1992; UNDP, 1995, 1997; Bradshaw and Wallace, 1996; Broad and Cavanagh, 1995–1996; Thomas, 1997). As Colin Leys (1996) has noted, the African continent is overwhelmingly shaped by poverty even as certain sectors of African state-societies are enjoying revived economic fortunes (*Economist,* 1997). The economic condition that Africa faces is in part related to its place in the modern world order and the historical lineage of colonialism, imperialism, and capitalism but is also to do with the internal political, social, and economic structures, institutions, and agents who have dominated the continents' "postcolonial" era (Callaghy, 1988; Azarya, 1988; Barratt Brown and Tiffen, 1992; Leys, 1996; Barratt Brown, 1995). For the hyperexploited classes in Africa, conditions are, if anything, worsening as the global economic norms of liberalization, deregulation, and privatization are implemented with little regard for their suffering (Tanzer, 1995; Bergsten, 1996; Dunning, 1993).[4] The imposition of such norms will reflect the particular circumstances of different state-societies, but it is clear that for the subordinate classes in Africa and elsewhere there is a general tendency toward undermining the provision of goods and services that are most likely to lead to the satisfaction of general needs: welfare, subsidized foodstuffs, public health and education resources, and so on (Bradshaw and Wallace, 1996; Thomas, 1997; Barratt Brown, 1995). Let us now turn to the specific relevance of class to the idea of human security in Africa.

Human Security and Class in Africa

Thus far we have considered some pressing reasons that questions of class should take prominence in any account of human security concerned with state-society relations. In particular, we have examined this issue through its implications for the satisfaction of human needs and the obstacles that class conflict presents in establishing a democratic social and political order. In this section we look at the relationship of class and human security within the context of African state-society relations and their relationship to wider global forces.

Class, States, and Democracy in Africa

A familiar criticism of the theoretical analysis of the state in orthodox security and international relations is that it tends to reify or naturalize the state. Chomsky, for example, has noted that there is nothing natural about modern nation-states. Indeed, the history of Europe, the birthplace of the modern nation-state, suggests that it might well be a highly unnatural form of political organization. The European continent has been littered with conflicts between states striving to expand or preserve their sovereignty at the expense of some other population and territory (Chomsky, 1993). This ongoing dilemma has become a global problem since the European powers began to spread into the rest of the world in the sixteenth century. Thus the history of the modern nation-state is one of violence and struggle against both foreign *and* domestic populations. It is not one of permanent or even consistent peace and security.

When we have this starting point in mind, it raises a number of problems for the orthodox security paradigm. The violence that states exert toward their own populations is reflected in the history of African states and continues to plague the continent. The recent experience of Rwanda provides us with an extreme example of state institutions deliberately working toward the destruction of vast sectors of society. As we have seen, though, the violence of state institutions toward domestic populations is not a problem unique to Africa (Moore, 1966, 1978), and African states are not unique in being perceived as artificial or unstable. The problems of African states may well have been exacerbated by a range of specific external and internal factors, most obviously colonialism and neocolonialism, but they are not specific to any one continent. Capitalism, colonialism, and imperialism have shaped and continue to shape the boundaries and institutions of African state-society relations, but it is also the case that the postcolonial internal developments within African states reflect the divisions of African societies, including and importantly, as Barratt Brown and Onimode observe, those of class (Young, 1995: Chapter 3; Onimode, 1988; Barratt Brown, 1995).

As the African state system has been shaped by both external and internal factors, so has the development of class relations in African states had both a local and a global aspect. At the local level, class divisions in African state-societies reflect those that have developed in nation-states in the wake of state-building processes (Barratt Brown, 1995: Chapters 3 and 7). Class relations in Africa are also part of the development of capitalism as a world economy that tends to construct conflicting classes. African nation-states have been marked by the uneven development of classes and the tendency toward military-state institutions that take a primary role in their construction (Clapham, 1996: Chapters 2 and 3). Again, these authoritarian political forms are not unique to modern Africa; nor do they preclude the fact that state managers and dominant classes, as mentioned earlier, tend to find that their interests and needs dovetail over time. Indeed, as Michael Barratt Brown has recently noted, African societies have long held strong democratic traditions that have been undermined in the past century by the Western political and economic transformation of the continent (Barratt Brown, 1995: 170–173).

In contemporary terms African states have been marked by an oscillation between periods of civilian, if not democratic, rule and the emergence of what has in practice been national security governments. The latter have been classic examples of the limitations of the orthodox security model with its assumption that the interests of state security are above and beyond those of so-called domestic politics. These militarized states have been guilty of the repression of subordinate and occasionally dominant social forces that have sought to challenge a range of state-led development processes. Although contemporary conflicts such as those in Nigeria cannot be seen as simply expressions of class, there seems little reason to doubt that class conflict plays a significant part in this situation. Indeed, Nigeria's current conflict reflects the complexities of both national and transnational class interests, as major oil corporations have long-established interests in the country and have helped to structure both Nigeria's internal and external development.

Contemporary Africa is marked by a stark contradiction between collapsing states and emerging capitalism. Class plays a major part in this latest struggle, as different social forces contest the meaning and practice of the development of democracy ('Nyong'o, 1992; Imam, 1992; Barratt Brown, 1995). A major obstacle to substantive political democracy in Africa remains the dramatic inequality between social forces in the continent. As Dahl (1985) noted, formal political democracy can exist in a society with such inequalities, as in practice the dominant social forces will monopolize political power as a mechanism for preserving their own interests. There is an apparent danger of this outcome for many African state-societies where there is no successful movement to empower the subordinate classes as actors in social and political life. To this end some writers have recently emphasized the need to reinvigorate civil society in Africa and elsewhere if democracy is to be reinforced (Clapham, 1993: 435–436; Harbeson and Rothchild, 1995: 3). The rationale behind this argument is that states have proven themselves to be unaccountable and inefficient institutions that are unresponsive to the needs of their populations.

Whereas the emphasis on civil society is an important development, there is a need to recognize that in countries gripped by stark disparities of social power such as those that bedevil most African nation-states, civil society is no simple panacea for the lack of democracy. On the contrary, it might well become the domain in which already powerful social forces extend their power over the rest of society and the state. Such an outcome has been noted by other writers and would do little to enhance the human security goals of democracy, needs satisfaction, and emancipation (Pasha, 1996). In order to make sense of the trends within Africa, we have to not only focus on the important internal social and political movements but also situate them within the context of wider processes of globalization.

Globalization, Class, and Needs in Africa

I have written about how we might understand globalization in more detail elsewhere (Wilkin, 1997) and for the purposes of this chapter wish only to consider the matter in the context of broad social, economic, and political processes of re-structuring in the world order (Wilkin, 1997). Specifically we need to consider the ways in which they impinge on needs satisfaction and democracy in Africa—of core concern for human security. Thus we turn to a consideration of globalization from above (GFA) and from below (GFB) and the implications for class as both a global and a local experience and category.

Globalization from above. This is taken to reflect the movement toward the imposition (in the case of many African states) and acceptance of what were referred to earlier as the new global liberal economic norms: liberalization, privatization, and deregulation. How these policies are implemented in concrete settings reflects the specific circumstances of each nation-state, its history, the balance of power between social forces, and so on. Globalization from above promotes policies that directly reflect class and class conflict. The overall aim of these policies is to help restructure global production in the world economy, in the process disempowering large sectors of the world's population. Since the late 1970s, resources and wealth have shifted from South to North and from rich to poor, widening and deepening the structural basis of class and social power in the world order and especially in Africa.

GFA undermines and exacerbates the already existing tensions in state-society relations by polarizing more starkly the class inequalities of social power that are a central concern of human security. In the context of Africa, for example, the introduction of global economic norms has largely come about through state institutions applying various forms of IMF or World Bank restructuring programs that threaten satisfaction of the most basic needs, such as subsided foodstuffs, medicine, and whatever public services exist that are fundamental to a secure society (Shaw, 1988; Callaghy, 1995; *Economist,* 1997; Barratt Brown and Tiffen, 1992; Barratt Brown, 1995: Chapter 3). Chossudovsky has traced the impact of these policies and noted the complex relationship between them and the gradual and eventually dramatic breakdown of societies in many African states (Chossudovsky, 1997, this volume).

In addition to reinforcing these class differences in Africa and elsewhere, globalization from above also diminishes the democratic character of national, regional, and international political institutions by placing key decisions over policymaking in the hands of ever further removed officials and institutions. Again, this isolation of the public from the decisionmaking process has generated a great deal of resistance throughout the world and over various issues from European integration to the completion of the last GATT round (Brecher, 1993; *Third World Resurgence,* 1993). The conclusion is that globalization from above tends to be antidemocratic and anti-needs-satisfaction in general terms while also reinforcing the unequal social power between classes. Its effects depend on the circumstances of particular peoples, histories, institutions, and so on.

Globalization from below. Globalization from below reflects the diverse and fragmented forms of *resistance and support* for the process of expanding the realm of private social power at the expense of the common good and the satisfaction of needs in general. (Both left- and right-wing political forces are part of GFB, and it is arguable that in many respects the grassroots right-wing movements have been most successful in recent decades.) The uneven impact of this global economic restructuring has been fundamental in generating resistance to its imposition in all areas of the world. In significant ways the struggle is one over the satisfaction of needs, the control of resources, and the possibility of substantive forms of democratic practice becoming embedded in the world order. In Africa this struggle is in part reflected in the reemergence of concerns over civil society as the possible site of progressive political change. Although there is a substantial difficulty with this notion, as mentioned earlier, there are tendencies toward both resisting and supporting the implications of GFA. Oppositional forces tend to be hostile to both state institutions and to untrammeled capitalist market relations (Brechar, 1993). What this illustrates is that the concern over democracy within contemporary Africa is both complex and largely driven by internal social forces (Clapham, 1993: 430). As the popular struggles over the last round of the General Agreement on Tariffs and Trade (GATT) and the imposition of general economic restructuring have illustrated, it is invariably (though not exclusively) the subordinate social forces that are both on the receiving end of the worst aspects of such policies and also actively opposed to them (*Third World Resurgence,* 1993). If human security is, as I maintain it must be, a concern with democracy and the satisfaction of human needs, then this struggle described as GFA and GFB is at the heart of the issue, in Africa and throughout the world order. Questions of class remain central.

Notes

1. As Chomsky, among others, has argued, the end of the East-West aspect of the Cold War does not necessarily mean the end of the exploitation of the resources and populations of the Third World by the Group of 7 (G7) countries, through either direct military intervention, the continuing economic intervention of their corporations, or through the workings of the international financial institutions. See Chomsky (1994). See Talbott (1996) for a contemporary defense of the idea of the national interest.

2. Classes avoid ruling directly wherever possible and instead seek to govern through the construction of blocs of social forces that cut across society to build a governing coalition. Within a social force, different factions of a capitalist class, for example, will struggle with each other to impose their views on the bloc as a whole. Thus, this is a fluid process of struggle and change that recognizes that interests are not static and unchanging. The term *social force* refers to the wider political movement that any dominant class has to build in order to rule by means other than direct and overt force. See Gill (1990) and Onimode (1988: 102).

3. This seems to me to be a central dynamic of globalization. See Wilkin (1997), UNDP (1997), and also Leys (1996: 22–25) for an overview of Africa in the global economy.

4. The liberalization of the world economy needs to be understood in the context of its skewed nature in recent decades, primarily through the GATT framework. As is often noted, this liberalization does not equate with a classic free-market model of economic organization. On the contrary, the liberalization of trade has been both skewed and controlled to serve the interests of both the major state powers and the transnational corporations (TNCs) that dominate global trade and investment. See Raghavan (1990) and Amin (1997). Thus "liberalization" is best seen as a code word for the process of a restructuring of the world economy that works largely in the favor of and is determined by the state managers and corporate interests of the G7 states.

3

Feminist Perspectives on Security in a Global Economy

J. Ann Tickner

Globalization, World Order, and Human Security

A central task for a different political economy is to reject the universalization of the categories of capitalism and to begin to see the world economy's various "barbarians" through their own eyes. An emphasis on local interpretations not only brings to the surface the violence encouraged by dominant representations, it also lets us see the limits that globalized representations put on the strategies that the less-advantaged have used to cope with the expansion of the world economy. (Murphy and Rojas de Ferro, 1995: 68)

Dominant representations of the contemporary global economy abound with declarations of endings and beginnings. With the end of the Cold War came the "end of history" and the "end of ideology" (Fukuyama, 1989). Beginnings are seen in metanarratives about a new era associated with the universalization of capitalism and the spread of Western liberal democracy. For its supporters, the spread of capitalism and democracy holds the promise of one world beyond ideological divides and international conflict. But cleavages still exist; according to certain international relations scholars, the East-West division of the Cold War era has been replaced by a North-South split between a peaceful group of liberal democratic states in the North and instability in the South, a divide sometimes referred to as "zones of peace and zones of conflict" or "mature and immature anarchies" (Singer and Wildavsky, 1993; Buzan, 1991b). Those who expect a positive future predict that these splits will diminish as the benefits of

trickle-down economic growth fueled by a growing open market economy lead to prosperity, democracy, and the diminution of conflict on a
global scale.

This neoliberal optimism has spawned a critical reaction. The end of
history is seen by some as a "world without alternatives," a world that exhibits a growing insensitivity to the plight of the powerless and an erosion
of the legitimacy of a "third way" to counter an ascendant liberal ideology that threatens the richness and complexity of global civil society
(Kothari, 1993: 120). Others see ethnic and social movements and local-
ized cultural reassertions from the world's "barbarians" as offering some
welcome resistance to the homogenizing forces of Western-led neoliberalism. Critics who focus on a growing inequality that they believe is exacerbated by the spread of liberal market forces frequently note that women
are often those most adversely affected by these trends; yet this critical literature has rarely incorporated gender as a category of analysis with which
to explain these negative impacts.

After elaborating on some of the arguments for and against globalization, this chapter will offer some feminist perspectives on these contending positions and their importance for human security. Gender will be introduced as an analytical category to explain why, as many critics note,
women's security is so often adversely affected by forces of globalization.
Consistent with critical security studies more generally, feminists define
security in multidimensional and multilevel terms—as the diminution of
all forms of insecurity including physical, economic, and ecological (Tickner, 1992; Peterson and Runyan, 1993). Unlike orthodox notions of security, feminist perspectives on security start with the individual or community rather than the state or the international system. Rejecting universal
explanations that, they believe, contain hidden gender biases, since they
are so often based on the experiences of men, feminists frequently draw on
local interpretations to explain women's relatively deprived position and
their insecurity. Consistent with their focus on social relations rather than
state relations, feminists seek to uncover how gender hierarchies and their
intersection with race and class exacerbate women's insecurities. Feminists frequently note the interrelationship between military, economic, and
environmental security; this chapter focuses on the economic dimensions
of human security. It also offers some evidence of how women are resisting globalizing forces when they perceive them as detrimental to their
lives. For feminists, these resistances are important for reasons that go beyond their practical achievements; they are also seen as generators of new
knowledge from the margins with which to counter the hegemonic liberal
consensus. This new knowledge is in part about asserting the needs of
women's human security.

Arguments for Globalization: Neoliberalism, Interdependence, and Orthodox Security

With the collapse of the socialist economies of the Eastern bloc and the adoption of export-led growth models by many states in the Third World, neoliberals are heralding a new era in which, they believe, the expansion and near universalization of a capitalist global market and the spread of liberal democratic norms will be accompanied by increased respect for human rights and political liberties. According to neoliberals, the globalization of markets will reduce inequalities within and between states and increase cooperation through economic interdependence and an interlinked global civil society that will gain strength as the competitive system of states is undermined. International institutions will be strengthened as states perceive that their interests are met better through cooperation than competition (Hurrell and Woods, 1995: 451–452). The core ideals of this version of liberalism, which was important in nineteenth-century Europe, include individualism, universalism, the defense of property rights, and the limitation of state intervention in the economy, which is best regulated by impersonal market forces.

In its contemporary manifestation, the global restructuration of the economy heralded by liberals is characterized by a reorganization of production evidenced by a shift from integrated corporations to networks of firms manufacturing components of the production process at different locations according to the availability of cheap labor and favorable tax rates. This is said to result in increased efficiency of production and presumably lower costs. This transnationalization of production is widening the availability of standardized consumer goods; markets are determining distribution on a global scale. In what has been termed a "post-Fordist" economy, the compact between labor and capital is being superseded by an emphasis on efficiency and competitiveness.

Applauding these trends and echoing the aspirations of nineteenth-century liberals, Kenichi Ohmae, a financial consultant who is frequently cited by advocates of globalization, writes of a "borderless world" in which nothing is overseas any longer. He sees an interlinked economy of 1 billion people in which transnational companies are bringing the promise of a better life with increased security and prosperity (Ohmae, 1991). According to Ohmae's liberal predispositions, these economic benefits have wider implications as both producers and consumers begin to think of themselves as "global citizens" operating in a world where boundaries have disappeared. This borderless economy creates a local/global dynamic whereby the importance of the state, both as an economic manager and a source of citizen identity, is eroding.

Ohmae's preferred minimalist role for the state—limited to providing the necessary infrastructure for competitive behavior in the global market—accords with neoliberal principles. He heralds a new age in which the military-based security associated with the Cold War is being replaced by global economic security supported by a new framework of global governance that will replace outdated, conflict-prone mercantilist behavior (Ohmae, 1991: xii–xiii). His advice to states in the South is to open their borders and shed the outworn vestiges of economic nationalism; this, he claims, is the only way to create sustained and widespread economic growth and prosperity, for in an interlinked economy, there will be no absolute winners and losers (Ohmae, 1991: 173–180).

In a similar vein, Francis Fukuyama has proclaimed the "end of history," an unabashed victory for Western economic and political liberalism marked by the total exhaustion of viable systematic alternatives (Fukuyama, 1989). With the demise of fascism and communism as the two major ideological challengers to liberalism in the twentieth century, Fukuyama sees an end of ideology, to be replaced by the growing "common marketization" of international relations and the diminution of the likelihood of large-scale conflict between states. With some regret Fukuyama sees struggles that call for courage and idealism being replaced by economic calculation.

Although liberals predict a more prosperous and peaceful world as liberal democracy and capitalism spread beyond the Western core, they acknowledge that divisions remain. According to the World Bank development report of 1989, in the late 1980s less than 25 percent of the world's population consumed over 80 percent of the world's annual consumable resources (Helleiner, 1994: 85). Most of this 25 percent are located in what Ohmae (1991) calls the "strategic triad" of North America, Europe, and East Asia. Many liberals realize that gains from economic globalization will not be evenly spread, but Ohmae and others claim that the benefits enjoyed by the core will trickle down to the rest of the global economy. Others are not so sure, however, and globalization has as many critics as it does supporters.

Arguments Against Globalization: Poverty, Inequality, and Global Insecurity

According to the UNDP *Human Development Report* of 1996, over the past three decades the world has become more polarized and the gulf between the poor and the rich has widened—the poorest 20 percent of the world's population have seen their share of global income decline from 2.3 percent to 1.4 percent in the past thirty years while the share of the richest

20 percent has risen from 70 percent to 85 percent (UNDP, 1996: 2). This growth of inequality, which for critics calls into question the liberal faith in trickle-down economies, is evidenced both within and between states. Critics suggest that recent trends in the global economy discussed above are responsible for these disturbing trends.

As transnational corporations choose their locations in the "borderless world," they play national governments against each other in order to get the best financial deals. Wages and environmental regulations are undermined as firms threaten to leave in search of cheaper labor and lower restrictions. As business perceives investment being inhibited by inflation, governments see the necessity of curtailing wages and public spending in order to provide a good business climate (Cox, 1994; also see Chossudovsky, this volume).

All of this means that in order to attract international investment, governments across the political spectrum have shifted to the right.[1] John Ruggie (1994: 523) sees this trend fueled by the logic of global capitalism as a decline of the postwar-embedded liberalism compromise, whereby governments countered the harsh effects of the market with social spending. The enormous increase of public debt is being financed in international financial markets, which means that governments become more accountable to external bond markets than to their own publics (Cox, 1994). Thus state autonomy is being eroded; in a globalized division of labor, the state no longer initiates action but reacts to worldwide economic forces, thus resulting in what James Mittelman (1997: 7) calls a politics of disillusionment. Mittelman sees a contradiction between the global preference for electoral democracy and the increasing economic polarization generated by a world capitalism that is not accountable to elected officials (Mittelman, 1997: 9). For many governments these trends are not a matter of choice but of necessity.

Certain states, however, have more power than others to influence outcomes and decisions; thus globalization affects different regions of the world in different ways (Hurrell and Woods, 1995: 456). Although liberals advocate a minimalist state, Saskia Sassen suggests that global capital needs the state to further deregulate, strengthen markets, and push for privatization, tasks in which the United States has taken a leading role (Sassen, 1996). Indeed, certain critics claim that far from witnessing a bypassing of the state by global capitalism, we are seeing very active states working to enhance the global and domestic interests of capital (Panitch, 1997: 85; Thomas and Wilkin, 1997). This changing role of the state is marked by a decrease in democratic accountability as well as the state's decreased ability to provide public goods (see Wilkin, this volume). According to Stephen Gill (1995: 400), we are witnessing the emergence of a politics of supremacy rather than a politics of justice. (See also Ray, this volume.)

Critics are more inclined to note these dimensions of political power in current trends toward liberalization; they too see a lack of viable alternatives, although they predict a more conflictual road ahead. Rajni Kothari sees the demise of the "third way" as part of the failure of southern elites to articulate an independent path of development and as their complicity in fostering a partnership with transnational capital (see also Mazrui, this volume); writing from a southern perspective, Kothari claims that the state is being disabled and disempowered (Kothari, 1993: 123–126). For Kothari, the consequences of the espousal of Western capitalist development in the South include a widening of poverty, serious environmental damage, an increase in ethnic conflict, and a declining sense of community.

Challenging this pessimistic view of a world without alternatives, James Richardson identifies an alternative to what he calls the liberalism of privilege—a radical liberalism concerned with justice and development from below. Rejecting orthodox liberalism's universalistic claims, this form of radical liberalism endorses the need for greater attention to the specific local and historical conditions of each particular development case. Richardson claims that the UN Human Development Program offers pointers toward an alternative to the established orthodoxy with its preferred approach of human development based on the satisfaction of basic needs. Yet noting the legitimacy of current liberal orthodoxy and its near universal espousal by ruling global elites, Richardson claims that radical liberalism lacks a generalized strategy for achieving its preferred program of human development (Richardson, 1997). Richardson also notes that a narrowing of the political debate to issues of economic management has caused an erosion of democratic political culture and a reduction in citizen participation.

Many of these critics of globalization note the disproportionate numbers of women at the bottom of the socioeconomic scale, the feminization of labor (Mittelman, 1997: 4), and the growth of women's social movements protesting the detrimental effects of global capitalism; yet their recognition of gender as a structure of inequality or a growing feminist literature on globalization has been slight. The chapter now draws on this literature to offer some feminist perspectives on the issues raised by both supporters and critics of globalization; also, it draws on gender analysis to offer some explanations for the insecurities faced by women, which feminists claim may be resulting from globalization.

Feminist Perspectives on
Globalization and Human Security

Feminist scholars tend to be skeptical of celebrations of beginnings and endings and historical turning points because there is evidence to suggest that times of "progress" are often regressive for women. For example, the "triumph" of capitalism in the former Eastern bloc has been accompanied by a sharp decline in both the economic status and the level of political participation of women (Moghadam, 1994). Given the increase in global inequality, the feminization of poverty, and the discriminations that women often face when they attempt to participate in the global market, feminist scholarship is questioning the triumphalist story of a borderless world that is being told by supporters of economic globalization. Feminists also reject theoretical projects that offer universal, essentialist, or reductionist explanations of multifaceted and complex social relations (Krause, 1996: 235). Many claim that neoliberalism's metanarratives about the triumph of rationality and the end of history have not moved us beyond ideology; rather, they are a disguise for a form of knowledge that tells only a partial story, a story that often does not include the experiences of many women and other marginalized people whose identification with a marketized version of global citizenship is minimal.

A Gendered Division of Labor: Generating Women's Insecurity in a Global Economy

Universalisms tend to conflate a masculine viewpoint with a general human standpoint (Braidotti et al., 1994: 37). When proponents of globalization speak of economic actors and global citizens, they are using terms that come out of a historical tradition of Western political and economic thought and practice based on experiences more typical of men than women. These terms focus our attention on the public world of the market and the state, traditionally inhabited by men, while rendering the private world of women virtually invisible. Fukuyama's prediction of a "common marketization" of international relations based on economic calculation reinforces this worldview, which portrays individuals solely as economic actors and which hides the complex social relations, including gender relations, within which individuals' lives are embedded. The market model, favored by liberals, is based on the instrumentally rational behavior of economic actors whose self-interested competitive behavior in the marketplace leads to an aggregate increase in wealth. Feminists claim that this representation of rational economic behavior is gendered masculine because it extrapolates from roles and behaviors historically associated with Western (elite) men;[2] it has been used, however, by liberal economists to represent the behavior of humanity as a whole.

If women's experiences were taken as the prototype for human behavior, this highly individualistic, competitive market behavior of "rational economic man" would not necessarily be assumed as the norm. Women in their reproductive and maternal roles do not conform to the behavior of instrumental rationality. Much of women's work in the provision of basic needs takes place outside the market, in households or in the subsistence sector. When women enter the workforce they are disproportionately represented in the caring professions or in "light" manufacturing industries, vocations or occupations that are chosen not on the basis of market rationality and profit maximization but because of values and expectations that are often emphasized in female socialization and expectations about appropriate roles for women (Tickner, 1992: Chapter 3).

Feminists claim that these different roles that have come to be seen as natural for men and women are the result not only of socialization but also of a gendered division of labor that had its origins in seventeenth-century Europe, when definitions of male and female were becoming polarized in ways that were suited to the growing division between work and home required by early capitalism. The notion of "housewife" began to place women's work in the private domestic sphere as opposed to the public world of the market inhabited by rational economic man. Gendered constructs such as "breadwinner" and "housewife" have been central to modern Western definitions of masculinity, femininity, and capitalism. Even though many women work outside the home, the association of women with gendered roles such as housewife, caregiver, and mother have become institutionalized and even naturalized, thereby decreasing women's economic security and autonomy.[3]

This public/private division has had consequences beyond the economic sphere. The historical legacy of Western democracy has also been problematic for women. With the development of a gendered division of labor, women were generally subsumed under male heads of households with no legal rights of their own, such as the right to own property or to vote. Historically, therefore, terms such as *citizens* and *heads of households* were not neutral but associated with men. In many parts of the world today women are still struggling for legal and social equality. In states where women have achieved formal or near-formal equality, feminists claim that this historical legacy still inhibits their political participation on an equal basis with men. When proponents of liberal democracy and marketization speak of the spread of human rights based on Western notions of individualism, feminists caution that both definitions of human rights and the kinds of violations that get attention from Western states and their human rights communities may also be gender biased.[4]

The development of the public/private divide and its implications for a gendered division of labor is a story based on Western experiences. It is important, however, that Western feminists not impose their own historical metanarratives when critiquing those of contemporary neoliberals, particularly when writing about the Third World.[5] It is true that forms of gender oppression and gender hierarchy exist in almost all parts of the world, but as a growing literature in postcolonial feminism reminds us, forms of patriarchy vary across cultural, racial, and class divides. Although admitting that feminist writing is still marginalized in the United States, Mohanty et al. claim that Western feminist writing on women in the Third World must be placed in the context of the global hegemony of Western scholarship (Mohanty et al., 1991: 55). Postcolonial feminists point out that Third World women face multiple oppressions based on racism and imperialism as well as patriarchy. Cautioning against a projection of Western feminist concerns, April Gordon (1996: 77) claims that despite the existence of patriarchy, women may actually feel a greater solidarity with their menfolk than with other women; Third World women have claimed that Western feminism's emphasis on the sexual division of labor creates an artificial competition between women and men that underestimates their common interest in economic survival. They also emphasize the importance of the local production of knowledge rather than relying on the validity of Western knowledge with its false claims of universalism (Mohanty et al., 1991: 11; see also Marchand and Parpart, 1995).

Nevertheless, it is also true that Western forms of patriarchy spread to much of the rest of the world through imperialism, where "civilized" behavior was often equated with the behavior of Western men and women, particularly behavior based on appropriate gender roles. Often native inhabitants of colonies were described in gendered and racialized terms—as childlike, emotional, and dependent—vestiges of which still appear in the discourse of the contemporary North/South divide and in liberal modernization programs (Scott, 1996). Even when devising schemes for the betterment of women's lives, development programs have often drawn on Western assumptions about the gendered division of labor. Although, as Gordon (1996: 82, 137) suggests, African women do not identify with the Western public/private dichotomy; development planning is permeated with sexist assumptions including the notion, often untrue, that households are nuclear with a male breadwinner and a woman who is primarily a housewife (see also Braidotti et al., 1994: 78).

Feminists attempting to understand the effects of globalization on women's security go beyond the economic emphasis of neoliberalism and focus on a broad array of social relations and institutional structures. Questioning the universalistic claims of Western knowledge, which, they claim, is primarily based on experiences of Western elite men, they argue for locally specific knowledge that takes into account various forms of oppression based on race and class as well as gender. Some of the feminist analysis outlined above will be drawn on below to better understand some of the inequalities and insecurities that women are facing in the process of globalization.

Understanding the Effects of
Globalization on Women's Security

Ohmae's top-down view of a borderless world with its emphasis on the globalization of production and finance hides the large inequalities, stressed by critics, that exist both within and between societies. Feminists have pointed out that although there are obviously significant differences in the socioeconomic status of women depending on their race, class, and nationality, women are disproportionately located at the bottom of the socioeconomic scale in all societies. Figures vary from state to state, but on average, women earn three-quarters of men's earnings. Of the 1.3 billion people estimated to be in poverty today, 70 percent are women; the number of rural women living in absolute poverty rose by nearly 50 percent over the past two decades (UNDP, 1995: 36). Women receive a disproportionately small share of credit from formal banking institutions. For example, in Latin America, women constitute only 7–11 percent of the beneficiaries of credit programs; although women in Africa contribute up to 80 percent of total food production, they receive less than 10 percent of the credit to small farmers and 1 percent of total credit to agriculture (UNDP, 1995: 4, 9). Consistent with human security's focus on social relations as sources of insecurity, feminists claim that these inequalities can be understood only by using gender as a category of analysis.

The new international division of labor has had significant effects on women. According to some commentators, the new world order is characterized by "gender apartheid" (Krause, 1996: 226). Krause claims that even in areas of the world where economic growth has been rapid, economic progress has not been matched by improvements in the position of women. Women who work in the wage sector are generally the most poorly paid, and women make up a disproportionate number of those working in the informal sector or in subsistence agriculture, areas of the economy that are often ignored by conventional economic analysis. According to Marianne Marchand (1996: 585), women have not been left outside global restructuring; they are participating while remaining invisible.

In the export processing zones (EPZs) of Asia, Africa, and Latin America more than 70 percent of the workforce is female. Certain feminists claim that women provide an optimal labor force for contemporary capitalism because they are defined as housewives rather than workers and thus can be paid lower wages on the assumption that their wages are supplemental to their family's income. Women's cheap labor dates back to the first industrial revolution in Britain and is particularly predominant in textiles, electronics, and what is termed light industries. Companies favor hiring young unmarried women who can achieve a high level of productivity at a lower wage; these women are frequently fired if they get married or pregnant. Because of expectations associated with traditional gender roles there is a belief that women possess "nimble fingers," have patience for tedious jobs, and sew "naturally"; thus, this kind of work is not seen as skilled and is remunerated accordingly (Enloe, 1989: 162). Moreover, as Enloe states, political activity does not go with female respectability; employers hire women on the assumption that they will provide a "docile" labor force unlikely to organize for better conditions.

Enloe (1989: 174) claims that a "modern" global economy requires traditional ideas about women, ideas that depend on certain social constructions of what is meant by femininity and masculinity. However, in spite of these assumptions about appropriate gender roles that characterize women as supplemental wage earners, estimates suggest that one-third of all households are headed by women, about half of which are in the Third World (Holcomb and Rothenberg, 1993: 55), and that this fact is frequently obscured by role expectations based on the notion of male breadwinners.[6]

Not all feminist scholars believe that the increase in employment of women in low-paying factory jobs is detrimental, however. Linda Lim (1990: 101–119) argues that negative stereotyping of women in export manufacturing in the Third World is based on outworn assumptions and generalizations from data collected in the 1970s during the earliest stages of the establishment of export factories. Lim claims that wages, hours, and conditions in factories in EPZs are generally better than in their domestic counterparts and, therefore, are much desired.[7] She also suggests that women workers in these industries tend to be better educated than average workers in their countries and that there is considerable diversity in terms of age and marital status. Even if this type of work is under remunerated relative to men or to wages in the industrial North, many argue that it may be the best option for women and better than no work at all; the extra cash flow can significantly enhance the income of very poor families. It also gives women more financial independence and higher status.

In her study of African women, April Gordon (1996) claims that paid work is an important source of power for women; like Lim, she sees no necessary connection between capitalism and the exploitation of women. Citing the African case, she suggests that a transition to capitalism, which, she predicts, is leading to the increased participation of women in the waged sector, will actually enhance women's position relative to men and break the hold of African patriarchy, which predates both capitalism and colonialism. For Gordon, therefore, patriarchy, not capitalism, is the real source of women's oppression. The authors of the 1995 UNDP *Human Development Report* also claim that women's status will be enhanced by entry into the workforce.

Although these claims may be true, Faye Harrison (1991: 174) questions whether workers in the Third World should be so underrewarded.

Receiving, on average, no more than one-sixth of the wages of their counterparts in industrial countries, Third World women represent a cheaper-than-cheap labor force, since they are usually rewarded at a lower rate than men. This leads Harrison to conclude that the interplay of class and gender is integral to capitalist development at the national and international levels.

Even in cases where women do benefit from entry into the workforce, women continue to suffer in all societies from the imposition of a double or even triple burden. In addition to their paid work, women continue to carry most of the responsibility for household labor and unpaid community work, which is seen as an extension of women's domestic role. Often men are reluctant to take on community work unless it is financially remunerated. Although there is a sense that women are not "working" when they are engaged in household or volunteer community labor, women are actually playing a crucial role in the reproduction of labor necessary for waged work; moreover, these reproductive tasks often constrain women's opportunities for paid work. The narrow definition of work as work in the waged economy tends to render invisible many of the contributions women make to the global economy. Although some feminists find this split between productive and reproductive work problematic, it does help to illuminate the often hidden and unrecognized income-earning work that women do due to gender role expectations (Holcomb and Rothenberg, 1993: 53).

In many parts of the Third World, women play an important role in agricultural production also; globalization has had varying effects on women's role in agriculture. Maria Mies (1986: 115) suggests that women are incorporated into the world market through agriculture in a number of ways; whereas they may undertake cash-crop production or work on plantations, frequently they work as unpaid family labor in small units that produce independently or on contract. Consequently, men are more likely to gain access to money, new skills, and technology and women continue to be defined as dependents or subsistence producers. In fact, as agriculture moves into the monetarized economy, often producing for export, women tend to get left behind in the subsistence sector, producing for family needs; this activity has the effect of subsidizing male workers who are directly linked to the global economy.

Another way in which women are subsidizing the global economy is through their work in the informal sector. In a study of Jamaica's informal economy in the 1980s during a time when Jamaica was undergoing IMF structural adjustment, Faye Harrison (1991: 177) noted that the informal sector was complementing large-scale industry by taking on tasks that the latter saw as unprofitable. Jamaica's export-oriented economy could not satisfy all local market demands, including for staple foodstuffs; these items were produced and sold in the informal economy at lower prices. Harrison claims that the presence of the informal sector with its large supply of cheap labor disproportionately composed of women, since women were unemployed at twice the rate of men, reduced labor costs for large corporations and provided cheap accessible goods for waged workers, thus allowing a depression of their wages. In general, the informal labor market is easier for women to enter, since it allows more flexible schedules that can be accommodated to reproductive work; therefore, female heads of households tend to be overrepresented in the informal sector, partially accounting for their relative poverty (Holcomb and Rothenberg, 1993: 65).

Although the feminist literature on globalization is split on the effects of capitalism on women's economic security, it is nearly unanimous in its claim that structures of patriarchy, evidenced in a gendered division of labor globally and within states, operate to constrain women's life chances, a claim that accords with human security's focus on social relations at both the global and local levels. Patriarchy is also built into domestic political structures that interact with the global market and international financial institutions in ways that can be detrimental to women. Therefore, feminists, like neoliberals, have also reacted negatively to the role of the state, but for different reasons.

The State's Role in a Globalizing Economy— Rendering Women Insecure?

Like critical approaches to security more generally, feminists have been suspicious of states as security providers. All states regulate gender relations in various ways through policies on family, population, education, and income redistribution. As long as there is an absence of women in positions of political power, feminists claim that most states are likely to represent the interests of men over women. Like certain critics of globalization discussed above, feminists also tend to be suspicious of the state's role in supporting global capital.

Mohanty et al. claim that the contemporary liberal state operates not as a neutral arbiter, as its supporters believe, but through "unmarked discourses" of citizenship and individual rights that mask patriarchal policies. She argues that the legacy of the colonial state in the Third World is more explicitly racially and sexually differentiated. Although the colonial state often transformed existing patriarchies, it instituted new ones; one important example is the colonial regulation of agrarian relations through the granting of property rights to men, which aggravated existing inequalities (Mohanty et al., 1991: 21).

It is in the area of structural adjustment programs (SAPs) that feminist literature on the effects of globalization on the Third World has had the most to say about the state. Even though SAPs are imposed in the name of liberalization, the state can significantly influence the redistribution of income and resources by determining the way in which SAPs are implemented. The goal of structural adjustment is to decrease demand and increase production and supply, particularly private-sector exports; many critics have claimed that SAPs fall most heavily on the poor when government welfare services and government bureaucracies shrink and subsidies decline, particularly those on food. It is often urban areas that suffer most from these effects; with more potential for growing food and with cash crops producing export earnings, rural areas sometimes experience an increase in income due to higher prices for market crops.

Feminists claim that whatever the variability of these policies, they are often gender biased. Since cash crops are typically controlled by men, increases in rural incomes may not benefit women equally. Since the public sector has traditionally provided many jobs for urban women, a freeze on wages and employment disproportionately affects women, particularly middle-class women employed as teachers, social workers, and nurses. When welfare services are cut it is usually women who take up the burdens of caring for children, the aged, and the sick, which means longer working hours with less pay.[8] Since the imposition of SAPs typically means a rise in food prices when states decrease or eliminate food subsidies, the impact falls disproportionately on women who must stretch family income by increasing their unpaid labor, earning a wage income, or reducing total family consumption, a cost that is typically borne by women and girl children (Elson, 1991: 44). The 1989 World Bank report on Africa casts women and the informal sector as the "safety net" in the transition to modern capitalism in Africa (Scott, 1996: 80), but women's unpaid labor is not infinitely elastic when women's health and nutritional status begin to suffer. Where households experience a decline in income, there is also an incentive for women to emigrate either to export processing zones or abroad, often as domestic servants.

Although they are quite critical of states' implementation of policies that often appear to be gender biased, certain feminists are increasingly looking to the state as a potential buffer against the detrimental effects of global capitalism. Whereas they would agree with critics of globalization that states and international institutions are often working in the interests of global capital, feminists are beginning to explore the possibilities of a reformed state that, since it does have the potential for democratic accountability, may be the most likely institution to effect redistribution and decrease inequality.

Diane Elson (1991: 51) outlines some strategies for modifying the effects of SAPs: claiming that there are always choices in states' allocation of resources, she suggests that in addition to self-reliance in food production, states could select public expenditure cuts that do not affect the least well off. These kinds of choices are politically difficult to implement; evidence suggests that there is a great deal of variability in state policies (see Guest, this volume). For example, the UN *Human Development Report* (UNDP, 1995: 40) reports that in Costa Rica under structural adjustment, job creation was achieved without lowering pay; a simultaneous effort to promote gender equality resulted in a rise in the ratio of average female wages to male wages from 77 percent to 83 percent between 1987 and 1993.

April Gordon (1996: 120–121) claims that the African state has done little to help women not because of capitalism but because capitalism is so weakly established; she believes that with democratization and increased opportunities for women in the economy, states are more likely to create new institutions based on gender equality. Likewise, Mona Harrington (1992) claims that the traditional role of the state in the West has been to temper economic power, redistribute income, and provide social support for those hurt by unrestrained economic processes. Noting the difficulty of regulating international economic power and the lack of democratic accountability in international institutions, Harrington argues for what she calls an inward-turning feminist liberal state that would protect the vulnerable at home rather than project power abroad.

This literature is split as to whether there is a necessary connection between capitalism and patriarchy, but all of it claims that patriarchal political structures, which it believes are present in most states, albeit in different forms, inhibit women's access to resources and political participation. Some feminists believe that capitalism has the potential to improve women's welfare; the majority see dangers in global markets that tend toward inequality and a lack of democratic accountability. Although most are critical of many contemporary state policies that they see as gender biased, certain feminists do see in the state the potential for political choices that can increase women's welfare. Given their limited access to formal political institutions, women are pressuring states or building alternate political, social, and economic structures through activities in grassroots movements. It is important that women not be seen as passive victims of globalization; women throughout the world are actively resisting forces that they see as detrimental to themselves and their families.

Women's Resistances— Promoting Human Security

In certain parts of the world the move toward open market economies is being accompanied by a trend toward democratization, a trend applauded by proponents of globalization both for its potential to enhance economic growth and prosperity and to promote human rights and political participation. As with the literature on economic globalization, the conventional social science literature on transitions to democracy has had little to say about women or gender. This is in part because this literature usually presents a top-down view of democracy and thus ignores activities outside the conventional political arena, in which women are more likely to be involved (Waylen, 1996: 117).

Since women are not well represented in formal representative political structures favored by proponents of liberal democracy, their demands for change are often situated in oppositional movements that pressure the state for redistribution of income or improved services at the local or national level. Movements that act more autonomously often focus around collective survival strategies such as communal kitchens or income-generating activities such as bakeries, craft workshops, agriculture and business cooperatives, and credit associations. Although many of these movements focus on women's practical daily needs, they are coming to see themselves as feminist in that they are focusing on women's subordination more generally as well as on strategies for its elimination (Waylen, 1996: 21).

Increasingly, those marginalized by the development process and the forces of globalization are carving out their own problem-solving paths (Braidotti et al., 1994: 115). In rural Africa, the recovery of subjugated knowledge is taking place through the revival of old methods of farming and local forms of organization. An important feminist critique of Western development models has taken place within DAWN (Development Alternatives with Women for a New Era); DAWN is a network that links women researchers from the South to provide guidelines for action based on research and analysis growing out of Southern women's experiences. DAWN's research methodology differs from economistic and positivist approaches in that it is bottom-up; starting from analyses of microlevel experiences of poor women and linking these experiences to the macroeconomic level, it works from the assumption that knowledge at each level should inform the other. Recognizing the political nature of the development process and the imbalances of power within and between states, this type of analysis rejects the separation of the public and private domains, and intuition from rationality. It claims to promote a new science of empathy that uses intuition and reason simultaneously (Braidotti et al., 1994: 116–117).

Southern feminists, such as those working in the DAWN group, recognize that Southern women face multiple subordinations based on sex, race, and class; to alleviate these oppressions DAWN promotes women's empowerment and self-reliance. It suggests that alternative development models may be needed depending on region and socioeconomic position. Empowering women to fight against oppressions caused by unequal gender relations accords with human security's focus on social justice even when it is in tension with the preservation of order, a concern of particular importance for traditional notions of security. Taking a somewhat different position, Gordon (1996: 80) claims, however, that it is necessary to deal realistically with the fact that global capitalism is hegemonic; therefore, feminists risk irrelevance if they do not fight to ensure women's rights and access to resources under the prevailing social conditions.

Whereas postcolonialist feminists are rightly concerned with the hegemonic voices of Western women, it is important that fragmentation not become an obstacle to collective action. Fearing further objectification and victimization of women in the South, Braidotti et al. propose an alliance between Northern and Southern women built on mutual respect and a recognition of multiple positionality. Based on an interchange of local knowledge arising out of specific situations, this type of model is very different from Western models that rely on elite knowledge emanating only from the North (Braidotti et al., 1994: 120–121).

Conclusion:
Women's Critical Security and World Order

Rather than celebrating a borderless world, feminists see boundaries—often gendered—between wealth and poverty that cannot be eliminated by market forces alone. Skeptical of claims about a new world order, feminist perspectives on globalization are unanimous in pointing to continuities in various forms of patriarchy that have had detrimental effects on women's economic security throughout much of history. Although they disagree as to whether there is a necessary connection between patriarchy and capitalism, most feminists believe that women continue to be disadvantaged relative to men by a global gendered division of labor wherein women disproportionately perform unremunerated subsistence or household tasks or low-paid work—roles that are effectively subsidizing global capitalism but are not contributing to women's economic security or well-being.

Suspicious of universal arguments about economic rationalization, feminists claim that the negative effects of this gendered division of labor on women cannot be understood without an analysis of the complex social relations, including gender relations, in which the lives of all human beings are embedded; many believe that women's oppression is caused not by impersonal market forces alone but by processes that result from conscious political, economic, and social choices. Feminists writing about contemporary globalization claim, therefore, that only when these processes are revealed and understood through forms of knowledge that come not from those at the center of the system but from the lives and experiences of those on the margins of the global economy can progress be made toward substantially reducing these gendered boundaries of insecurity and inequality.

Notes

1. The 1997 election results in the United Kingdom and France, where Labor and Socialist governments were returned to power, suggest that support of the electorate for the shift to the right may be eroding.

2. Defining gender as a social construction, feminists claim that certain characteristics such as rational, independent, powerful, and public have stereotypically been associated with masculinity, whereas their opposites—emotional, dependent, weak, and private—have been associated with femininity. Note that these characteristics are relational in that they depend on each other for their definition. They are also unequal; masculine characteristics are typically seen as more valuable by men and women alike. And since these characteristics are socially constructed it is quite possible for women to display masculine characteristics and vice versa, although men risk more by displaying femininity. Although gender, as opposed to biological sex, is a social construction that varies across time, place, and culture, it comes to be seen as natural, thus making gender hierarchies difficult to overcome. Sandra Harding claims that we appeal to these gender dualisms to organize and divide our social activities among different groups of humans (Harding, 1986: 17–18).

3. For further elaboration of the origins of the gendered division of labor see Mies (1986, Chapter 2).

4. Since basic needs and welfare provision so often fall to women, as will be discussed further on, the preference by Western liberal states for political over economic rights may be gender biased. Also, since human rights violations are usually defined as violations by officials of the state, domestic violence has generally been outside the international human rights agenda.

5. I realize that the term *Third World* is controversial. In the development literature, it has frequently been replaced by terms such as *South* to avoid its association with underdevelopment and inferiority as well as the ambiguity caused by the disappearance of the category Second World; many feminists continue to use the term, although with a somewhat different meaning. Mohanty et al. (1991: 2–7) uses the term to include minority women in the West as well as the South. While cautioning against subsuming the very diverse histories and struggles of women of color under one label, Mohanty and other postcolonial feminists use the term to introduce transnational issues of race and class into feminist analysis.

6. In one town in Mexico in the late 1970s, one-third of women employed by garment manufacturers were heads of households (Safa, 1986: 66). Holcomb and Rothenberg (1993: 55) note that statistics on the number of female-headed households in the world are notoriously unreliable. They do tend, however, to be among the poorest of the poor.

7. That women (and men) in the global workforce are still being seriously exploited is undeniable, however. The *New York Times* (March 28 and 31, 1997) reported that in Vietnam, more than 90 percent of Nike workers are girls or young women aged 15–28; their wages are below the cost of three small meals per day. All workers interviewed reported physical complaints and hunger; at one factory, women were punished by being forced to run around the factory in the hot sun because they had not worn regulation shoes to work.

8. For example, in Jamaica under structural adjustment, social services expenditures fell 44 percent in real terms between 1981 and 1983 and between 1985 and 1986 (Elson, 1991: 47).

4

Security and Community in a Globalizing World

Jan Aart Scholte

What are the bases of and prospects for community in Africa at the end of the twentieth century, particularly in view of processes of globalization that have been enveloping the contemporary world? Has globalization tended to undermine previously prevailing structures of social solidarity, perhaps even to the point of rendering any form of community unviable? Alternatively, and more positively, might globalization also have opened up possibilities for novel constructions of community? Could these arrangements in turn contribute to wider and deeper conditions of security, in both local and world politics?

As is amply demonstrated throughout this book—and in the emergent field of critical security studies more generally—security involves a much broader span of issues than traditional notions of international security have allowed. Especially since the end of the Cold War, prevailing concepts of security have extended beyond military-strategic matters alone to encompass guarantees of subsistence, democracy, human rights, cultural identity, and ecological integrity. Indeed, many citizens of the 1990s are prepared to compromise certain older security priorities (e.g., the preservation of sovereign statehood) in order to achieve a more holistic—often called *global*—security.

Implicitly if not explicitly, much of this expanded conception of security touches on the problem of community. Increasingly, it is recognized that security—in a deeper sense than the absence of armed conflict and the survival of a state's territorial integrity—entails, inter alia, that people enjoy an experience of social cohesion. Thus human security depends in part on a confidence of belonging with concomitant expectations that persons will receive support from and contribute support to a collectivity with which they are affiliated. In recognition of this priority, the 1995 World

59

Summit for Social Development took building solidarity as one of its three principal themes. Some commentators may hope that the third exhortation of the French Revolution (less its sexist quality) is belatedly starting to receive due attention next to long-championed *liberté* and *égalité*.[1]

Recent heightened interest in community also arises from widely held concerns that contemporary globalization is destroying many bases of social solidarity. (Scholte, 1996a: 565–607). For example, this trend has smothered many traditional local communities in a flood of foreign direct investment, electronic mass media, and global consumer culture. At the same time, globalization has challenged "modern" national communities by undermining the structures of geography (territorialism) and governance (sovereign statehood) that have in the past so buttressed the nationality principle. Nor has globalization thus far brought much realization of cosmopolitan designs for a universal world community. On the contrary, global relations have frequently tended to increase awareness of cultural differences and to fuel conflictual identity politics. In sum, then, although community was often precarious in the territorialized international world of the past, it is perhaps even weaker in the globalizing world of the present.

This predicament, where none of the old formulas of community seem viable, has prompted some creative theorists and activists to attempt to redesign the bases of social solidarity. Thus globalization has created both a requirement and an opportunity to develop alternatives—to universalist cosmopolitanism on the one hand and to culturally relativist communitarianism on the other. This development is to be welcomed insofar as the former has historically implied the violence of imposed homogenization and the latter has frequently implied the violence of exclusion. A third way could build a nonuniversalist, nonculturalist, nonviolent model: new relations of community that could form a linchpin of global security.

This chapter aims to help us toward such alternatives and looks in particular to Africa for clues. Africans have experienced some of the greatest implosions of community in the current period of globalization but have also devised some innovative responses to the challenge of reforging social solidarity. The continent is a part of the world where territorially based state-nations (i.e., national solidarities connected to states) have in most cases had limited opportunity to consolidate and where destructive aspects of globalization have seriously constrained the possibilities of developing alternative forms of community. Nevertheless, Africa also offers some inspiring examples of local self-help, intercultural cohesion, and transborder solidarity networks, for example, in countless community-based organizations, in postapartheid South Africa, and in regional women's associations.

In undertaking this investigation I must straightaway stress that I am neither African-born nor an Africanist by training. My contribution comes as a student of globalization who has been developing arguments concerning the general causes, course, and consequences of this currently unfolding world-historical process. (Scholte, 1996b: 43–57; Scholte, 1997a: 427–452). For the rest I look to Africa for inspiration—to be educated rather than to educate.

The chapter takes three main steps to explore, with respect to Africa, the community dimension of security in the contemporary globalizing world. The first section briefly reviews the principal models of community that have operated in the modern world system, namely, cosmopolitanism and communitarianism. Both approaches are found to have severe limitations. The second section elaborates different ways that contemporary globalization has affected community in Africa. The spread of transborder relations is shown, on the whole, to have weakened state-nations while encouraging a growth of various substate, regional, and transworld forms of community. The third and final section considers whether and how, in the light of African experiences, globalization might offer opportunities to create new forms of community, arrangements that would provide more substantial cohesion and thus greater security. Although it is too early to draw definitive conclusions on this last point, already some promising possibilities for nonuniversalist postidentity communities can be noted in Africa.

Frameworks of Community

With considerable—but not excessive—simplification, we can distinguish two principal approaches to community in the modern world system: cosmopolitanism and communitarianism (Brown, 1992: Part 1; Phillips and Wallerstein, 1985: 159–171). The general features of each model are described briefly below, together with certain shortcomings. Some recent alternative conceptions of community are noted at the end of this section. Admittedly this summary discussion will not do full justice to the variety and detail of theories of community or to the sophistication of some of the formulations. Nevertheless, the critical overview will provide a conceptual context for the subsequent discussion of community in Africa under circumstances of globalization.

Cosmopolitanism

In brief, cosmopolitanism posits the existence of a (latent) single community of humankind and urges that people accord their highest respect and loyalty to this universal community, above any other social collectivity. For cosmopolitans, constructions of social cohesion that divide humanity (e.g., by nationality, race, or gender) are acceptable only insofar as they do not inhibit—and preferably promote—the actualization of the universal human community. Thus, from a cosmopolitan perspective, the state, religious groups, and other "partial communities" have no value that is separate from and prior to the all-encompassing world community.

For cosmopolitans with a religious approach, the basis for universal solidarity lies in devotion to a common God. Meanwhile secularists derive cosmopolitanism from a scientifically discoverable "human nature"; thus all people are the same before they are different and belong together before they belong apart. In their different ways, both religious and secular cosmopolitans believe that a universally shared understanding of the world and a universal moral code will secure an all-inclusive human community. This common morality of humankind (whether articulated in the Ten Commandments, the Universal Declaration of Human Rights, or some other pronouncement) takes priority over any norms that are particular to a specific group.

It should be stressed that although some cosmopolitans have argued for the creation of a world state, this outcome is not intrinsic to cosmopolitanism. The point for cosmopolitans is to realize universal social cohesion among humankind. The institutional form that underpins this solidarity is a secondary question, and it has multiple possible answers. These include anarchy, federalism, and a universal church as well as a centralized world government.

Several strands of cosmopolitan thinking can be distinguished in contemporary history. For their part, adherents of certain world religions such as Christianity and Islam have promoted the principle of a universal human community rooted in a particular faith and creed. The task is therefore to bring all nonbelievers into the City of God, or the *umma* (community of Muslims). From a secular perspective, Kantian arguments have defined cosmopolitanism in terms of (1) a world order founded on a federation of republican states and (2) a duty of all persons to accord hospitality to strangers. Meanwhile utilitarian-liberal arguments have maintained that a single "open" world market will yield the greatest happiness for humankind as a whole. In contrast, Marxist arguments have proposed that a worldwide solidarity of workers, based on class interest, provides the means for achieving universal human emancipation. A similar logic informs some feminist arguments that worldwide women's solidarity opens the way to a society free of inequality, oppression, war, and underdevelopment.

As will be elaborated later in this chapter, contemporary history in Africa shows a number of cosmopolitan impulses, for example, in humanitarian assistance and calls for global distributive justice. It will also be seen that globalization has played a considerable part in encouraging these tendencies. However, at the present juncture we should note that cosmopolitan notions of a universal community of humankind have several major problems.

First, both religious and secular constructions of cosmopolitanism posit the existence of certain essential truths that apply across all cultural contexts; however, many people throughout the world reject this premise. Cosmopolitan projects are unworkable unless a consensus exists on this epistemological point. From the perspective of the late twentieth century, no such consensus is in prospect. Nor is it clear that such a development would be desirable given the loss of cultural diversity involved.

Second, in the absence of a universal agreement on universal norms, universalistic claims have in practice reflected particularistic experiences and interests. In most (albeit not all) cases, affirmations of purportedly universal standpoints have emanated from centers of structural power in the modern world system. Thus cosmopolitan arguments can usually be traced to the North, to professional classes, to European languages, to white persons, and to men. These attributes do not as such invalidate the views being expressed; however, the structurally and culturally specific sources of cosmopolitan arguments do put into question their claims to universal relevance. Indeed, cosmopolitans have rarely arrived at their position following extensive, open, respectful, and reciprocal exchanges with persons of different heritages, religions, classes, races, genders, sexual orientations, ecological settings, and so on.

Third, lacking a basis in dialogues about and negotiations of difference, modern cosmopolitan projects have easily become acts of domination. Thus, for example, many conversions to universalist religions have been effected in the context of colonial rule. Similarly, the leaders of poor and vulnerable countries have often adopted a universal model of development when grants, credits, supplies, and equipment from the North are attached. Any community of humankind forged through such unequal, top-down relations constrains the capacities of persons in subordinated positions (i.e., the majority on earth) to define themselves and shape their destiny. It would seem difficult to reconcile an undemocratically constituted cosmopolitan community with a maximization of human security.

Communitarianism

The principal alternative approach to community in the modern world system, communitarianism, in some respects constitutes a defensive reaction against an imposition of cosmopolitan projects. Communitarian arguments define social solidarity primarily in terms of divisions of humanity and entertain appeals to a transcendent community of humankind only insofar as such propositions do not compromise the interests of a given group. For communitarians, heterogeneity comes before homogeneity: fundamental differences between peoples are more important in producing social cohesion than an underlying commonality of humankind as a whole. Communitarians do not understand "we" in an all-inclusive sense but in contradistinction to "them." Communities are framed with reference to sharply drawn lines between "inside" and "outside."

Communitarianism is best known as an argument for the moral worth of the modern sovereign territorial state. This structure of governance allegedly provides the highest available guarantee of social solidarity, which is mainly achieved by uniting a state's permanent population around a banner of nationhood. The nationality principle holds that persons find social cohesion through particular shared experiences (e.g., of language, customs, sensibilities) that distinguish them from other similarly constituted groupings. State and nation have been deeply intertwined in the modern world system, so much so that we often conflate the two terms. On the one hand, the state has taken a leading role in nation-building—through school curricula, conscription, production of national symbols, and so on. Concurrently, promises of national self-determination have given modern states their principal source of legitimacy. Through this relationship of powerful reciprocal reinforcement, territorial state-nations rose in the course of the nineteenth and early twentieth centuries to become the foremost framework of community in the world system. This predominant position has been reflected, inter alia, in our habit of discussing modern world politics with a vocabulary of "international relations."

Yet communitarian assumptions have informed other types of sectoral solidarities besides nationalism. The logic of mutually defining us/them, inside/outside groupings has manifested itself not only along lines of national/foreigner but also in oppositions of black/white, coreligionist/nonbeliever, East/West, proprietor/proletarian, and so on. Such alternative communal groupings have long existed in the modern world system in a subordinate position to state-nations. More recently, however, globalization has intensified identity politics in which communities based on gender, race, sexuality, age (more particularly youth), class, and so on have increasingly challenged the primacy of the nationality principle (Scholte, 1996b: 581–589).

Nonterritorial constructions of sectoral communities can appear to exhibit certain cosmopolitan tendencies. After all, they notionally incorporate blacks, gays, and other groups the world over. However, in common with nations, these alternative forms of social solidarity rest on group distinctions and exclusions rather than on notions of an all-inclusive community of humankind. Their primary logic is thus one of world-scale communitarianism as opposed to cosmopolitanism.

Like cosmopolitanism, communitarianism has faced major problems in practice. To begin with, this approach makes the unviable assumption that humankind can be neatly divided into mutually exclusive identity communities. For communitarianism to produce reliable conditions of community, interacting persons must all draw their distinctions between "us" and "them" along the same lines. Yet prospective members of a community almost never have a shared understanding of that community's boundaries; thus the group is at best only loosely cohesive.

For instance, it has historically proved almost impossible to achieve a tight and stable match between nation, state, and territory. On the one hand, many persons who identify themselves with a particular nation have fallen outside the jurisdiction of the corresponding territorial state. The many examples of this phenomenon include overseas Chinese, expatriate Indians, and the Somali diaspora. Conversely, many persons who reside inside a country have not identified with the corresponding national project. For instance, some would-be members of a state-nation have instead accorded their primary allegiance to a substate ethno-nation (e.g., Kikuyu) or to a suprastate region-nation (e.g., Europe) or to one of the transstate diasporas mentioned above. As we will see later, contemporary globalization has intensified the trend toward competing state, substate, and regional nationalisms in Africa.

These problems of ambiguous, overlapping, and contending definitions of "inside" and "outside" become even greater when nonterritorial identities are added to the equation. In practice, a person has, in addition to nationality, multiple dimensions of identity that are not fixed to a particular place: gender, religion, profession, kinship, and so on. The precise mix of identity ingredients varies considerably from person to person, and individuals emphasize different aspects in different contexts of their lives, even from one moment to the next.

Thus definitions of group affiliations are rarely as singular, clear, and fixed in practice as communitarianism supposes in theory. Effective community cannot be constructed on the basis of unidimensional and stable identities, since a person invariably has multiple and fluid identities. Communitarianism demands that people are what they are not, which is hardly conducive to genuine security.

Indeed, an insistence on communitarianism has invariably resulted in violence, both toward the "we" and toward the "them." In respect of the "inside," communitarianism has implied conformity and in the process often suppressed difference. Thus the history of state-nations is littered with instances where governments have used force against indigenous peoples, class movements, and other alternative loci of group loyalty in order to create and sustain (purported) national unity. On broadly similar lines, some feminists have sought to impose an artificial unity on women the world over. For their part religious fundamentalists have suppressed diversity within the faith. Earlier this century, West and East opposed difference within their respective Cold War blocs. And so the list of enforced unities continues.

In respect of the "outside," meanwhile, communitarianism has often consolidated the solidarity of "we" through a denigration of "them." In these instances unity is achieved across the diversity within a nation, class, religious group, or whatever by constructing "the other" in terms of inferiority, evil, or threats. For example, many nationalists have deplored the invasion of their language by foreign words or the "infection" of the national population with foreign genes. The logic of communitarianism thus tends to be negative, and the cohesion of the group becomes correspondingly artificial and shallow.

Communitarianism has also often built community through violence with exclusions of the "other." In this vein states have blocked various cross-border movements of people, goods, finance, and so on in the name of national interest. With communitarian logic, different racist groups have sought a removal of blacks, Arabs, whites, Hispanics, or whatever "other." For their part, some radical feminists have defined their solidarity in part through a segregation from men. On some occasions these exclusionary measures are defensive reactions, particularly by subordinated circles against feared erasure by a dominant group. Although this motivation is understandable, violence has in such instances begotten violence, which is in the longer term no formula for security of community.

Alternatives?

Thus far we have established some fundamental flaws in the two principal conventional approaches to constructing community in the modern world system: universalist cosmopolitanism and culturally relativist communitarianism. To be sure, in practice many people do not adhere rigidly to these models and handle questions of community with a shifting mix of cosmopolitan and communitarian impulses. For example, a person may at one moment espouse universal human rights through Amnesty International and at the next turn invoke ethnonationalism to demand Scottish independence. These contradictions tend to make the attainment of community along cosmopolitan or communitarian lines even more elusive.

However, these two perspectives do not exhaust the possible frameworks of community. Several other approaches are also available, although they have to date usually taken a backseat to the leading two schools of thought. Yet the pursuit of alternatives that neither suppress nor exclude difference might yield greater opportunities to build substantive social solidarity and thus enhance human security.

A first nonuniversalist, nonculturalist approach to community shifts the emphasis to a microlevel, where social solidarity is based on face-to-face contacts and directly supplied mutual services. This localist answer to the challenge of forging social cohesion champions grassroots activity in so-called community-based organizations (CBOs). Its advocates maintain that the "third sector" of voluntary associations seals bonds of social solidarity that the state and the market cannot adequately provide (Etzioni, 1995).

Microcommunities have much to commend them. For one thing, localism offers an inclusive framework, encompassing all persons in a given neighborhood or district. Second, this local solidarity normally develops out of positive acts of mutual assistance rather than negative acts of denigration or exclusion of outsiders. Third, authoritarian dynamics of the sort that usually accompany cosmopolitanism and communitarianism are on the whole less likely to afflict localism inasmuch as centers of power at the grassroots are usually readily identifiable and always close at hand to be challenged. Fourth, small-scale and face-to-face contacts in microcommunities can be conducive to conflict resolution through dialogue and accommodation rather than suppression of weaker parties.

However, localism has its shortcomings as well. First, it would be wrong to assume that a local context ipso facto guarantees community. Some proponents of localist alternatives are inclined to romanticize the grass roots as being somehow inherently more genuine and generous than other constructions of community. Yet graft and oppression can infest the most intimate of associations. Local programs enhance community only when they are carefully designed, well run, adequately resourced, and democratically accountable.

Second, even the best constructed and operated local entity is inadequate on its own as a formula for community. Most people in contemporary society cannot fulfill all of their material and affective needs within the confines of their immediate environs. Many services cannot be provided locally, and most persons reach out to a wider world to develop various dimensions of their identity. Hence an effective design of community must incorporate multiple contexts besides the local.

Cosmopolitanism and communitarianism have failed as designs for larger-scale social cohesion because each has depended on violence: they cannot attain community without negating it. Both approaches impose homogeneity on situations of heterogeneity, and both tend to assume that once attained, communities will be static. The challenge for theories and practices of community is therefore to secure social solidarity among large, heterogeneous populations in contexts of continual social change.

It would contradict the preceding observations if we were now purportedly to solve the problem of community with a single and fixed formula. However, in the present context of a globalizing world the following set of five general suggestions could provide a constructive starting point. The particular formulation is mine, but the ideas are broadly drawn from contemporary critical theory and postmodernism.

First, social solidarity is more likely to flourish when the parties to it have person-to-person relationships with one another. Bonds of nationality, race, gender, and other social categories rest on anonymity, but partners in a veritable community are subjects rather than objects for each other. Such intimacy has traditionally been attained in households and other immediate territorial locales. In addition, however, contemporary developments in communications technologies such as the telephone and electronic mail have allowed close relationships to form regardless of the number of miles between persons. With such connections it is possible to have a global community of, say, AIDS sufferers as well as a local community in an African village.

Second, both within microcommunities and in their relations with the wider world, people should recognize, respect, and celebrate difference— both within and among themselves. All social groupings from township to nation to profession and religious communion contain diversity as well as commonality, and a veritable community cannot be constructed out of the similarities alone. Moreover, the accommodation and, indeed, promotion of difference should be seen as a positive opportunity for creating social solidarity rather than—following conventional assumptions—as a hindrance.

Third, a deeper security of community is available through a fundamental shift in mentality from "othering" to reciprocity. Social cohesion can then be approached in terms of connection points rather than dividing lines. Community is made from hybridity, not myths of self-contained groups. No purity can be diluted if it has never existed in the first place. Hence the challenge is to build community out of combinations and to develop interculturality in circumstances of respectful dialogue and with every attempt to compensate for power inequalities among the partners.

Fourth, community will advance circumstances of security when parties have a sense of responsibility for one other. Veritable social cohesion rests on more than stories of a glorious collective past and future. It requires also concrete acts of solidarity in the here and now, particularly toward the needy and vulnerable. This is not to resurrect hierarchical and paternalistic charity of the kind that has underlain feudalism and liberal imperialism, for example. Moreover, parties in seeming need must always retain the right to refuse proffered "help." Still, constructive interculturality requires critical responsibility, an ethic of care, a will among all partners in a community to advance one another's welfare in mutually acceptable ways.

Fifth, alternative ethics of community must accord a central role to restraint. It should not be imagined that new emphases on intimacy, a celebration of difference, interculturality, and responsibility will eliminate difficulties of communication and divergent material interests. However, the mode of conflict management can change from the proclivity toward violence, which has marked cosmopolitanism and communitarianism, to an alternative priority for restraint. The challenge is to develop politics of persuasion without compulsion.

The preceding remarks sketch no more than a general—what some might call postmodern—perspective on community. Putting these guiding principles into practice is problematic, of course. For one thing, old habits of cosmopolitanism and communitarianism can sabotage the effort and have to be resisted at every turn—while still respecting the rule of restraint. Moreover, implementation must vary between contexts across time and space; the formula is in this sense neither singular nor fixed. Some of these challenges are explored in relation to Africa later in this chapter.

The sorts of new thinking about community just mentioned have appeared concurrently in history with the unprecedented spread, intensification, and acceleration of globalization. Indeed, as later discussion in this chapter will elaborate, arguments for localism and interculturality have arisen partly in reaction to globalization. Now we turn to an elaboration of the connections between globalization and community in Africa.

Failures of Old-Style Communities

As noted in the introduction to this chapter, many social commentators have worried that globalization is making conventional designs of community unworkable. On the one hand, although in terms of social geography the world has in some respects become a single place, cosmopolitan designs are far from being realized. On the other hand, the spread of transworld flows has made communitarian solidarities even more problematic than they were when territorial distance and borders could provide some degree of buffer between groups.

The present section explores these difficulties with reference to contemporary Africa. On this continent, as elsewhere in the world, the growth of supraterritorial relations has sometimes reinforced but more usually emphasized the inadequacies of social cohesion focused on humankind, state-nations, substate ethno-nations, suprastate region-nations, and transborder groups. To be sure, developments in the character of communities in Africa cannot be wholly explained as a consequence of globalization, but the growth of transborder connections has often figured significantly.

Cosmopolitanism

Prima facie globalization would seem to answer cosmopolitan hopes. After all, global communications give people all over the world an unprecedented intimacy with one another. Global products and global consciousness encourage cultural homogenization on a world scale. A global financial system and global ecological degradation present humankind with common interests worldwide. As Anthony Giddens has observed, with globalization "humankind in some respects becomes a 'we,'" facing problems and opportunities where there are no 'others' (Giddens, 1991: 27).

These general trends are also reflected in an increase of cosmopolitan conceptions of community in and toward Africa. For one thing, global organizations (official, commercial, and voluntary) have, together with bilateral donors and locally based partners, ensured that a universalist discourse of development has dominated the policy agenda in postcolonial Africa. Elite circles in particular have generally assumed that Africa must participate in a common human project of mechanization, commercialization, individualization, and rationalization—in short, of modernization.

A second major way that transborder relations have promoted cosmopolitanism in regard to contemporary Africa has come in the context of revealingly named "humanitarian" assistance. Global mass media in particular have played a key role in mobilizing the so-called world community to provide emergency relief in disaster situations. In July 1985, for example, satellite transmissions brought the Live Aid pop concerts simultaneously to half the countries of the world and yielded almost $4 billion in donations for twenty drought-stricken countries of Africa. Similar scenarios have unfolded—albeit with less spectacle—in respect of Biafra in the late 1960s, the Sahel in 1972–1974, Somalia in the early 1990s, Rwanda in the mid-1990s, and so on. Electronic mass communications have on such occasions produced empathy with previously distant strangers and a universalist ethic of care. Transborder organizations like the evocatively named Médecins sans Frontières have then effected much of the relief effort.

Globalization has further promoted cosmopolitan tendencies in Africa through the growth in the second half of the twentieth century of a substantial transworld human rights movement. Universalism is of course inherent in the concept of *human* rights, even when it is argued that there are African and other cultural variants of the underlying norms (An-Na'im and Deng, 1990). African states have since the 1960s acceded in large numbers to UN-sponsored covenants and conventions on human rights as well as the region-specific African (Banjul) Charter of Human and People's Rights, signed in 1981 and operative since 1986 (Hamalengwa et al., 1988). Outside official circles, the Anti-Apartheid Movement, launched in 1959, was one of the world's first major transborder human rights campaigns. Amnesty International now counts sections and groups in fifteen African countries, plus individual supporters in several dozen more.

Cosmopolitan tendencies have furthermore underlain global campaigns for world-scale distributive justice vis-à-vis Africa. Among states, this striving had its strongest expression in 1970s calls for a new international economic order (NIEO). On this occasion governments throughout Africa joined with regimes across the so-called South to demand reforms in global institutions and regulations that would produce a redistribution of world wealth in favor of poor countries. The NIEO campaign fizzled out in the early 1980s, but African states have continued to advocate global distributive justice in a (now substantially weakened) Third World coalition. Meanwhile nongovernmental organizations (NGOs) based in the North as well as the South have implicitly invoked cosmopolitan assumptions in their promotion of distributive justice for Africa. For example, Africa-based lobbies such as Afrodad and Uganda Debt Network have collaborated with North-based associations such as Eurodad in transborder campaigns to lessen iniquitous debt burdens in Africa.

A final area where globalization has increased cosmopolitan impulses involving Africa lies in transworld environmentalism. Global ecological issues have prompted the creation of a number of associations and campaigns in which Africans work together with environmentalists across the world in the (supposed) interest of humankind as a whole. For example, Rainforest Action Network includes members in ten African countries, and Earth-Action Network has member organizations in forty-two African countries.

The various programs just reviewed all have laudable aspects; nevertheless, they also exhibit the general objectionable qualities of cosmopolitanism discussed earlier. To begin with, in each case transworld collaboration has generally demanded that all parties endorse one particular understanding of development, human rights, sustainability, and so on. Africans have rarely held much initiative in constructing the essential truths on which the "universal community of humankind" should be based. As a result, we cannot be confident that the purported common interests of humanity in fact reflect the needs and priorities of most Africans.

Indeed, African participation in cosmopolitan projects is generally limited to a small elite. For example, planning for development has generally entailed a small African cadre working with externally based institutions. African membership of human rights and environmental movements is also extremely small and weak. Campaigns for a more just world economic order likewise have rarely given an active role to the victims of the injustices. In short, cosmopolitan initiatives involving Africa have generally had very shaky democratic foundations.

In fact, cosmopolitan strivings—however well intentioned their proponents might be—have in many instances produced acts of subordination. Thus orthodox discourses on development and human rights have tended to marginalize alternative perspectives. Humanitarian assistance has often created a mentality of dependence among recipients. African development and environmental NGOs are usually largely dependent on North-based funders and tend to respond to externally generated agendas.

A final major objection to cosmopolitan projects in respect of Africa is that they have delivered few concrete results. Four decades of "development" have borne little fruit for many Africans and bypassed others altogether. Time after time, the cosmopolitan sentiments that drive humanitarian assistance toward Africa have dissipated after the television crew leaves. For its part, the human rights movement has to date constructed little effective monitoring and enforcement machinery in Africa. Campaigns for global distributive justice have presided over a substantial growth in world inequality, from which Africa has suffered more than any other continent. As mentioned earlier, global environmentalism has concentrated on climate conventions and trade in endangered species, whereas types of ecological degradation that have more immediate and more threatening impacts on Africans are relatively ignored. In sum, although cosmopolitanism may have comforted liberal souls in elite circles, it is doubtful that it has improved human security for the majority of Africans.

Tethered State-Nations

Regarding communitarianism, in many ways globalization has pulled the rug out from under the modern national project in Africa. The continent was a late entrant in the world-historical game of creating territorial communities that matched state jurisdictions. As a result, the artificiality of national solidarities was generally more glaring in Africa than elsewhere in the world when globalization intensified in the mid–twentieth century. As will be elaborated, certain dynamics of globalization have subsequently undermined state-nations in Africa still further.

Colonial territorial boundaries in Africa usually bore no relation to the preexistent cultural geography. Moreover, to the limited extent that colonial administrations in Africa engaged in nation-building, they generally did so mainly to further the growth of modern states and not to promote social solidarity per se. For their part, the colonized usually invoked the nationality principle primarily as a tool in the struggle against European rule and less as a foundation for long-term social solidarity in the respective territories. In any case, anticolonial campaigns in Africa were usually too brief and insufficiently intense to forge a deep and lasting sense of national unity. Emergent modern elites in Africa employed the discourse of nationalism chiefly to gain recognition in the wider world of tellingly named inter*national* relations. However, this talk of nationhood usually did not reflect real-life sentiments of community in the majority of the colonized populations.

Hence at the moment of decolonization—which roughly coincided with the acceleration of globalization—state-nations in Africa were generally weak. Since then, the spread of transborder relations has in general exacerbated the African state's incapacity to execute an effective national project. Globalization has had this implication in three main ways: by making sovereign statehood impossible, by fostering the growth of supra-territorial constituencies, and by discouraging interstate warfare (Scholte, 1997b: 13–30; Scholte, 1997a: 440–452). Elsewhere in the world the rise of supraterritoriality has provoked many nationalist reactions (Scholte, 1996a: 589–590), but this dynamic has operated little in Africa.

Historically, the modern state's attribute of sovereignty has played an important role in the formation and perpetuation of national communities. A crucial relationship of mutual reinforcement operated—especially from the late eighteenth to the mid–twentieth century—between assertions of state sovereignty on the one hand and affirmations of national self-determination on the other (Hobsbawm, 1992). The state claimed supreme, comprehensive, and exclusive rule over its territorial jurisdiction; and the native (however defined) population of that territory correspondingly claimed a singular and unique national character. The state was accorded a monopoly of governance, and the nationality principle was accorded a par-allel monopoly of community. Of course social organization was often not so clear-cut in practice, but sovereignty bound nation and state tightly to-gether at the heart of world order, particularly in the first half of the twen-tieth century.

Owing to globalization, this dynamic of nation-building has not fig-ured in Africa nearly as much as it did elsewhere in the world at earlier historical junctures. By the time African states obtained legal sovereignty, the growth of transborder relations was making the principle impractica-ble. African states have been sovereign in name only. Most postcolonial governments in Africa have been dependent on, for example, global cur-rencies and credits, transworld languages such as English and French, global products for much military and other technical equipment, and as-sistance from transborder NGOs. Also in the face of globalization, gov-ernments in Africa have, like states everywhere, become increasingly in-volved in multilateral (as opposed to unilateral sovereign) governance through a variety of regional and worldwide arrangements. Indeed, in a sign of globalizing times, the Organization of African Unity (OAU) has subtly relaxed its previous uncompromising insistence on the sanctity of inherited state borders and the principle of nonintervention in internal af-fairs. Thus, for example, the OAU supervised a cease-fire in Rwanda in 1991 and became involved in the referendum on Eritrean independence in 1993 (Jonah, 1994: 10–12).

For these reasons and more, the parallelism between statism and na-tionalism has had a limited role in African history. It has been incongru-ous—and to that extent difficult—for African governments to espouse the principle of a single, distinctive, and exclusive national community for their respective territories when their states have not exercised supreme and exclusive authority over those jurisdictions.

The spread of transborder relations has further compromised the African state's promotion of national solidarity insofar as governments have often ruled with an eye not only to their territorial constituency but also to supraterritorial interests. Indeed, a regime in Africa might even give top priority to, for instance, providing an attractive investment climate for transworld companies or ensuring inflows from global financial markets or securing assistance from global governance agencies. In many cases ruling circles in Africa derive much of their power and wealth from supraterritorial channels. To that extent contemporary African elites have perceived less urgency to forge national solidarity in their respective countries than did, say, governing classes in other parts of the world before the onset of globalization.

Globalization has also hampered the consolidation of national communities in postcolonial Africa insofar as the growth of supraterritorial interests has introduced major disincentives to interstate warfare. In earlier times armed conflicts between states substantially reinforced national solidarity in countries of Europe, the Americas, and much of Asia (Hayes, 1966: Chapter 6; Finer, 1975). Yet the more than fifty states of Africa have—in spite of widespread violence of other kinds—on the whole only rarely engaged in warfare against each other since the 1950s. Apart from a handful of armed anticolonial struggles (e.g., in Algeria and former Portuguese-ruled territories), Africans have therefore not undergone the nation-building experience of interstate, inter*national* war.

Globalization does not provide a sole explanation of the relative absence of war between states in Africa and worldwide. However, historically unprecedented levels of global interconnections among people—and in particular the emergence of transborder official, business, and professional classes—have presented major countervailing forces against armed violence between states. In postcolonial Africa there has been far more warfare *within* than between states. Thus in Africa war has more often damaged than enhanced the development of state-nations while frequently promoting the growth of substate nations of the kind described in the following section.

Indeed, it would seem that only a minority of Africans today look to the state as their chief, let alone exclusive, bearer of community. Recent cuts in government provision of employment and services—largely in the context of SAPs—have eroded the state's precarious social base still further. Large proportions of African populations now regard the state as irrelevant or as a house of banditry or as a purveyor of indifference and cruelty (Cheru, 1989). Extreme critics attack the contemporary state in Africa as a "curse," as being "as hateful to many of the people inside it as the old colonial state was before" (Davidson, 1992; Cheru, 1989: 206). Frequently the leadership of African states has been culturally closer to a global modern elite than to the rural majority populace. In the rare exceptions to this rule, the governors in question have usually become army-backed tyrants like Jean-Bedel Bokassa in his self-styled central African empire or Samuel Doe in Liberia (Kokole, 1996: 131). When we take these circumstances in sum, it is little wonder that Africa has led the contemporary world in so-called collapsed states, including at various times Chad, Ethiopia, Liberia, Sierra Leone, Somalia, Uganda, and more (Zartman, 1995).

On the whole, then, the state-nation has not provided contemporary Africa with an effective framework of social cohesion, and a good part of the cause lies in globalization. Apart from Somalia, states are unlikely to vanish altogether from the African scene, but they seem just as unlikely to provide Africa's inhabitants with the security of community. Epitomizing this failure, a group of refugees from Rwanda sheltering in Uganda recently refused to sing "their" national anthem when "their" ambassador paid a visit (*The New Vision* [Kampala], July 26, 1997). Indeed, the roots of state-nations are generally so shallow in Africa that people have not—as in many other parts of the world—been able to draw on state-centered nationalism to express resistance to globalization.

To be sure, a few states in Africa have during the time of globalization deepened a sense of national solidarity in their populations. Such a trend is discernible in Eritrea and Namibia, for example, where long and ultimately successful armed decolonization struggles have been followed by concerted efforts at national reconciliation. Presidents Nelson Mandela of the Republic of South Africa (RSA) and Yoweri Museveni of Uganda have also worked with some effect to rally different ethnic and religious elements around a state-centered national banner. However, as will be elaborated later, the secret of their success probably lies in their avoidance of a communitarian approach to building social solidarity.

Ethno-Nations

As briefly noted, many Africans have in contemporary times of globalization rejected the state-nation and instead looked to smaller ethnic (or tribal) groupings as their basis for social solidarity. In this way developments in Africa have, as elsewhere in the world, manifested a dynamic whereby globalization has unfolded concurrently with—and encouraged—localization (Swyngedouw, 1989: 31–42; Hall, 1991: 19–39; Bird et al., 1993; Friedman, 1994; Robertson, 1995: 25–44). The spread of supraterritoriality has not been the sole impetus behind resurgent ethnonationalism in Africa, but it has ranked as an important contributory cause of this communitarian turn.

The contemporary worldwide rise of substate ethnonationalism has found fertile ground in Africa insofar as only a few states on the continent (e.g., Lesotho, Somalia) have had anything approximating a monoethnic population. It is more usual for a country in Africa to house multiple cultural heritages, dozens of languages (e.g., more than sixty in Côte d'Ivoire), several religions, and other types of diversity. If we take ethnonationalism to its conclusion, Africa would be fragmented into several hundred territorial units rather than the fifty-some states of today.

Although many ethnic traditions in Africa have a long ancestry, they did not define mutually exclusive and competing "tribes" until colonial times—and often largely as a consequence of colonial policy (Davidson, 1992: 100–101). Since decolonization, substate ethnonationalism (sometimes more pejoratively called tribalism) has posed a powerful challenge to state-nations in many African countries. Some of these movements have sought to capture an existing territorial state for narrow communal interests; others have pursued greater autonomy within or outright secession from their state.

As already noted, globalization does not provide a single-factor explanation for the rise of ethnonationalism in Africa; however, the spread of transborder networks has in at least two broad ways helped to create an environment conducive to the pursuit of these substate nations. First, as elaborated earlier, transborder relations have tended to undermine the state-nation as a locus of community. In this light, contemporary ethnonationalism in Africa may be understood as a response to the (globalization-induced) eclipse of sovereign statehood and the resultant search for other, more reliable frameworks of social solidarity. Moreover, where globalization has encouraged a government to ignore or positively disadvantage part or even most of its resident population, a turn to tribalism can signal an attempt to disengage from the territorial state.

A second way that the spread of supraterritoriality has fueled ethnonationalism in Africa is more affective in nature. To paraphrase Raimondo Strassoldo, the contemporary worldwide rise of smaller-scale communities can be appreciated partly as a psychological search for enclaves of familiarity and intimacy at a time when globalization has exposed persons to unfathomable expanses of locations, people, things, and ideas all at once (Strassoldo, 1992: 46). In this light, substate nationalisms in Africa constitute more than attempts to secure such material welfare as the central government often fails to provide. These programs generally also seek to carve out spheres of cultural distinctiveness and political autonomy in reaction against top-down and homogenizing tendencies in globalization. Moreover, in circumstances where globalization has unsettled established social structures, ethnonationalism holds out the (illusory) promise of providing the emotional security that is (allegedly) gained from rediscovering and sustaining one's (supposed) primordial identity.

In practice, however, ethnonationalism has added little to human security in Africa. On the contrary, these substate nationalist strivings in

Africa have often turned violent, provoking civil war in Angola, Burundi, Ethiopia, Liberia, Nigeria, Sudan, Uganda, Western Sahara, and elsewhere. In one of the more horrifying scenarios, an extreme communitarianism brought genocide to Rwanda in 1994 with a massacre of 800,000, mainly Tutsis. Ethnonationalism has also contributed substantially to major problems of displaced persons and refugees in Africa.

Toward Region-Nations?

Next to a growth in substate nationalism, globalization has also encouraged a worldwide move to communitarianism writ large through the formation of suprastate communities on regional lines. The chief examples of this trend toward (as yet incipient) suprastate nations lie in Western Europe, the Americas, and Southeast Asia; however, regionalism has not entirely bypassed Africa (Mistry, 1996; Teunissen, 1996). Several regional trade agreements and currency areas appeared south of the Sahara in the aftermath of decolonization. The past decade has, moreover, seen aspirations to develop wider and deeper regional solidarity. Principal initiatives in this regard include the formation of the Arab Maghreb Union (AMU) in 1989, the creation of the Southern African Development Community (SADC) in 1992, and the launch of the Common Market for Eastern and Southern Africa (COMESA) in 1994. On a continental scale, the 1991 OAU summit agreed to create the African Economic Community (AEC) on the lines of the European Union (EU). Although the Abuja Treaty received the required number of ratifications to enter into force in 1994, concrete steps in the envisioned thirty-four-year process toward an AEC have thus far been limited (Naldi, 1992: 203–243; Ajomo and Adewale, 1993).

By no means has globalization been the only force propelling suprastate regional projects in Africa and elsewhere in the contemporary world, but transborder relations have encouraged the trend in several general ways (Hine, 1992: 115–123; Hettne and Inotai, 1994; Gamble and Payne, 1996: 247–264). For one thing, technologies of global communication make possible a tight coordination of activities on large regional scales. Second, regional common markets provide convenience and economies of scale for the distribution and sale of global products. Third, regional customs unions facilitate the development of transborder production processes, where different stages in a production process are sited in different countries in accordance with endowment and cost advantages. Fourth, and in a more reactive sense, regionalism can be a macronationalist, neoprotectionist defense against the turbulence associated with globalizing capitalism and the imposition of global culture. Calls to turn the EU into "Fortress Europe" well illustrate the latter dynamic.

None of these regionalizing impulses of globalization have operated very strongly in Africa, and to this extent it is not surprising that on the whole, regionalism has to date not proved a very promising formula for community in the continent. Various projects like the Economic Community of West African States (ECOWAS), launched in 1975, have made only slow progress. Other schemes of regional integration in Africa have remained paper agreements (like the Economic Community of the Great Lakes Countries) or have collapsed altogether (as the East African Community did in 1977). The Organization of African Unity has done comparatively little in thirty-five years of existence to make good its name. Indeed, Julius Nyerere, the former president of Tanzania, is reported to have quipped that "the OAU exists only for the protection of African Heads of State" (El-Ayouty, 1994: 179). As for the AEC, one critic has—it would seem rightly—dismissed the initiative as "a mere copy, though on a larger scale, of the existing unworkable integration arrangements in [Africa]" (Aly, 1994: 89).

In any case, most regional initiatives in Africa have had a chiefly commercial motivation with little parallel drive to deepen social cohesion among the populations of participating countries. Exceptionally, the Economic Community of West Africa (CEAO) has included the Solidarity Fund, which has given poorer members priority access to credits and guarantees, and the Community Development Fund, through which the richer member states have paid fiscal compensation to the others (Mistry, 1996: 89–90). Meanwhile, apart from a few transborder professional associations, development NGOs, and women's organizations, very little civil society has emerged on regional lines to give a social complement to prospective common markets in Africa.

In short, it is questionable whether regionalism—certainly on its own—offers a viable formula for community in contemporary Africa. At best, regional solidarities might provide a secondary layer of community behind a primary emphasis on state-nations, substate associations, and other constructions. However, according to present trends the significance of regionalism for Africa is more as a mechanism of exclusion from the North (in the form of the EU, the North American Free Trade Area, and Asia-Pacific Economic Cooperation) than as a mode of inclusion and reciprocity within the continent itself.

Transborder Communities

State-nations, substate groupings, and regional units all broadly conform to a territorial logic of community; in addition, though, globalization has propelled the development in Africa of certain transworld solidarities of the kind described in the first part of this chapter. Such a trend is not surprising inasmuch as a growth of supraterritorial spaces might be expected to encourage the formation of communities whose membership is likewise not defined by territorial location, distance, and borders. Among the transborder groupings mentioned earlier, those connected to race, religion, and gender have had the most relevance in contemporary Africa.

Transborder solidarity of race—and more particularly of black Africans with other black people the world over—first developed in the late nineteenth and early twentieth centuries. The intercontinental Pan-Africanist Movement held its first conference in 1893, and in the mid-1920s the Universal Negro Improvement Association, under the leadership of Marcus Garvey, encompassed over 900 chapters across five continents (Leanne, 1994: 86–89). In more recent times, the acceleration of globalization has helped to revive notions of transworld black solidarity. For example, global communications and organizations have greatly facilitated contacts between the diaspora and the "roots." Meanwhile global marketers have promoted brands of black music, black fashion, and other symbols of a transworld black culture. Sometimes these global connections have also fostered a growth of transborder black solidarity. For instance, blacks throughout Africa and further afield were united in the struggle against apartheid, and the aforementioned African–African American summits have, inter alia, generated substantial contributions from black Americans to education efforts in Africa.

Religious bonds have provided the cement for certain other transborder solidarities in the Africa of the late twentieth century. For example, the contemporary worldwide upsurge of Islamic revivalism has touched Africa through the Muslim Brotherhood in Egypt, the National Islamic Front (FIS) in Algeria, the government of Omer el-Bashir in Sudan, and other entities. In addition, global Islamic relief organizations have contributed humanitarian assistance to various countries in Africa. In Christian circles the Roman Catholic Church and the World Council of Churches are among the institutions that have likewise sponsored solidarity between Africans and coreligionists in the world at large. In addition, a number of evangelist Protestant preachers have beamed their sermons from the United States straight onto African television screens, and in the case of Morris Cerullo, have also included stops in Africa on their world tours.

Transborder women's solidarity is a relatively more recent development in Africa, having no significant antecedents before the 1970s. Since then, African women have formed several continental associations such as the African Women's Economic Policy Network (AWEPON) and the Council for Economic Empowerment of Women in Africa (CEEWA). Women's groups from Africa have figured prominently in the four World Conferences of Women held since 1975 and in other global conferences of the 1990s.

Innovative though many of these initiatives have been, on the whole transborder communities remain quite weak in Africa. Indeed, several supraterritorial solidarities—for example, of workers and homosexuals—have played little role at all in the continent. For one thing, only small numbers of (primarily elite) Africans have participated in these networks. Even those activists have usually devoted only a small proportion of their efforts to transborder campaigning both because their resources are limited and because immediately pressing local problems exhaust most of their energies. Transworld solidarity networks have also lacked depth in Africa insofar as they have overestimated the degree of similarity among blacks, believers, and women the world over. For example, although Africans and African Americans share certain general phenotypical features and a broad experience of structural inequality, in the details of everyday life the two groups have little in common. Likewise, many African women's organizers have major clashes of perspective with their sisters from other continents. On the whole, then, transworld communities in Africa tend to be loosely cohesive and only intermittently active. Certainly on their own, these groups have not developed sufficient bonds of solidarity to create secure circumstances of community in Africa.

Beyond Cosmopolitanism and Communitarianism

The preceding section has shown that traditional formulas for community offer very little promise of human security for contemporary Africa. Cosmopolitan projects have almost invariably placed Africans in a subordinated position. With regard to communitarian designs, state-nations in Africa have rarely served collective interests, ethnonationalism has frequently turned violent, region-nations have been largely irrelevant on the continent, and transborder solidarities have been weak.

All of this suggests that Africans would do well to experiment with alternative constructions of social solidarity. A "new localism" of community-based associations and critical interculturality was mentioned in an earlier section as a potentially positive innovation in the construction of social cohesion under globalization. As is elaborated in this section of the chapter, Africans have on a number of occasions already begun to explore these possibilities to transcend cosmopolitanism and communitarianism.

A New Localism

Microcommunities at village and district levels have thrived in much of contemporary Africa. CBOs (also called voluntary development organizations—VDOs) have proliferated in many countries. (Many Africans invoke the terms CBOs and VDOs rather than NGOs in order to avoid any possible inference that such associations are directed against the state.) These grassroots initiatives have nurtured social solidarity through the collective provision of local needs in respect of sanitation, education, health care, improvements in agriculture, and so on. Much of this activity is small scale and informal, but other CBOs in Africa have developed into fairly large programs that attract attention far afield. An example of a high-profile grassroots association is the tree-planting Green Belt Movement in Kenya with over 50,000 members organized in over 2,000 local community groups (Ndegwa, 1996: 81).

Many governments in Africa have regarded CBOs warily as potential rivals. Sometimes state authorities have banned these local associations or placed them under close surveillance. In contrast, in the 1990s governments have attempted to forge partnerships with (and capture?) CBOs. An important step was taken in this direction when representatives of over 500 official and grassroots groups promulgated the African Charter for Popular Participation in Development and Transformation at Arusha, Tanzania, in February 1990 (UN Economic Commission for Africa [UNECA], 1990; Onimode, 1992: 113–122). A number of African states have subsequently formally adopted the Arusha Charter, and the 1990 OAU summit commended "popular-based political processes" (Ake, 1996: 134).

In another sign of acknowledging localism, several governments in Africa have pursued significant programs of decentralization in the 1990s. States including Benin, Eritrea, Ghana, and Uganda have delegated tasks or devolved decisionmaking authority over certain realms of policy to lower-level authorities (Manor, 1995: 81–88). In this way, too, some rulers in Africa have concluded that the success of their state is linked to fostering local communities in tandem with national solidarity.

Globalization has facilitated the contemporary growth of micro-communities in Africa in some of the same broad ways that the trend has contributed to the rise of ethnonationalism. Hence many Africans have turned to CBOs as a self-help measure to compensate for an incompetent or indifferent state. In addition, many people have promoted the new localism in order to restore a sense of intimate community that they cannot find in globalized spaces. As already suggested, most Africans cannot integrate transworld solidarities of race, gender, and religion into their everyday lives.

Globalization has also fueled the new localism insofar as many CBOs and VDOs in Africa have relied on substantial financial, technical, and moral support from supraterritorial organizations. Many of these grassroots initiatives have obtained sponsorship from transborder development NGOs such as Innovations et Réseaux pour le Développement (IRED), Netherlands Organization for International Development Cooperation (NOVIB), and Oxfam. Other support has come from official global governance agencies like UNDP, UNICEF, and the World Bank. In Uganda, for example, indigenous civil society associations such as Action for Development (ACFODE) and Development Network of Indigenous Voluntary Associations (DENIVA) that nurture grassroots activism have depended almost entirely on transborder funding. Similarly, local community welfare organizations in Liberia have worked on postwar rehabilitation and development with the aid of UN agencies and global NGOs. Meanwhile, the Movement for the Survival of the Ogoni People (MOSOP), created in 1990, has avoided dissolution by the Nigerian state in good part thanks to transworld support from environmental, human rights, and religious organizations as well as the Body Shop retail chain (Boele, 1995).

Interculturality

As noted earlier, as promising as localist initiatives can be, they are not faultless and cannot by themselves meet all the material and affective prerequisites of community. Hence the locality will invariably interlink to one extent or another with national, regional, and transworld networks. The challenge is to forge community out of these multiple and overlapping spheres. Does contemporary Africa include instances where the postmodern principles advocated earlier are practiced?

In some ways Africa might present one of the world's most auspicious contexts for such innovations. To begin with, the failings of cosmopolitanism and nationalism are probably nowhere more striking than in Africa; the search for alternatives has correspondingly greater urgency. More positively, African cultures have traditions of discussion, conciliation, magnanimity, and power-sharing that broadly parallel the suggestions made earlier for a different politics of community (Kokole, 1996: 137–139; Deng, 1996: 226).

One outstanding instance of alternative approaches to community has come in the Republic of South Africa since the dissolution of apartheid. Yesterday's warriors against racism have been magnanimous in victory. Indeed, elements from the old regime were invited into the new government elected in 1994. Amnesties and the inquiries of the Truth Commission have further advanced conciliation in the country. Threats of violent ethnonationalism from the Nkatha Freedom Party and the Afrikaner Resistance Movement have been defused. Various civic associations thrive as expressions of diversity. CBOs are active in giving voice to the poor. The foregoing comments are not meant to suggest that all is well with community in the RSA. However, the degree to which old bitter divisions have given way to social cohesion is remarkable.

The situation in Uganda under the National Revolutionary Movement (NRM) has received less attention in the world press than South Africa, but notable developments in rebuilding community have occurred since

Yoweri Museveni assumed the presidency in 1986 (Khadiagala, in Zartman, 1995: 33–47). The NRM ended years of ethnic-clientelist authoritarianism in Uganda, and in spite of a devastating civil war, its approach once it controlled the state was conciliatory. Many of its former enemies were taken into government, and traditional monarchs have seen a number of their powers restored. The NRM's "movementism" has thus far banned political parties as divisive, but parliament includes designated seats for various interest groups (labor, women, etc.) as well as territorial constituencies. Grassroots participation was secured at the outset of NRM rule through so-called resistance committees. More recently it has continued through over 10,000 CBOs and a program of decentralization begun in 1992. The government's *Poverty Elimination Action Plan,* published in 1997, resulted from two years of consultations among ministries, global governance agencies, bilateral donors, CBOs, national civic associations, and transborder NGOs. Destitution and inequality remain great in Uganda, but the time of military tyranny and unbounded ethnic strife has ended.

The South African and Ugandan cases do not exhaust the signs of innovation in contemporary Africa. As mentioned, a number of African governments have embarked on new partnerships with grassroots associations, often in collaboration with global governance agencies. In Ethiopia, meanwhile, the Tigre-dominated transitional government made an abortive attempt in 1993 to recognize cultural diversity, to permit a corresponding degree of regional autonomy, to create a multiethnic army, and so on (Keller, 1995: 138).

Clearly there should be far more security of community in Africa. Interculturality in the RSA and movementism in Uganda might yet go the way of the Ethiopian false start. Indeed, it would be naive to suggest that authoritarian and exclusionary tendencies are absent under Mandela and Museveni. To cite just one shortcoming, in Uganda the promising initiative of the Ministry of Gender and Community Development has been severely underfunded. Nevertheless, the experiments being pioneered in these situations did not—and possibly could not—occur before the current era of accelerated globalization.

Conclusion

The argument in this chapter has rested on four main points, namely that community is integral to security; community can be constructed in a variety of territorial and nonterritorial contexts; the principal modern approaches to forging community, cosmopolitanism and communitarianism, are fundamentally flawed; and globalization has opened opportunities to develop alternative and perhaps deeper conditions of community. These four theses have been explored in relation to contemporary Africa, where it has been seen that security in relation to community has generally been quite fragile. In Africa, community has mainly been pursued through various cosmopolitan, state-national, ethno-national, regional, transborder, and local frameworks. The politics of community have produced considerable violence. However, various voluntary development organizations and certain governments have in the 1990s attempted to forge community in new ways.

Globalization has encouraged the development of alternative relations of community inasmuch as transborder flows have (1) broken the near monopoly of the state and nation on political organization and (2) increased awareness of cultural diversity and hybridity. However, it remains to be seen whether the resultant opportunities to create new dynamics of community will be fully exploited. After all, cosmopolitanism and communitarianism can extend from the old territorialized world to colonize supraterritorial spaces as well. It is to be hoped that the South African, Ugandan, and other experiments can demonstrate the feasibility of postmodern communities and encourage others to follow.

Note

1. I owe inspiration for this observation to Peter Waterman.

5

Justice and Security

Aswini Ray

The first problem facing anyone interested in justice and security is the relative insensitivity of international relations and orthodox security to the question of justice, both at the diplomatic plane and within the mainstream scholarly discourse. Historically, the guiding principles of international relations and orthodox security have been stability, predictability, and order at the cost of justice. This historical inheritance is among the discipline's original sins. This chapter explores the reasons for the abiding continuity of some of the recurrent sins of international relations, in the context of the increasing process of globalization, and the implications for security. Suggested remedial measures would follow logically from these explanations.

Diplomacy and Laws of War as Injustice

International law, particularly relating to the treatment of prisoners of war, rather than international diplomacy, has apparently manifested some concern for justice, at least by implication. But on closer scrutiny, such a deduction appears to be a somewhat idealized version of reality. Paradoxically within it, the "laws of war" appear more sensitive to the principles of justice, and equality, than the "laws of peace," the latter reflecting a bias in favor of the interests of the dominant and the powerful within the global power hierarchy. Such humanitarian laws of war as those of the Geneva Conventions on prisoners of war (POWs) seem to have been inspired more by the pragmatism of their signatories and the need to avoid reciprocal retribution than the concern for universal justice. At any rate, the same signatories showed no particular concern for justice in their demands for reparations after World War II, despite the considerable suffering of the people of the defeated states, who were also victims of their ruling elite's revanchist policies. The war-crimes trials at Nuremberg and Tokyo were more examples of victors' justice than universal justice, as the Indian

85

judge Radhabinod Pal stated in his lone dissenting judgment at Tokyo. The trial did not include those responsible for the tragedy inflicted on the people of Hiroshima and Nagasaki, which in terms of human costs was not strikingly different from the Nazi crimes. Besides, retribution as deterrence may be legitimate in international law but is difficult to reconcile with principles of justice when directed against individuals obeying orders of war.

After the end of the Cold War, Iraq's invasion of Kuwait and the orchestrated UN-sponsored "police action" against Iraq are dubious examples of respect for universal principles of justice. The UN's collective action did conform to the requirements of international law within UN Charter provisions; indeed, General Schwartzkopf, its commander in chief, boasted postvictory that he had thrown Iraq back to the Stone Age—presumably beyond his brief—and he was made a national hero and certainly was not tried for war crimes. Even the UN sanctions against defeated Iraq, at the cost of enormous sufferings to its people, have not received much attention either within international diplomacy or in the international relations scholarly discourse. No one has demanded any sanctions, or even just compensations, for the colossal blunder of Vietnam or Grenada. Elsewhere across the world, victims of the superpowers' Cold War rivalry, like the "boat people" of Vietnam and refugees from beleaguered Afghanistan— among the more sensational recent examples—still search for sanctuary. Empirically, it seems that states generally abiding by such elementary principles of justice such as equality before law in their domestic politics tend to be less scrupulous about such principles in their international conduct. The concern for justice within international law, as Geoffrey Best puts it, is "justice in no common or comfortable clothes: it was a sense of justice inseparable from a sense of the morally ambiguous proclivities of states and the justifications of raison d'etat; the mixedness of human nature; and the ultimate paradox that Antigone could be thought right and wrong at the same time" (Best, 1995: 77).

Conceptual innovations and theoretical insights, to the extent attempted within international relations, have been largely concerned with systemic stability within the historically rooted "statist fetishism" around legitimacy, balance of power, collective security, and, more strikingly, balance of terror with the goal being to ensure order and the enforcement of law rather than justice. Even the Cold War global system, despite its manifest amorality and abiding distortions when viewed from the standpoint of universal justice (Ray, 1989b: 13–28), was thought to be stabilized through confidence-building measures among the superpowers when, paradoxically, it collapsed without warning. The trauma of the unpredicted breakdown of the Cold War has not been followed by sufficient soul-searching within the international relations community around its inability to either anticipate or explain the traumatic destabilization of the global order.

The causal nexus of the breakdown remains unexplored. In view of the temporal disjunction between the two, whether the end of the Cold War hastened the collapse of the Soviet Union or the collapse of the Soviet Union ended the Cold War is still unclear (Ray, 1996: 114). Instead, we hear the heralding of the "end of history" (Fukuyama, 1989). The respectability of such patently ahistorical obiter dicta within the mainstream discourse of international relations (IR) is equally puzzling. Even after the dramatic shock to the credibility of this policy science—a credibility said to rest on its predictive capacity—post–Cold War trends indicate the continuity of the same mind-set: ahistorical predictions about a possible new "clash of civilisations" (Huntington, 1993: 22) and its consequent policy implications regarding a new diabolical "other" as well as an imaginary crisis of impending doom and the consequent search for instruments to enforce universal order within one's own rules of the game. "We are in for abnormal times. Our best hope for safety in such times, as in difficult times past, is in the American strength and will—the strength and will to lead a unipolar world—unashamedly laying down the rules of the world order and being prepared to enforce them" (Krauthammer, 1991: 33). Despite the traumatic setback to its central concern of the Cold War era, mainstream international relations, at both the diplomatic and the scholarly plane, still remains unrepentant. Like the eternal Bourbons, the tendency is to "learn nothing, forget nothing" of history.

This persistence regarding ahistorical realism in international relations calls for some explanations, at any rate by those concerned with their professional self-esteem. We who are outside the mainstream of international relations owe it to ourselves to accept the challenge to empirically substantiate that the prioritization of order and stability at the expense of justice is conceptually as flawed in the domain of international relations as it is in the realm of national politics—more so in the era of increasing globalization. To do that, we need to explore the possible reasons for the continuing operational disjunction between the concern for justice at the national plane and concern for justice at the international plane, even by democratic states with established traditions of justice as the guiding principle of orderly governance.

Democratic States and International Justice

During the colonial era, for example, while almost all of Africa and Asia still remained enslaved under colonial rule, even Abraham Lincoln expressed his disapproval of slavery only within his nation-state when he pointed to the incongruity of "a nation consisting of half slaves and half free" citizens. The European democracies in that era also limited their concern for liberty, equality, and fraternity, the Universal Declaration of the Rights of Man, and the ideals of the Magna Carta to their respective nation-states. For example, Britain in this era waged the opium war against China in support of the East India Company's right to smuggle opium. In India, the colonial power organized the amputation of the fingers of silk weavers to promote British textiles. The massacre of peaceful protesters at Jalianwallabagh (Amritsar) is a more telling example. Even the postcolonial states, after flying the flag of a global struggle for freedom and justice, have swiftly conformed to the prevalent international standards of justice, if not lower standards in some cases. Through the Cold War, most of the states within the global system, irrespective of their record of justice at home, generally conformed to the two superpowers' standards of international conduct, some more successfully than others. "The reluctance of democracies to extend their models of governance to inter-state relations," as David Held argues, has led to a striking paradox within the global system: "The increase in the number of democratic states has not been accompanied by a corresponding increase in democracies among states" (Held, 1995: 417, 418). Despite the widespread legitimacy of the human rights issue, it is still, as in the Cold War era, used as a diplomatic tool rather than for the emancipation of humanity toward universal freedom and dignity.

If this disjunction is rooted in the structural proclivities of all sovereign states, then (1) it must be reflected in the mainstream theories of the state and in those of the human and social sciences concerned with normative questions of ethics, equity, and justice within sovereign states; and (2) remedial measures lie in restructuring the organizing principle of the state and its sovereignty, and the concept of raison d'état.

If, empirically, this disjunction is more pronounced in nondemocracies than democracies—as seems to be the case—then encouraging democracies within states, as actors within the global system, assumes some importance in the interest of promoting even some incremental justice in international relations. This approach seems to be the new orthodoxy of the international funding agencies of development, which are pursuing it with the same zeal with which they promoted Third World modernization during the Cold War, mainly through the military and state bureaucracy. The mainstream scholarship of international relations has replicated this sharp shift in focus. That, among the available options, democracy remains the least unjust form of governance is part of universal common sense, and the post–Cold War concern with universalizing democracy and human rights is certainly welcome in the direction of reversing IR's Cold War inadequacies, both at the scholarly and diplomatic plane. However, present policies assume a consensus that is far from certain on the meaning of democracy, and visible and endemic operational complexities exist in the context of the process of globalization and its impact on critical security. These complexities are discussed further on; the immediate impact of the present emphasis on elected governments—as distinct from "liberal democracies"—at the microlevel of states in the periphery provides its own lessons about policy priorities.

In the context of the disjunction in the concern for justice at the national and international levels, the democracy variable is empirically contestable. Let us assume, for example, that wars are the most extreme manifestation of unjust international conduct; the conclusion that undemocratic regimes have relatively greater proclivities for such injustice is based on extremely limited temporal and spatial experience and yet is a theoretical generalization of contemporary international relations.

In the colonial era, most of the major wars were among the European democracies or initiated by them in their colonies in Asia and Africa. The most significant exception was World War II, obviously plotted by undemocratic regimes in Europe and Japan. Since then, however, throughout the Cold War era, although the theater of most wars has dramatically shifted from a predominantly European location to the Third World, the largest number of actual wars have involved the United States, whether directly or by proxy (Kende, 1978). Two equally distinguished examples of democracies, England and France, initiated wars jointly against Egypt and separately against Argentina, Iceland, Indo-China, and Central Africa. If we consider preparations for war such as armaments stockpiling or trading in arms, involvement in low-intensity insurgency operations, subversion of popular regimes, intelligence operations, and "proxy wars," the record of the "free world" throughout the Cold War most impressively undermines the assumption of democracy as a critical variable in the context of our present concern. Even within the Third World, the record of democratic states like India, Israel, or Nasser's Egypt do not lend support to the assumption of the democracy variable.

The assumption that open democratic systems make it more difficult to conduct secret preparations for a surprise war is also only partially true. Most such states, as the United States in the McCarthy era, have devised institutional or extrainstitutional arrangements based on the privileged status of national security to insulate their security activities from democratic scrutiny. Secret nuclear weapons aside, even rockets, missiles, and the chemical and bacteriological weapons of democratic states remain insulated from the post–Cold War global regimes' technologically sophisticated monitoring instruments. The record privileging national security in more established democracies is as impressive as in nondemocracies. For example, the U.S. policy of global "military alignment" as an instrument of the Cold War along with "security checks" on U.S. citizens, was announced through a presidential decree (National Security Council Resolution 68). Also, the war in Vietnam, involving 500,000 troops, was never declared by the Senate, the only body with the constitutional authority to do so. Similarly, the Anglo-French war against Egypt, and even Britain's military nuclearization, were never even discussed in their cabinets, much less in the public arena. Such significant examples undermine claims of just behavior in the sovereign states' international conduct. Within these democracies, the prioritization of national security over human security has been at the cost of the transparency of the extended sphere of their raison d'état, as in the United States in the McCarthy era.

Rather than revealing a connection between democracy and just international conduct, these examples, along with many others, tend to indicate a close positive correlation between the possession of military power and the proclivities for its misuse. Democracies usually employ such power in their international relations either directly or as deterrence; nondemocracies use it in both national and international domains and more often against their own people. Even on the basis of the arguable assumption that wars are the most extreme form of unjust international conduct of states, the historical record of democracies does not qualify them as being the least unjust form of governance—however desirable they may be otherwise—or as self-sufficient instruments for promoting justice in international relations.

The absence of war may be a necessary, if never sufficient, condition for peace; war's absence is less central to justice. "Peaceful" nuclear explosions, environmental degradations, the dumping of dangerous wastes and pollution in the seas or in space, the use of industrial gases and chemicals that affect the ozone layer, and discrimination against aliens are no less unjust than wars. Even on such issues, the record of Western democracies is too varied to generalize democracies as a reliable variable for our purpose.

The increased international demand for democracy is linked in complex fashion to our concern with human security and globalization at both the micro- and macrolevels. It is to these issues that we now turn. Remedial measures must be effected at the operational plane for mainstream scholarship of international relations to be liberated from its present amoral roots and used as an intellectual instrument for the promotion of universal justice.

Globalization, Security, and Justice

The breathing space created for normative concerns within international relations by the sudden collapse of the Cold War system is refreshing. Although such an opportunity cannot be wasted, it is prudent not to overestimate its salience or durability. IR's past sins have ruled out many options for justice whether in the Kantian, Gandhian, or Rawlsian sense, at least in the foreseeable future. It may be more realistic to direct our concern toward optimizing incremental potentials for justice as long as the new milieu lasts. The terra firma of international relations and the current state of its intellectual resources compel such modesty. There are simply too many historical liabilities ruling out infinite options.

The process of globalization did not begin with the so-called end of history or with its historical distortions across the globe. Each successive phase of this long historical process has left its trail of social, economic, political, and humanitarian complexities, creating a web across the world with varied contemporary relevance in the different regions. These complexitites have been documented, even quantified, in the respective disciplines: for example, by Ferdinand Braudel and his French Annales School on the impact of the globalization process on maritime trade in the Mediterranean region; Ashin Das Gupta on Asia; Immanuel Wallerstein with his "world systems" analyses; Andre Gunder Frank and Regis Debray on Latin America; Ali Mazrui, Samir Amin Cesaire, and Frantz Fanon on the African experience; and Ashish Nandy and Partha Chatterjee on India. Some of their theoretical frameworks or prescriptive implications may be controversial, but as sources of empirical reality they remain as valid as official documents.

From such sources it is evident that the process of globalization through military conquests, religious proselytization, and maritime trade had considerable historical relevance centuries later during the emergence of the European nation-states, and during their subsequent transformation as secular democracies in more recent times. Similarly, globalization through mercantile capitalism leading to the Spanish and Portuguese immigration to South America and within the Soviet system in Central and Eastern Europe as well as Central Asia during the Cold War has varying levels of relevance in each of these region's post–Cold War problems. At the subaltern level, globalization through the African slave trade, through indentured Indian labor, and through mercenary soldiers in British colonies in Asia, Africa, and the Caribbean—as well as the more recent globalization of the criminal underworld (hand in glove with military-civilian oligarchies of the Cold War) and of transnational banks like the liquidated BCCI, both of which are involved in drug traffic and money-laundering— have varied salience for contemporary problems in the different regions of the world and for the human security concerns of individuals, groups, and communities of sovereign states. Admittedly, the globalization ushered in by the Cold War has been significantly different from that in previous phases, in terms of its scale and momentum. This is because of the unequaled levels of economic, military, technological, and communication power at the disposal of the cold warriors. But whereas the Cold War territorially limited the process of globalization within two ideological divides—

just as globalization was limited within different colonial systems in the preceding era—the collapse of the socialist system universalized the capitalist market. This market is an extension of the global power structure and is under one hegemonic power, as envisaged at the outset of the Cold War (Horowitz, 1971).

This context has spawned the neoliberal ideological offensive within international relations for a new economic globalization through "structural adjustment" of the national economies away from the military-strategic preoccupations of the Cold War (see Chossudovsky, this volume).

With the sovereign state still relevant as the unit of analysis, the post–Cold War power hierarchy remains skewed in favor of the dominant few early starters, as in the previous era, and the Cold War developmental model linking the military-bureaucratic oligarchies of the Third World in a clientelist relationship to the "power state" of the Western industrial democracies (Hayter, 1971). The global market and its subsidiary regional trading groups also generally reflect this power hierarchy as do the World Bank and the IMF as institutions monitoring the globalization process of structural adjustment; their head executives are still nominated by the U.S. president and approved by the U.S. Senate on behalf of the world capitalist market. The fund-strapped UN system of worldwide security has been forced to conform to the same hierarchy by the hegemonic power—its richest member, largest contributor, and biggest defaulter.

Within this empirical reality, the new ideology of globalization seeks to legitimize the hegemony of the world market over state sovereignty; and its extension to the microlevel of the national markets as a substitute for the state is unlikely to have strikingly different consequences for justice and human security within the global system. The new rationality, insulated from any special concern for universal justice, is more likely to reinforce at the global level the experience of early capitalist development within the European national economies—and with greater distortions in the absence of any sovereign global authority as a substitute for the state. At any rate, the disjunction in the concern for justice at the national and international planes may even increase within this version of globalization, as trends already indicate.

The earlier experience in England remains immortalized by Charles Dickens in *A Tale of Two Cities*: "It was the best of times, it was the worst of times"; and later in czarist Russia by Tolstoy in *Anna Karenina*: "All happy families are alike; each unhappy family is unhappy in its own way." Despite the absence of quantitative data, such powerful portrayals of social reality are also valid for the global plane in the post–Cold War era of globalization.

Such empirical reality within the nineteenth-century European nation-state also spawned its "realists" in liberal theory and social policies; and, reinforced by Darwin, they advocated unfettered market justice through laissez-faire despite the inherited social inequalities of the ancien régimes. But mainstream Western social and human sciences, drawing on their historical reservoir of moral and intellectual resources, rejected Darwin's relevance to social policies on normative grounds without prejudice to his biological theory. They thus laid the foundations for liberal democracy, the welfare state, and the socialist state within their respective concepts of justice.

Despite its temporal and spatial limits, this historical experience still remains largely unexplored in terms of its relevance to international relations and, more specifically, to our concern for justice within the global system. Paradoxically, whereas the empirical base of realism as national security was rooted in a reconstructed version of the European experience, the neoliberal mystique of market justice is almost singularly rooted in the unique American experience. The inadequacy of this unique empirical base for social policies has been underscored in recent times in Europe by the political reassertion of the welfare state through the electoral victories of the Social Democrats. Its relevance for the rest of the world appears more remote in view of the sharper asymmetry with the American experience. As universal principles, a realist version of national security and a neo-liberalist version of market justice appear to be flip sides of the recurrent reality within international relations—the universal being defined by the powerful at the cost of justice. The appropriation of these principles by those in power has manifested itself also at the level of concepts with built-in policy priorities and consequent hierarchies, distinguishing the mainstream of international relations scholarship from its also-rans at the operational and scholarly plane.

For example, the universalization of the post–World War II era as the postwar era was a conceptual trivialization of the concerns of the vast majority of humanity in the postcolonial era. The concept structurally prioritized between the sharply asymmetrical concerns of postwar reconstruction in Europe—and Japan, the abiding exception of Western modernity outside the West—and the postcolonial agenda of nation-building. Most of the postcolonial states were not nation-states in the same sense as in the West and Japan (Ray, 1989b). The former were states in search of nationhood, consisting of disparate communities, administratively united by the contingencies of colonial policing and appropriation with a brutalized state apparatus as their colonial inheritance. Many of these disparate communities cut across the new frontiers of their sovereign states, within which they were inadequately integrated by concrete ties of society, market, infrastructure, and a culture of imagination. Consequently, the postcolonial agenda of nation-building at the social, economic, political, institutional, and humanitarian plane constituted states' human security concerns rather than a realist version of national security directed against a potential external threat (Ray, 1989a). This realist version of mainstream international relations spawned the "Third World," to which the Cold War was extended, as in the case of the earlier two "world wars." The historical asymmetry in the priorities of postwar reconstruction and postcolonial nation-building were operationally manifested when the Cold War global system enabled relative security, economic prosperity, and political stability in North America, Europe, and Japan at the cost of wars, threats of war, and domestic repression in the Third World. This development was also accompanied by such economic growth as was possible through foreign aid to regimes of military and civilian oligarchies (Ray, 1996).

The end of the Cold War has yet to manifest itself through any dent to these entrenched ancien régimes within the Third World or within many countries of the former Second World despite their "democratic" transformation through elections. This may explain the continuity of wars, ethnic divisiveness, religious fanaticism, social violence, crime, drugs, and threat of famine in these regions coexisting with the economic prosperity and political stability of the victors of the Cold War. Consequently, the end of this history cannot be a cause for universal celebration or inspire universal confidence about the apparent concern for justice within the new global order. The process of globalization of the Cold War era, built on the historically inherited global asymmetry of power of the earlier phase, has reinforced its structural asymmetry with new distortions. The new globalization through economic liberalization and cultural homogeneity has spawned fresh complexities at the cost of justice and human security within the global system.

For example, globalization through transnational corporations has created networks of interdependence within a hierarchy of nation-states. Global transnationals still fly their national flags, with the state as their ally, within a relationship of mutual reinforcement rather than aggrandizement (Hymer, 1979; Barnet and Muller, 1974). General Motors, IBM, Rolls Royce, Siemens, Sony, and Toyoto, for example, are still states' respective national flagships and as diplomatic instruments have assumed greater legitimacy in the era of globalization. Such corporate power, controlling technology, management, and capital, as well as consumer preferences, make for leverage on many weaker states with raw materials and labor as their only bargaining power. Obviously, this inequality cannot be the basis for global interdependence.

The Bretton Woods system of the postwar capitalist world created an international economic order with a built-in, self-generating propensity for the continuous transfer of capital from the South to the North (Brandt Commission, 1980). Complementing the Cold War global system and its information and intellectual hierarchy, the economic order sharpened the North-South inequalities inherited from the colonial era. Within the diplomatic space of the bipolar divide of the Cold War, the "voting bloc"

(Henry Kissinger) of its Third and Second Worlds initiated the creation of the UN Conference on Trade and Development (UNCTAD) and the UN International Development Organization (UNIDO) and finally the UN resolution for a more just new international economic order and new information order. The collapse of the Second World aborted these potential instruments of incremental justice within the Bretton Woods system through the democratic principles of the UN system. The new economic order after the Uruguay Round has been more in conformity with the post–Cold War power hierarchy. The flag of global "free trade" proclaims this hierarchy as stridently as the flag of the "free world" proclaimed the military alliances in the preceding era.

Within the new dispensation of the Intellectual Property Rights Convention, forced on the Third World by the international financial institutions (IFIs), some Oriental traditional medicines have already been appropriated by Western patents, such as Neem and Turmeric, despite Indian protests. In return, Western consumer preferences, American culture and taste, have flooded the world market, undermining self-esteem among younger generations regarding their heritage. Within this process of globalization through free trade, the global cultural attractions of the West are more a product of its technology and communication than necessarily their aesthetic content.

By profitably communicating Western consumer preferences as the main metaphor of a superior lifestyle, the new globalization process has accentuated the global hierarchy of power while making the transnationals more difficult to bargain with—it has made the green card, along with the greenback, the most subversive instrument of national sovereignty across the world. Within the countries of the erstwhile Third and Second Worlds, the middle-class professional elite and the working class are now divided between those who have the green card and those aspiring to have it. Those outside this contest now seek to retrieve their self-esteem, some through local enclaves of American-style malls, plazas, and discos and others by symbolic gestures of protest against them, together creating new social and political tensions. The conflict between tradition and modernity, continuing through the colonial era and accentuated by the Cold War process of globalization, has been sharpened within the Third World by the seductive appeal of the homogenized version of Western modernity profiled through its powerful communications and technology. Religious fanaticism, ethnic divisiveness, and regional tensions, stoked as instruments of the Cold War, have found new symbols of the "other" to survive.

But the most adverse impact of this process of globalization is in the sphere of human resources, encompassing technology, management, education, health, and the creative arts. Sieved through increasingly harsher and selective immigration policies of the industrial states committed to free trade, the best talents in most spheres of creativity—after acquiring their skills in the subsidized educational institutions of the Third World— have been attracted to the promised West. In the new process of globalization, the Third World is a major source of low-paid skilled labor for the industrial countries and their transnationals. Apart from the substantial capital transfer on this account, which replicated the colonial and Bretton Woods global division of labor, the long-term impact on the global intellectual hierarchy cannot be seen as conducive to universal justice.

Despite the adverse impact of this historical continuity in the process of globalization, the end of the Cold War, rather than bringing any change in the content of globalization per se, has enabled concerns around democracy, human rights, gender quality, and the environment to surface within the mainstream of international relations. Some of these spheres of concern have also spawned global networks of nongovernmental organizations (NGOs) with motivated and skilled cadres. In some cases, they are coordinated by global institutions within and outside the UN system.

Whereas these aspects of the globalization process need encouragement, our assessment of their salience and durability must be tempered by the understanding that they have arisen in conjunction with the end of the Cold War. Within the historical process of globalization motivated by capitalist accumulation, these concerns, or their globalization, are no more the inspiration for the new globalization process than the schools, hospitals, roads, and democratic upsurge in the colonies were for the colonial process of globalization or for the modernization of the Third World during the Cold War.

Yet the globalization of such concerns has opened new options for justice in international relations, particularly in such states where democratic politics are limited. For example, gender justice, human rights, and environmental groups now have global constituencies working against gender discrimination in the workplace, child labor, and deforestation.

This observation is also valid for the democratization process of the Third and Second Worlds, encouraged by the coordinated policies of the donor agencies in the Western world. Though such agencies are still selective in excluding some OPEC countries, their present approach is a welcome change from their earlier support for Third World modernization through military, civilian, and feudal oligarchies, along with their revivalist religious and ethnic domestic support bases. But the operational potentials of the democratic transformation of entrenched oligarchies through external pressures are limited and predictable according to comparable historical experiences. Even under more favorable circumstances of economic growth, the democratic transformation of European ancien régimes took place over a long period of time. The existing global system, rigidly controlled by the rich and the powerful, is not conducive to the democratic transformation of its periphery.

For example, when IFI conditionalities compel the new democracies to withdraw financial subsidies for the public distribution of essential commodities such as food to the poor or public transport and education or force industries to retrench surplus labor without any safety nets, these measures, apart from raising questions of justice, do not facilitate the resolution of resultant social conflicts through democratic institutions. Even in the sphere of defense budgets, the transition from the human security–led development of the Cold War era to the new path of development-led human security, has not been easy within even those states with long liberal democratic traditions, as the postwar experience of the United States would testify (Horowitz, 1971; Mills, 1978). These historical liabilities within the "junkyards" of the Cold War global system recurrently manifest the disjunction in the concerns for justice at the domestic plane and at the international plane. There is the sense in which the democratization of the post–Cold War global system, and its peripheral states, is dialectically linked to the promotion in international relations of universal human security.

Conclusion

Perhaps there is a new opportunity for international relations on the scholarly and practical planes to direct attention toward building a global consensus. Ideally this focus might emerge through a network of NGOs working with normative principles and institutions that have considerable legitimacy despite their operational inadequacies.

Four proposals immediately come to mind: first, democratization of the UN system, particularly the UN's social, economic, and humanitarian institutions; second, the enforcement of the Universal Declaration of Human Rights, both through the United Nations and through NGOs; third, regional development with external funding, based on the Human Development Index at the national level as the operational version of entitlement as justice; and fourth, NGOs monitoring the process.

But to be an effective catalyst for the operational plane, the scholarship of international relations needs to have a critical look at the state of the discipline and its resource base. To be able to undermine its statist fetishism, international relations scholarship must utilize alternate sources of information and data. The state and the mainstream media, even within the free world, have proved to be particularly vulnerable to disinformation around raison d'état, as evidenced during the McCarthy era in the United States. Alternatively, the social and human sciences could be explored as possible resource bases of international relations. NGOs could be new sources of empirical data.

Equally important for understanding in international relations are the creative and visual arts. For example, Picasso's *Guernica* as an evidence of Nazi atrocities or Chaplin's films as the social reality of economic depression or the Hiroshima war memorial, despite being unquantified, are no less convincing means for understanding international relations than official archives. Similarly, Satyajit Ray or Mrinal Sen are no less convincing accounts of Indian social reality than the quantified official data of governments. It requires creative imagination to incorporate these accounts into the scholarship of international relations; they have more potential than the official records have so far provided. Realism in international relations has stoked power politics and has ultimately led to the accumulation of bombs and missiles in both the practical intellectual arsenals. If this dominance is too powerful to be undermined by scholarship, perhaps we should question the quality of the scholarship.

PART 2
African Experiences

6

Security in the Senegal River Basin

Anne Guest

This study is an empirically based attempt to assess the impact of global forces on a particular area of West Africa—the Senegal basin. Until recently the middle basin of the Senegal River, though divided between Senegal and Mauritania, contained a cohesive and functioning society. Running through this chapter is a narrative of the way in which events initiated at the national or global levels made an impact on the security of this society to the extent that from 1989 to 1992 Senegal and Mauritania broke off diplomatic relations over disputes originating in the valley.

Also running through this chapter is an examination of the nature of global influence. For most African countries global influences in the form of colonization have determined their historical identity and continue to mold their present development. Senegal and Mauritania are no exception to this. Independence, when it came in 1960, was relative, not absolute. How does this imperial type of global influence compare with the more recent phenomenon of globalization? Are we looking at two distinct forms of influence, or is globalization a continuation of postcolonialism under a different name?

The perspective on security adhered to here mirrors the views expressed elsewhere in this volume in that it is a concern with what Caroline Thomas has referred to as human security. More pointedly it is a concern with the factors that enable the construction of secure societies within which the range of human needs might be met. Thus it is a concern with the satisfaction or otherwise of the needs of peoples that are both general and particular. As this chapter illustrates, the satisfaction of such needs is often dependent on the role of the state and the degree to which state institutions and managers are responsive to the needs of their communities as opposed to the demands of other forces, in this case, those of international financial institutions.

The idea of security addressed here, then, is one that focuses on the social, political, and economic conditions that generate the possibility of secure social orders. As a consequence it draws attention to an array of factors that are local, regional, and global. In this chapter, for example, the security of the peoples of the Senegal River basin reflects the struggles among local people, national governments, and state managers and the pressures exerted by various international organizations. The evidence presented suggests that there is nothing inevitable about the outcomes of such struggles and illustrates the significant degree of autonomy that state managers and national governments retain to pursue policies that could be more in line with the needs of their local populations. The point is that a concern with human security is an attempt to focus on the centrality of state-society relations in the world order, as they provide the conditions from which secure societies might be established.

Background:
The Senegal River Basin—Society and Geography

The Senegal River rises in the highlands of Guinea, flows down through rapids and waterfalls to the far west of Mali, and then forms the boundary between Senegal and Mauritania as it progresses 857 kilometers through the flatlands of the middle valley until it reaches the delta and the sea at St. Louis. The middle valley has always been the focus of socioeconomic activity on the river, as it is the only stretch of the river where agriculture is sufficiently viable to support extensive communities. Here, in the middle valley, life is almost entirely dependent on the waters of the river. Rainfall is barely sufficient to raise one crop, and droughts are common at this southern tip of the Sahara.

It is clear that despite a high degree of risk, the people in this valley were able to build a society that ensured that their human security needs were met. How was this done? The answer lies in the tightly knit interdependent socioeconomic system that developed, from the beginning of this century, once the French colonists had shifted their attention away from the slaves and gum arabic the valley could provide and into groundnuts, which could be grown only in the basin to the south. The valley system revolved around the rhythms of the year, and especially around the availability of water. When the rains fell in May and June the less fertile ground beyond the floodplain of the river *(dieri)* was planted with millet, maize, and sweet potatoes. In October, after the flood, the fertile floodplain *(oualo)* was planted with sorghum and vegetables. These agricultural activities were supplemented by fishing and trading and were woven into the yearly rhythms of pastoralists. Their herds of cattle, sheep, and goats grazed the Sahelian grasslands beyond the valley until the crops had been gathered, then were brought into the valley to clear off the stubble and manure the ground.

It was a fragile system. Both nature and humans could upset it. A failure of the flood or the rains could result in a dearth of fish and a shortfall of crops. More widespread drought—affecting the grazing outside the valley—brought the animals onto the cultivated land too early, before the crops were harvested. This could lead to disputes between farmers and herders. But underlying the fragility was a toughness that came from the ability to adapt. The system was never static. When, for example, the French demanded taxes in cash at a time when the valley was still a barter economy, a strategy was evolved of sending the young men to France to earn the money that was needed. The emigration of the young men of the valley became one of the survival strategies adopted not only to pay taxes but also to provide a buffer against bad harvests.

The ethnic composition of the valley mirrored the interdependent pattern of the economy. Two distinct racial groups—African and Maure—inhabited the valley. The Africans were the predominant group numerically. Most of the Maures did not choose to live in the valley, as they were nomadic peoples roaming the vast hinterland of Mauritania with their camels. They made their living from their animals and by trading across the Sahara. Nevertheless, many Maure families claimed to own land in the valley.

The Africans were divided into five main ethnic groups—the Toucouleur, Wolof, Soninke, and Bambara, who were principally farmers, and the Peul, who were herdspeople. Despite the boundary line between Senegal and Mauritania—which had been drawn down the middle of the river in 1960—all of these groups continued to move to and fro across the river, the Peul with their animals, the farmers to cultivate plots on the opposite bank. Villages stretched across the river, which was viewed more as a link than as a boundary.

The organization of authority in the valley was hierarchical and patrimonial. There were two traditional authorities: religious—the marabouts and imams—and secular. The authority of the religious derived from Allah, since most of the inhabitants of the valley were Muslim, and that of the secular authorities from their reputation as wise old men with the ability to predict the flood and set the time for planting. Gradually the religious authority was being challenged by the secular ideas brought by the émigrés returning from France, but the authority of the wise old men remained intact.

This, then, was the system that enabled the inhabitants of the valley to survive. It was finely tuned to the harsh geographical conditions of the valley, using interdependence and adaptation to reduce the risks to survival. From 1972 significant new risks threatened the critical security of the valley people. Looking at the nature of these risks and their external causes, we can see three periods: 1972–1981, the era of the development plans for the valley and the first serious challenges to the critical security of the people; 1981–1989, a time of intensification of the risks and the first clear connection between these risks and globalization; and 1989–1992, the time of conflict in the valley and attempted pacification. Each period will be examined in some detail to determine the origin of the critical state in which the valley now finds itself.

Human Security in the Senegal River Basin

Developing the Valley: 1972–1981

The year 1972 is crucial because in this year agreements were signed that committed the governments of Senegal, Mauritania, and Mali to a cooperative development of the valley.[1] The plan set out by the conventions of March 1972 (Convention Relatif au Statut du Fleuve Sénégal and Convention Portant Création de l'Organisation pour le Mise en Valeur du Fleuve Sénégal, OMVS) was to build two dams, one in the upper part of the river where it flowed through Mali and the other in the delta region between Senegal and Mali. The upper dam—the Manantali—would hold back the annual floodwaters in order to generate hydroelectric power and to provide a continuous feed for irrigated agriculture in the valley. It was envisaged that the land of the middle valley would be divided into neat parcels (perimeters) that would be served by irrigation and drainage channels. On these rice would be grown to feed the urban populations of Senegal and Mauritania, and cotton and sugarcane to provide a surplus for export. The hydroelectric power would supply the urban populations. In addition it would allow the exploitation of mineral reserves in the remote areas of the west of Mali and the north of Senegal.

The lower dam—Diama—was intended to prevent seepage of saline water up the river, thus making more land available for irrigated agriculture. In addition to these perceived benefits of the two dams, Mali was hoping that the constant regulated depth of water in the river would allow navigation up to its border. Mali was a land-locked country in desperate need of access to the coast.

These were the plans. What were their implications for the security of the people in the valley? First, there were the risks common to anyone living downstream of a big dam. These are

- an increase in waterborne diseases such as bilharzia and malaria
- a severe reduction in the amount of fertile silt brought down with the floods and deposited on the land

- a disturbance of the natural ecology of the valley. In the case of Senegal the forests, which were an invaluable source of material for many uses, were unable to survive without flooding.

In addition it is clear that the socioeconomic system of the valley did not fit into the new plans. The absence of a flood would make the cultivation of the fertile oualo soils, and thus of the food crops—maize, sorghum, millet, vegetables—impossible. In its place the farmers were expected to manage an irrigation system to produce rice, which they did not eat and had never grown. Rice cultivation would involve

- buying seed (hitherto farmers had saved their own seed from year to year)
- learning how to use and maintain irrigation channels
- buying machinery, as the work was more intensive and there was a shortage of labor power in the valley
- obtaining credit, as the costs of seed, machinery, and possibly fertilizer could not be met until the first harvest had been gathered
- learning to market outside the valley with all its attendant risks of price fluctuation and with the added disadvantage of very poor communications to the valley area.

What was being proposed was an agricultural revolution for the farmers and total exclusion for the pastoralists, since their animals did not fit into the perimeter scheme at all. As if this were not enough, the switch from flood to irrigation would remove the authority of the old seers who had predicted the flood and advised on times to plant.

The obvious question is whether the governments of Senegal and Mauritania ever seriously considered the human security of the people in the valley. The conclusion must be that they did not. In the years immediately following independence the valley area was all but ignored by these governments. The valley lay to the extreme north of Senegal and the extreme south of Mauritania, and neither government had the capacity to control the peripheral areas of its territory. Nor did the economic benefits of the river valley seem important in the early years of independence, when Senegal could rely on groundnuts and Mauritania on iron ore to keep their economies afloat. The river valley was therefore ignored until circumstances changed and the valley suddenly became the hope for the future.

Evidence of the governments' neglect of their people's futures lies in the fact that no feasibility studies of the likely effects of the development plans on the existing socioeconomic system were made before the 1972 agreements were signed. The only study of this kind was produced in 1980, when construction of the dams was well under way. This *Étude socioeconomique du Bassin du Sénégal* was criticized for lack of any extensive

research and for twisting evidence to suit the convenience of the development body—the OMVS (Adams, 1985: 157–159, 173–175).

The one concession the governments did make to the needs of the valley people was to set up parastatal organizations to advise the farmers on
seeds, fertilizers, and machinery and on managing irrigation channels, marketing, and seeking credit. These organizations—Société d'Aménagement
et d'Exploitation des Terres du Delta (SAED) in Senegal and Société Na-
tionale de Développement Rural (SONADER) in Mauritania—were viewed
with suspicion by the farmers, since they originated with the governments
that had created the problems in the first place (Conac, Savonnet-Guyot,
and Conac, 1985: 567–580). Nevertheless, some farmers did begin to seek
advice and begin the adaptation process. Small irrigation perimeters were
particularly successful; farmers used them in dry years and reverted to traditional practices when there were good rains (Woodhouse and Ndiaye,
1991: 6; Diemer, Fall, and Huiberg, 1991). As long as this mixture of old
and new styles of cultivation remained a possibility, the ability of the people of the Senegal valley to adapt in order to survive mitigated the risks
threatened by the development plans.

There came a time when even this strategy was threatened, but before
we go to the next period in the investigation, it is important to look at why
the governments of Senegal and Mauritania, in making the development
plans, appeared to neglect the needs of their people to such an extent. Was
this neglect due to external pressures, and if so, what form did these pressures take?

Three distinct pressures can be identified, all of which were reflected
in the stated objectives of the OMVS, which were

- to secure and improve the incomes of the maximum number of inhabitants
- to establish a more stable ecological balance between man and his environment, not only in the basin, but also in most of the territories in
  the Sahelian zone of the three States
- to reduce the vulnerability of the States' economies in the face of climatic factors and exterior factors
- to accelerate the economic development of the three States and increase interstate cooperation. (Omar and de Waal, 1994)

The three pressures were the climate, the competitive economic environment created by the Bretton Woods system, and the legacy of skewed
economies left by French colonialism, which put the river basin countries
at a severe disadvantage in the competitive market (see Chossudovsky,
Tickner, and Thomas, this volume). By 1972 the three had come together.

Both Senegal and Mauritania had been developed by France as mono-
group economies oriented to Europe. Senegal grew groundnuts and Mauritania produced iron ore. In the early years of independence groundnuts and

iron ore performed well on the world market, but by the late 1960s prices began to fall. Low rainfall intensified into drought in 1972. The groundnut crop was poor and in Mauritania the nomadic Maures—who composed 78 percent of the population—found it increasingly difficult to maintain a living in the desert.

From the earliest days of independence, the river basin states had realized that the solution to their generally weak condition was not to fight—since they did not have the means—but to cooperate (Zartman, 1966). President Keita of Mali said in 1961: "We are convinced that the States of Africa will never be independent, in the full sense of the word, if they remain small States, more or less opposed to one another, each having its own policy, its own economy, each taking no account of the policy of other" (address to Chatham House, June 7, 1961). Cooperation was seen as the answer to incomplete independence.

The commitment to cooperation throughout Africa as a whole can be gauged by the number of cooperative agreements that were made. Some, such as the Mali Federation (1960) and the Union Africaine et Malgache (1960) aimed at political integration and were not successful. Others, such as the customs unions, which evolved into the Communité Économique de l'Afrique de l'Ouest (1970) provided a useful tool of regional integration. The Organization of African Unity set up in 1963 provided an overall umbrella.

Cooperation in the Senegal basin was aimed at diversifying the economies of the participating countries by adding rice and minerals to their repertoire and making them less dependent on oil imports. To this end the state leaders were prepared to sacrifice sovereignty over territory, giving up their individual rights to sections of the river in order to develop it in cooperation.

What part did France play in this scenario? Having brought about the conditions of weakness, did France still pull strings in Senegal and Mauritania? Immediately following independence France had made cooperation accords with all its former colonies. These covered four areas: defense, economics and finance, culture, and technical assistance. The agreements that were reached varied from country to country. Senegal was willing to be used as a base for French troops in West Africa; Mauritania asked for French troops to be removed. Both countries joined the West African Monetary Union (UMOA), and thus the franc zone, in which the common currency (CFA franc) was guaranteed by the French franc (Chipman, 1989: 208–209). However, Mauritania left the zone in 1973 and established its own currency, the ouiga. Two years later Mauritania pursued its independence further by nationalizing the Société des Mines de Fer de Mauritanie (MIFERMA), the largely French-controlled company that operated the iron ore mines (Belvaude, 1989: 113–114). In taking this stand Mauritania was aiming to reduce its dependence on France and to counterbalance

French with Arab influence. Senegal followed this route with more caution. In 1972 France was still providing 53 percent of the aid that was sent to Senegal (Barge, 1979: 274–276), and the personal relationship between Senegalese and African presidents meant that extraordinary appeals for funds were usually heard.

Despite the continuation of French aid and personnel in Senegal and to a lesser extent in Mauritania, France does not seem to have been able to exert *direct* pressure to achieve its wishes. This became most evident when the funding of the development plans was under discussion. The development plans provided for two dams, one in Mali in the upper part of the valley and the other between Senegal and Mauritania in the delta. The global assessment of the plans, which was commissioned from a British consultant, Sir Alexander Gib, and partners and produced in 1978, found that the combination of the two dams made no sense economically (Gib and Partners, 1978). Either dam would be economically viable, but together they canceled out each other's benefit. Despite this assessment, the basin states were adamant that they wanted two dams. Their reasons were geopolitical, since each country wanted some stake in a dam. In order to obtain funding for both dams the river basin states played off the French preference for the lower dam (Diama) against the German preference for the upper dam (Manantali) and managed to obtain promises of funds for both (Vlachos, Webb, and Murphy, 1986: 32). There is no doubt that the river basin states were able to take advantage of a benign donor environment and of rivalry between different European states to gain what they wanted.

It seems that Senegal and Mauritania, in response to a hostile global economic environment and difficult climatic conditions, decided to cooperate to develop the Senegal basin. Despite a commitment in their agreements to secure and improve the incomes of the maximum number of inhabitants of the valley, the governments failed to assess the effects of development on the security of the people and quickly lost sight of the needs of the people in order to focus on the economic needs of the state. The part of France in this seems to have been more structural—in creating the conditions of economic weakness—than direct. France was not able to control the decisions of either Senegal or Mauritania.

Global Forces and Increased Risk— Generating Insecurity: 1981–1989

In this second period the construction of the dams proceeded, funded by a mixture of European and Arab states and Arab and African development banks. The Diama dam was completed in 1986 and the Manantali dam in 1987. The preparation of land for irrigation was not as successful. In Senegal only 13 large perimeters and 643 small perimeters had been prepared by 1988, a total of only 38,270 hectares of land out of the 240,000 available (Crousse, Mathieu, and Seck, 1991: 19–23). In the meantime the mixture of the old and new agriculture continued under increasing pressures.

The first of these was directly due to the further deterioration of the economic situation in Senegal and Mauritania. Renewed drought in 1978 coincided with oil price rises and a further fall in the price of commodities. Senegal was forced to seek help from the World Bank in 1979, and its first SAP was drawn up to run from 1980 to 1985. Mauritania agreed on its first stabilization program with the IMF in 1981. A condition of the stabilization and structural adjustment programs was that the governments of Senegal and Mauritania cut their social budgets and trim their spending on bureaucracy. Among the first casualties were SAED and SONADER. Although these parastatals had never been popular with the farmers in the valley, their removal left the farmers without any access to information or credit. It also broke the one line of communication between the governments and their people. From 1981 the people of the Senegal valley had to face the additional risks posed by the development plans on their own.

In fact their response was as tough and flexible as their responses to other challenges in the past had been. In this case the adaptive strategy they adopted was the increasing use of self-help groups both to ease day-to-day survival and to form networks of communication that acted as springboards for political activism. This adaptation was partly possible because of the gap that had opened in the traditional authority structures as a result of the development plans. The old seers of the patriarchal structure had lost their authority, and their place was taken by the women and by younger men with experience working in France. The catalysts in this process were the "foreigner" who came to work in the valley—an English social anthropologist, Adrien Adams, who married a Soninke farmer (Adams, 1977, 1985)—and NGOs from Holland, France, and the United States (Miller, 1985: 88–89). Gradually a new political awareness emerged among the valley people.

A second source of pressure in the valley arose from the need to repay external funders. As the construction of the dams reached completion, the governments of the river basin states knew they would be expected to begin repaying loans. This—along with IMF and World Bank conditions that emphasized exports and market competition—meant that the potential of the development schemes must be realized as fast as possible (see Tickner and Thomas, this volume). The generation of power (one way of realizing potential) was dependent on the installation of turbines at the completed Manantali dam. The dam was not completed and funding for the turbines was not available, so the burden fell on the other way of realizing potential—irrigated agriculture. In order to press ahead with rice production it was necessary to rationalize landholding in the valley. This was the nub of the problem for the farmers.

The rights to land had evolved over many years and arose from three distinct traditions—African common law, French Roman law, and Muslim law. These three operated piecemeal across the valley with the result that 41 percent of legal disputes in Mauritania were said to stem from land ownership problems (Boutillier et al., 1962). On the whole African common law was the dominant legal system, but the versions on the right (Mauritanian) and left (Senegalese) banks of the river were different.

African common law made a distinction between land held by right of grant *(de maitre)* and land held by right of cultivation *(de culture)*. Many of the farmers in the valley had no legal title to the land they worked, but it was accepted that certain pieces of land were attached to their family as long as they were being cultivated (Boutillier and Schmitz, 1987).

In Senegal, the noble Toucouleur had owned most of the land de maitre and collected rents from the farmers. Since the land yielded little, they had grown more careless about collecting the minimal amounts of rent and were not, therefore, badly affected by Senghor's 1964 Loi sur le Domaine National, which nationalized 97 percent of agricultural land in Senegal. In 1972 this law was followed up by one to create "rural communities" that would be responsible for land allocation. This system seemed to work well for the farmers, who were now responsible to a rural council rather than a landowner. On the whole there was wider access to land than before. Because the laws were enacted before the development plans made the land valuable, the landowners were not dismayed. Many found that they could still use their influence via the village councils.

More potentially damaging to the existing farmers in the middle valley was the Senegalese decree of June 30, 1984 (No. 64-573), affirming the right of government to allot land to private enterprise. This decree raised fears of entrepreneurs taking over large tracts of land for industrialized agriculture. This fear has not yet proved legitimate in the middle valley, although there was an unsuccessful attempt by the marabouts of the groundnut basin to mobilize their followers to move into the valley in 1993.

The situation in Mauritania was considerably more serious than that in Senegal owing to other severe tensions within the country. Mauritania was a land of two races, black Africans and Maures, or Arabs. The Maures were the dominant race, forming 78 percent of the population and absorbing the majority of government posts. Before the droughts of 1972–1974, the Maure were largely nomadic, living with their herds in the semidesert that formed the principal part of Mauritania. The black Africans inhabited and cultivated the river valley at the extreme south of the country. Their land and occupation were not prized by the Maures. The drought changed all that. In 1970, 72 percent of the population of Mauritania was nomadic; by 1975 only 27 percent. Some had gone to the city (up from 14 percent to 31 percent), but many arrived in the valley (14 percent to 42 percent) (Mauritanian government statistics).

The arrival of the Maures in the valley caused immediate problems. The blacks had no title to their lands in most cases since they relied on a right acquired by cultivation—de culture. The Maures claimed that the land belonged to them de maitre even though they had never been near it. The situation became more tense as the potential for profit from the development plans became evident. The Maures had lost their livelihood in the desert and intended to replace it by irrigated farming in the river valley.

In addition there was another group in Mauritania that had recently lost its livelihood and was competing for the land in the river valley as the most promising economic goods left in the state of Mauritania. This group was the *haratines,* or freed slaves. Slavery was abolished in Mauritania in 1980. Most slaves were black Africans by origin. However, they shared the cultural identity of their masters, the Maures, and thought themselves superior to the black Africans of the river valley. In any dispute with the black population their former masters invariably took their side.

In 1983 the Mauritanian government passed a land act to regularize the landholding in the valley. The act stated that any land that was undeeded or unimproved was the property of the state and could be ceded to those committed to improve it. Much of the black African land *was* undeeded. At least a third of it was said by the government to be unimproved, as the cycle of cultivation required that land should lie fallow for two or three years to allow recovery. The African farmers—on the whole—considered the law an attempt to oust them in favor of the Maures and haratines.

Their fears seemed to be confirmed when the law was applied in the valley for the first time. A prefect at Boghe issued a decree on May 10, 1988 (No. 119/DB), abolishing rights de culture and giving nine lots of land thus freed to Maures who had recently arrived from the north. The land had been cultivated by black Africans from both Mauritania and Senegal (the practice of cultivating on both sides of the river had continued to this point).

The responses to this action revealed how far the governments of each country had distanced themselves from the security needs of the valley people and how far the political consciousness of the people had grown. On the left (Senegalese) bank, a meeting was organized by one of the marabouts—Thierno Mountaga Tall—under pressure from the people (*Africa Confidential*, 1989: 3–4). It was declared at this meeting that the land-rights problem was a problem not just for the farmers but for the whole nation. The government was warned of grave consequences if the increasing pressure on the area was not addressed. Conflict was becoming a distinct possibility. The faith of the farmers in government activity on their behalf was very low. They returned home to organize self-defense committees—*patriotes sénégalais.*

The Senegalese government was sufficiently impressed to consult with Mauritania, which agreed to try and make some kind of land settlement.

The Aleg Accords, which they drew up jointly in August 1988, were the only attempt in the history of the development of the river basin to address the problem of integrating the farmers of the valley into the new landownership patterns required by irrigated agriculture.

But it was too late. The conflicts over land between herders and farmers and between black Africans and Maures were intensifying. An incident between black farmers and Maure herders on an island in the river in April 1989 began a three-year period of sporadic violence across the river during which diplomatic relations between Senegal and Mauritania were suspended.

Global Forces and State Autonomy: 1989–1992

What is significant from the point of view of the investigation of the connection between globalization and the security of the people in the region is that the violence was extended from the valley into two further areas. First it manifested in the capital cities of each country, where—it was later alleged—young men without jobs (due to IMF austerity programs) alighted on the considerable communities from the neighbor country as the cause of their misfortunes and ransacked their businesses and in some cases killed the proprietors. This violence led to an exchange of nationals on May 1, 1989, in which 500,000 Mauritanian Maures and 30,000 to 40,000 Senegalese laborers were returned to their own country.

The second area into which the violence erupted was within Mauritania itself. On May 5, 1989, the Mauritanian government turned on its own black population and killed 77 people. Others were deported across the river. By the end of 1990 it was estimated that 150,000 black Mauritanians had been removed to Senegal and 60,000 to Mali. Those deported lost all their possessions including any form of identification. Even after the peace settlement of 1992, 50,000 black Mauritanians were lodged on the left bank of the river, unable to return to a country that refused to acknowledge them.

Obviously the situation in the valley had become one of extreme challenge to the security of the people. In addition to the insecurity created by new agricultural systems, lack of government support, and continuing droughts, the competition for land had reached a critical phase. The conflict removed the black farmers from the right (Mauritanian) bank and concentrated 50,000 additional people on the left bank.

How much of this pressure on the valley and the severe threats to the security of the farmers who lived there could be attributed to the forces of globalization? Could the triumph of liberal ideology be blamed for the fate of the people of the Senegal valley? The evidence suggests that the new style of external pressure—in the form of IMF and World Bank conditions—did leave the Senegalese and Mauritanian governments with less room to maneuver. The paternalistic and idiosyncratic help of the old colonial power had allowed room for bargaining—as the funding of the two dams has shown. The new forces of globalization left fewer bargaining chips.

This conclusion can be supported by two sets of events in 1992 and 1993. The first concerns the attempts to seek funding, this time for the turbines that were to produce the power from the Manantali dam. The dam was completed in 1987, but no funding had been agreed on for the turbines because Senegal and Mauritania could not agree on whether the power distribution line should run along the right or left bank of the river. As long as they continued to argue, the donors refused to commit any money. This was a very different scenario from 1974, when the donors had agreed to fund two incompatible dams.

In 1989 a settlement between Senegal and Mauritania on the route of the power line had been reached and representatives had been dispatched to seek funds, but the outbreak of hostilities between the two countries put the missions to donors on hold. During the course of the dispute the two countries reversed the agreement of 1989, opting for a solution that gave each a stronger geopolitical position vis-à-vis the other. The donors, led by Canada and the World Bank, were not prepared to accept this. At a meeting in 1992 they told the river basin states that unless they abandoned their style of "belligerent" regional cooperation there would be no money. Senegal and Mauritania were forced to back down.

The second set of events demonstrating the increased influence of global forces on the river basin states concerns the very rapid progress toward democratization that took place alongside the peace process. As Senegal and Mauritania began to move toward a resolution of their dispute, it was clear that outstanding difficulties—such as loss of property and the massive displacement of persons from Mauritania to Senegal—could be resolved only by large sums of money, which neither country had. In 1991 Western and Arab states pledged the necessary funds, but only on condition that Senegal and Mauritania make a serious commitment to democracy. In Senegal's case, direct pressure from the United States forced President Abdou Diouf—who already ran a democratic country—to accept the leader of the opposition party into his cabinet.

In Mauritania the changes had to be more radical. President Ould Taya had resisted the call for democracy in the former French colonies that President Mitterrand had made at the Franco-African Summit in June 1990. In April 1991 he capitulated and announced that a constitutional referendum would be held and would be followed by multiparty elections. The government that took power following the elections in April 1992 was the first to be democratically chosen in Mauritania since 1961.

The insistence that the governments should become democratic would seem to be a hopeful development for the people of the valley. Unfortunately this was not the case. The style of democracy with which the proponents of liberal democracy were satisfied was more show than substance (see Wilkin, this volume). In 1992 the British embassy in Senegal concluded: "The absence of effective participation in the political system by the rural population could explain the fact that Senegalese democracy has not—so far—led to any real social and economic progress" (briefing paper for European Community, July–December, 1992, para. 12).

This seems to imply that the people were not taking advantage of the chance of democratic participation that was on offer. The reality was somewhat different. It has already been noted that political consciousness in the valley had grown. The problem was that it was not recognized by the governments. In 1992 the peasant associations from the valley made an appeal to the Senegalese government to work with them to solve difficulties about land allocation, the release of an artificial flood, and the health problems caused by waterborne diseases—all the human security problems brought about by the development plans. They had still not received a reply by April 1994 (Knight, 1994: 194–198).

It is clear from these two sets of events that external agents were having a considerable effect on some of the choices available to the governments of Senegal and Mauritania by 1991. What is also clear is that Mauritania had less maneuvering space than Senegal. Mauritania had made the mistake of remaining neutral toward Saddam Hussein because of the strong pro-Iraq Ba'athist party among its Maure population. It was punished for this by a withdrawal of all aid, both Western and Arab. The IMF refused to negotiate a new structural adjustment program until October 1992. The strength of the IMF can be gauged from the fact that until it put its seal of approval on Mauritania, no other donor came near the country. Mauritania had to survive without any external funding for two years. This applied to Arab as well as Western sources of aid. The first delegations from the Saudi Development Fund and the Arab Development Funds did not arrive in Mauritania until May 1993.

In contrast, Senegal retained the ability to play the external agents against each other. In 1992 the World Bank withheld the next tranche of its loan to Senegal because President Diouf had declared that the well-being of his people was of more importance than World Bank conditions. An official U.S. Agency for International Development (USAID) report in 1990 had come to the conclusion that the Senegalese economy would never adapt because it could attract such a high level of funding (Elliott Berg Associates, 1990). Where did this funding come from? Principally from France, which Senegal—unlike Mauritania—had continued to cultivate, but also from a spectrum of other sources: Canada, the United States, and the Arab states. These funds enabled Senegal to maintain independence from France as well as from the World Bank. In 1993 an exasperated French specialist in postcolonial affairs raged against Senegal's manipulation of

France (Bayart, 1993a: 52). He described the Senegalese economy as being clinically dead and suggested that France was unable to pressure Senegal because of its own need to appear to have influence in Africa.

This account suggests that a clever government could still be effective as a gatekeeper between its own people and external pressures, and that one way it could do this was by playing off the old personal type of influence left over from the colonial age against the new, more impersonal global ideology of liberal democracy. Senegal was able to do this; Mauritania was less successful.

Further, the account suggests that it was still possible for a successful government, such as Senegal, to pay attention to the security needs of its people *if it chose*. The history of the development of the Senegal valley in this chapter has shown how the governments of Senegal and Mauritania chose the economic interest of the state rather than the human security of the valley people. However, there is an upbeat addendum to the narrative. It concerns a debate over the "artificial flow."

By 1987, when the Manantali dam was completed, it had become obvious that the farmers in the valley were not making the switch to irrigated agriculture as rapidly as their governments had imagined. A survey was commissioned from Sir Alexander Gib and partners to estimate whether it would be possible to generate electricity *and* release water from the dam as an artificial flood until the farmers had gotten used to irrigation (Gib and Partners, 1987). The report concluded that it would not. There was insufficient water for both purposes, and since electricity gave the highest return, it should have priority. Not surprisingly, the findings of the report were welcomed by urban consumers in Senegal and Mauritania; multinational corporations (MNCs) in Europe; the United States, Korea, and Japan; and financial institutions that had lent money for the project. They wanted quick returns on their investments and saw "integrated development," that is, the complex interweaving of farming, herding, fishing, and trading that had sustained the valley in the past, as an uncertain bet. The report failed to give any value to returns from these subsidiary activities and ignored the contribution of the flood to the fertility and ecological balance of the valley.

In 1990, the Institute of Development Anthropology (IDA), an American NGO, conducted the only serious socioeconomic surveys of the valley that have been made in its history of development (IDA, 1990). The IDA concluded that it *was* possible to use the dam both for power production and to enhance the traditional agricultural practice of the valley by allowing the release of an artificial flood each year. Its findings were based on an economic valuation of the traditional valley occupations, which the Gib report had ignored.

For those waiting for the bonanza of rice, cotton, and sugarcane, the IDA report—supporting the continuation of the traditional agricultural system—

was not welcome, but for the people of the valley it offered the possibility of a future of greater security than ever in the past. The IDA made a strong case to the Senegalese government in 1993 and was heard. Had the people of the valley become visible to their governments at last?

Against this hopeful scenario in Senegal is the less savory situation in Mauritania. Here the racial tension over the land in the valley has moderated, but only because many of the African farmers remain in exile in Senegal. The Mauritanian government will listen to the Maures who farm the valley, since the government is predominately Maure and the valley is the prime site for economic goods in the state. But it continues to pay scant attention to the needs of its African population.

Conclusions:
Human Security and the Limits to Globalization

The conclusions to this account are brief. There is no doubt that there have been significant external pressures on the countries sharing the Senegal river basin. The pressures exerted by France, as former colonizer, appear to have been more personal, more easily manipulated, and thus less heavy than those of the representatives of the global neoliberal ideology. The two types of influence remain distinct and sometimes in opposition. It is the contention of this chapter that despite these external influences, the governments of the two countries have retained sufficient power throughout to attend to the security needs of their people. The case of the artificial flood demonstrates that the economic needs of the state are not incompatible with the needs of the valley farmers. The governments of Senegal and Mauritania could have chosen at any point to listen to their citizens and modify their schemes accordingly. They chose not to do so. Although the forces of globalization may reduce the choices of African governments, in the case of the Senegal valley, the greatest immediate challenge to the security needs of the people appears to have come from their own governments.

Note

1. Mali continues to be a party to the development schemes to this day. In this account Mali will take a backseat, as it does not own land in the middle valley.

7

Human Security and Economic Genocide in Rwanda

Michel Chossudovsky

The Western media has presented the Rwandan crisis as a profuse narrative of human suffering while carefully neglecting to explain the underlying social and economic causes. As in other countries in transition, ethnic strife and the outbreak of civil war are increasingly depicted as something that is almost inevitable and innate to these societies, constituting a painful stage in their evolution from a one-party state toward democracy and the free market. The brutality of the 1994 genocide and massacres have shocked the world community, but what the international press failed to mention was that the civil war was preceded by the flare-up of a deep-seated economic crisis. It was the restructuring of the agricultural system that precipitated the population into abject poverty and destitution.

The deterioration of the economic environment, which immediately followed the collapse of the international coffee market and the imposition of sweeping macroeconomic reforms by the Bretton Woods institutions, exacerbated simmering ethnic tensions and accelerated the process of political collapse. In 1987, the system of quotas established under the International Coffee Agreement (ICA) started to fall apart; world prices plummeted; and the *Fonds d'Égalisation* (the state coffee stabilization fund), which purchased coffee from Rwandan farmers at a fixed price, started to accumulate a sizable debt. A lethal blow to Rwanda's economy came in June 1989, when the International Coffee Agreement reached a deadlock as a result of political pressures from Washington on behalf of the large U.S. coffee traders. At the conclusion of a historic meeting of producers held in Florida, coffee prices plunged in a matter of months by more than 50 percent.[1] For Rwanda and several other African countries, the drop in

117

price wreaked havoc. With retail prices more than twenty times that paid to the African farmer, a tremendous amount of wealth was being appropriated in the rich countries.

A major concern, as chronicled elsewhere in this volume, is with the causes of human insecurity and suffering in the contemporary world order. This chapter is concerned explicitly with the underlying economic factors that generated the conditions for the ensuing social conflict that emerged in Rwanda, as it has much to tell us about the impact of global economic policies on the developing world and on the security of its societies. This conflict also forces us to confront the complex question of the responsibility for the events that devastated Rwanda and continue to do so. If, as argued elsewhere in this volume, security is in part a concern with the satisfaction of human needs as well as the construction of stable societies, then Rwanda's plight highlights the malign impact of neoliberal policies on the current world order in stark and brutal fashion. The lesson to be drawn is that the goals of human security are fundamentally challenged by the neoliberal policies that have shaped the global political economy since the 1970s.

The Legacy of Colonialism

What is the responsibility of the West in this tragedy? First it is important to stress that the conflict between the Hutu and Tutsi was largely the product of the colonial system, many features of which still prevail today. From the late nineteenth century, the early German colonial occupation had used the *mwami* (king) of the Nyiginya monarchy installed at Nyanza as a means of establishing its military posts. However, it was largely the administrative reforms initiated in 1926 by the Belgians that were decisive in shaping socioethnic relations. The Belgians explicitly used dynastic conflicts to reinforce their territorial control. The traditional chiefs in each hill *(colline)* were used by the colonial administration to requisition forced labor. Routine beatings and corporal punishment were administered on behalf of the colonial masters by the traditional chiefs. The latter were under the direct supervision of a Belgian colonial administrator responsible for a particular portion of territory. A climate of fear and distrust was installed, communal solidarity broke down, and traditional client relations were transformed to serve the interests of the colonizer.

The objective was to fuel interethnic rivalries as a means of achieving political control as well as preventing the development of solidarity between the two ethnic groups, which inevitably would have been directed against the colonial regime. The Tutsi dynastic aristocracy was also made responsible for the collection of taxes and the administration of justice. The communal economy was undermined, and the peasantry was forced to shift out of food agriculture into cash crops for export. Communal lands were transformed into individual plots geared solely toward cash crop cultivation (the so-called *cultures obligatoires*) (Rumiya, 1992: 220–226; Guichaoua, 1989).

Colonial historiographers were entrusted with the task of transcribing as well as distorting Rwanda-Urundi's oral history. The historical record was falsified: the mwami monarchy was identified exclusively with the Tutsi aristocratic dynasty. The Hutus were represented as a dominated caste (Nahimana, 1993).

The Belgian colonialists developed a new social class, the so-called *nègres evolués,* recruited among the Tutsi aristocracy. The school system was put in place to educate the sons of the chiefs and provide the African personnel required by the Belgians. In turn, the various apostolic missions and vicariats received under Belgian colonial rule an almost political mandate, and the clergy was often used to oblige the peasants to integrate the cash-crop economy. These socioethnic divisions—which have unfolded since the 1920s—have left a profound mark on contemporary Rwandan society.

Since independence in 1962, relations with the former colonial powers and donors have become exceedingly complex. Inherited from the Belgian colonial period, however, the same objective of *pushing one ethnic group against the other* (divide and rule) has largely prevailed in the various military, human rights, and macroeconomic interventions undertaken from the outset of the civil war in 1990. The Rwandan crisis has become encapsulated in a continuous agenda of donor roundtables (held in Paris), cease-fire agreements, and peace talks. These various initiatives were closely monitored and coordinated by the donor community in a tangled circuit of conditionalities and cross-conditionalities. The release of multilateral and bilateral loans since late 1990 has been made conditional on implementing a process of so-called democratization under the tight surveillance of the donor community. In turn, Western aid in support of multiparty democracy has been made conditional (in an almost symbiotic relationship) on the government reaching an agreement with the IMF, and so on. These attempts were all the more illusive because after the collapse of the coffee market, *actual* political power in Rwanda largely rested, in any event, in the hands of the donors. A communiqué of the U.S. State Department issued in early 1993 vividly illustrates this situation: the continuation of U.S. bilateral aid was made conditional on good behavior in policy reform as well as progress in the pursuit of democracy (see Wilkin, this volume).

The model of democratization based on an abstract model of inter-ethnic solidarity envisaged by the Arusha peace agreement signed in August 1993 was an impossibility from the outset, and the donors knew it. The brutal impoverishment of the population, which resulted from both the war and the IMF reforms, precluded a genuine process of democratization.

The objective was to meet the conditions of "good governance" (a new term in the donors' glossary) and oversee the installation of a bogus multiparty coalition government under the trusteeship of Rwanda's external creditors. In fact, multipartism as narrowly conceived by the donors contributed to fueling the various political factions of the regime. Not surprisingly, as soon as the peace negotiations entered a stalemate, the World Bank announced that it was interrupting the disbursements under its loan agreement (*New African*, June 1994: 16).

The Economy Since Independence

The evolution of the postcolonial economic system played a decisive role in the development of the Rwandan crisis. Although progress was indeed recorded after independence in diversifying the national economy, the colonial-style export economy based on coffee *(les cultures obligatoires)* and established under the Belgian administration was largely maintained, providing Rwanda with more than 80 percent of its foreign exchange earnings. A rentier class with interests in the coffee trade and with close ties to the seat of political power had developed. Levels of poverty remained high; yet during the 1970s and the first part of the 1980s, economic and social progress was nonetheless realized: real GDP growth was of the order of 4.9 percent per annum (1965–1989); school enrollment increased markedly; and recorded inflation was among the lowest in sub-Saharan Africa, less than 4 percent per annum (UN Conference on the Least Developed Countries [UNCLDC], 1990: 5; République Rwandaise, 1987).

Although the Rwandan rural economy remained fragile, marked by acute demographic pressures (3.2 percent per annum population growth), land fragmentation, and soil erosion, local-level food self-sufficiency had, to some extent, been achieved alongside the development of the export economy. Coffee was cultivated by approximately 70 percent of rural households, yet it constituted only a fraction of total monetary income. A variety of other commercial activities had been developed, including the sale of traditional food staples and banana beer in regional and urban markets (Guichaoua, 1987). Until the late 1980s, imports of cereals including food aid were minimal compared to the patterns observed in other countries of the region. The food situation started to deteriorate in the early 1980s with a marked decline in the per capita availability of food. In overt contradiction to the usual trade reforms adopted under the auspices of the World Bank, protection to local producers had been provided through restrictions on the import of food commodities (UNCLDC, 1990: 2). They were lifted with the adoption of the 1990 structural adjustment program.

The Fragility of the State and Society

The economic foundations of the postindependence Rwandan state remained extremely fragile; a large share of government revenues depended on coffee, with the risk that a collapse in commodity prices would precipitate a crisis in the state's public finances. The rural economy was the main source of state funding. As the debt crisis unfolded, a larger share of coffee and tea earnings had been earmarked for debt servicing, putting further pressure on small-scale farmers.

Export earnings declined by 50 percent between 1987 and 1991. The demise of state institutions unfolded thereafter. When coffee prices plummeted, famines erupted throughout the Rwandan countryside. According to World Bank data, the growth of gross domestic product (GDP) per capita declined from 0.4 percent in 1981–1986 to –5.5 percent in the period immediately following the slump of the coffee market (1987–1991).

The IMF–World Bank Intervention

A World Bank mission traveled to Rwanda in November 1988 to review Rwanda's public expenditure program. A series of recommendations had been established with a view to putting Rwanda back on the track of sustained economic growth. The World Bank mission presented the Rwanda government with policy options consisting of two scenarios. Scenario 1, entitled No Strategy Change, contemplated the option of remaining with the old system of state planning; Scenario 2, labeled With Strategy Change, was that of macroeconomic reform and transition to the free market. After careful economic simulations of likely policy outcomes, the World Bank concluded with some grain of optimism that if Rwanda adopted Scenario 2, levels of consumption would increase markedly over 1989–1993 alongside a recovery of investment and an improved balance of trade. The simulations also pointed to added export performance and substantially lower levels of external indebtedness. (A 5 percent growth in exports was to take place under Scenario 2 as compared with 2.5 percent under Scenario 1.) These outcomes depended on the speedy implementation of the usual recipe of trade liberalization and currency devaluation, alongside the lifting of all subsidies to agriculture, the phasing out of the Fonds d'Égalisation, the privatization of state enterprises, and the dismissal of civil servants.

The With Strategy Change (Scenario 2) was adopted; the government had no choice. A 50 percent devaluation of the Rwandan franc was carried out in November 1990, barely six weeks after the incursion from Uganda of the rebel army of the Rwandan Patriotic Front.

The devaluation was intended to boost coffee exports. It was presented to the public as a means of rehabilitating a war-ravaged economy. Not surprisingly, exactly the opposite results were achieved, exacerbating the civil war. From a situation of relative price stability, the plunge of the Rwandan franc contributed to triggering inflation and the collapse of real earnings. A few days after the devaluation, sizable increases in the prices of fuel and consumer essentials were announced. The consumer price index increased from 1.0 percent in 1989 to 19.2 percent in 1991. The balance-of-payments situation deteriorated dramatically, and the outstanding external debt, which had already doubled since 1985, increased by 34 percent between 1989 and 1992 (World Bank, 1994b: 383). (The outstanding debt had increased by more than 400 percent since 1980—from US$150.3 million in 1980 to US$804.3 million in 1992.) The state administrative apparatus was in disarray, state enterprises were pushed into bankruptcy, and public services collapsed. Health and education collapsed under the brunt of the IMF's imposed austerity measures. Despite the establishment of a social safety net (earmarked by the donors for programs in the social sectors), the incidence of severe child malnutrition increased dramatically and the number of recorded cases of malaria increased by 21 percent in the year following the adoption of the IMF program, largely as a result of the absence of antimalarial drugs in the public health centers. The imposition of school fees at the primary school level was conducive to a massive decline in school enrollment (Gervais, 1993: 36).

The economic crisis reached its climax in 1992, when Rwandan farmers in desperation uprooted some 300,000 coffee trees (Economist Intelligence Unit, 1994: 10). Despite soaring domestic prices, the government had frozen the farmgate price of coffee at its 1989 level (125 RF per kg) under the terms of its agreement with the Bretton Woods institutions. The government was not allowed (under the World Bank loan) to transfer state resources to the Fonds d'Égalisation. It should also be mentioned that a significant profit was appropriated by local coffee traders and intermediaries, serving to put further pressure on the peasantry.

In June 1992, a second devaluation was ordered by the IMF, leading— at the height of the civil war—to a further escalation of the prices of fuel and consumer essentials. Coffee production tumbled by another 25 percent in a single year. Because of overcropping of coffee trees, there was increasingly less land available to produce food, but the peasantry was not able to easily switch back into food crops. The meager cash income derived from coffee had been erased, yet there was nothing to fall back on. Not only were cash revenues from coffee insufficient to buy food, the prices of farm inputs had soared and money earnings from coffee were grossly insufficient. The crisis of the coffee economy backlashed on the production of traditional food staples, leading to a substantial drop in the production of cassava, beans, and sorghum. The system of savings and loan cooperatives that provided credit to small farmers had also disintegrated. Moreover, with the liberalization of trade and the deregulation of grain markets as recommended by the Bretton Woods institutions, heavily subsidized cheap food imports and food aid from the rich countries were entering Rwanda with the effect of destabilizing local markets.

Under the "free market" system imposed on Rwanda, neither cash crops nor food crops were economically viable. The entire agricultural system was pushed into crisis; the state administrative apparatus was in disarray due to the civil war, but also as a result of the austerity measures and sinking civil service salaries. This situation inevitably contributed to exacerbating the climate of generalized insecurity that had unfolded in 1992. As the Rwandan economy collapsed under a range of global and local pressures, the state institutions became increasingly unable and unwilling to meet the basic needs of their population. The fragility of state-society relations was exposed under such conditions. The combined impact of the historical legacy of colonialism and the divisions it imposed on Rwandan society, when coupled with the vulnerability of such a weak economy forced to confront global market forces, proved to be central factors in the unraveling of Rwandan state-society relations. General insecurity has been the result of these developments.

The seriousness of the agricultural situation had been amply documented by the Food and Agriculture Organization (FAO), which had warned of the existence of widespread famine in the southern provinces. The International Committee of the Red Cross (ICRC) had estimated in 1993 that a million people were affected by famine (*Marchés Tropicaux*, April 2, 1993: 898). An FAO communiqué released in March 1994 pointed to a 33 percent decline in food production in 1993 (*Marchés Tropicaux*, March 25, 1994: 594). A report released in early 1994 also pointed to the total collapse of coffee production due to the war but also as a result of the failure of the state marketing system, which was being phased out with the support of the World Bank. Rwandex, the mixed enterprise responsible for processing and export of coffee, had become largely inoperative.

The decision to devalue (and the IMF stamp of approval) had already been reached on September 17, 1990, prior to the outbreak of hostilities, in high-level meetings held in Washington between the IMF and a mission headed by the Rwandan minister of finance, Mr. Ntigurirwa. The green light had been given: as of early October, at the very moment when the fighting started, millions of dollars of so-called balance-of-payments aid (from multilateral and bilateral sources) came pouring into the coffers of the Central Bank. These funds administered by the Central Bank had been earmarked by the donors for commodity imports, yet it appears likely that a sizable portion of these "quick disbursing loans" had been diverted by the regime and its various political factions toward the acquisition of military hardware from South Africa, Egypt, and Eastern Europe. (There has been no official communiqué or press report confirming or denying the channeling of balance-of-payments aid toward military expenditure. According to the Washington-based Human Rights Watch, Egypt agreed with Kigali to supply $6 million worth of military equipment. The deal with South Africa was for $5.9 million. See *Marchés Tropicaux,* January 28, 1994: 173.) These purchases of Kalachnikov guns, heavy artillery, and mortar were undertaken in addition to the bilateral military aid package provided by France, which included, inter alia, Milan and Apila missiles (not to mention a Mystère Falcon jet for President Habyarimana's personal use) (*New African,* June 1994: 15; also *Archipel* 9, July 1994: 1). Moreover, since October 1990, the armed forces had expanded virtually overnight from 5,000 to 40,000 men, inevitably requiring (under conditions of budgetary austerity) a sizable influx of outside money. The new recruits were largely enlisted from the ranks of the urban unemployed, of which the numbers had swelled dramatically since the outset of the collapse of the coffee market in 1989. Thousands of delinquent and idle youths from a drifting population were also drafted into the civilian militia responsible for the massacres. And part of the arms purchases enabled the armed forces to organize and equip the militiamen.

In all, from the outset of the hostilities (which coincided chronologically with the devaluation and the initial gush of fresh money in October 1990), a total envelope of some $260 million had been approved for disbursal (with sizable bilateral contributions from France, Germany, Belgium, the European Community, and the United States). Although the new loans contributed to releasing money for debt servicing as well as equipping the armed forces, the evidence would suggest that a large part of this donor assistance was neither used productively nor channeled into providing relief in areas affected by famine.

It is also worth noting that in 1992 the World Bank, through its soft-lending affiliate, the International Development Association (IDA), had ordered the privatization of Rwanda's state enterprise, Electrogaz. The proceeds of the privatization were to be channeled toward debt servicing. In a loan agreement cofinanced with the European Investment Bank (EIB) and the Caisse Française de Développement (CFD), the Rwandan authorities were to receive in return (after meeting the conditionalities) the modest sum of $39 million, which could be spent freely on commodity imports (*Marchés Tropicaux,* February 26, 1992: 569). The privatization carried out at the height of the civil war also included dismissals of personnel and an immediate hike in the price of electricity, which further contributed to paralyzing urban public services. A similar privatization of Rwandatel, the state telecommunications company under the Ministry of Transport and

Communications, was implemented in September 1993 (*Marchés Tropicaux*, October 8, 1993: 2492).

The World Bank had carefully reviewed Rwanda's public investment program. The *fiches de projet* having been examined, the World Bank recommended scrapping more than half the country's public investment projects. In agriculture, the World Bank had also demanded a significant *downsizing* of state investment, including the abandonment of the inland swamp reclamation program, which had been initiated by the government in response to the severe shortages of arable land (and which the World Bank considered unprofitable). In the social sectors, the World Bank proposed a priority program (under the social safety net) predicated on maximizing efficiency and reducing the financial burden of the government through the exaction of user fees, layoffs of teachers and health workers, and the partial privatization of health and education.

The World Bank would no doubt contend that things would have been much worse had Scenario 2 not been adopted—the so-called counterfactual argument. Such reasoning, however, sounds absurd, particularly in the case of Rwanda. No sensitivity or concern was expressed as to the likely political and social repercussions of economic shock therapy applied to a country on the brink of civil war. The World Bank team consciously excluded the noneconomic variables from their simulations.

Whereas the international donor community cannot be held directly responsible for the tragic outcome of the Rwandan civil war, the austerity measures, combined with the impact of the IMF-sponsored devaluations, contributed to impoverishing the Rwandan people at a time of acute political and social crisis. The deliberate manipulation of market forces destroyed economic activity and people's livelihoods, fueled unemployment, and created a situation of generalized famine and social despair. The lessons of Rwanda are complex but important if the idea of human security is to have any practical importance in international politics. The combined impact of global neoliberal economic policies, coupled with the general weakness of the Rwandan state to resist them, led to a situation in which the conditions necessary for the disasters that subsequently befell Rwanda were firmly in place. The unraveling of state-society relations and the polarizing of social forces illustrate clearly the ways in which untrammeled market forces serve to undermine the possibility of stable social orders.

Conclusions:
Economic Genocide and Human Security

To lay the blame solely on deep-seated tribal hatred not only exonerates the great powers and the donors, it also distorts an exceedingly complex process of economic, social, and political disintegration affecting an entire state of more than 7 million people. Many countries in sub-Saharan Africa face Rwanda's predicament (in Burundi, for example, famine and ethnic massacres are rampant). And in many respects the Rwandan devaluation of 50 percent in 1990 appears almost as a laboratory test case, as well as an omen for the same devaluation of the CFA franc implemented on the instructions of the IMF and the French Treasury in January 1994.

It is also worth recalling that in Somalia in the aftermath of Operation Restore Hope, the absence of a genuine economic recovery program by the USAID mission in Mogadishu—outside the provision of short-term emergency relief and food aid—was a major obstacle to resolving the civil war and rebuilding the country. In Somalia, because of the surplus of relief aid, which competed with local production, farmers remained in the relief camps instead of returning to their home villages. What are the lessons for Rwanda? As humanitarian organizations prepare for the return of the refugees, the prospects for rebuilding the Rwandan economy and society outside the framework determined by the IMF and Rwanda's international creditors seem to be extremely bleak. Even in the event that a national unity government is installed and the personal security of the refugees can be ensured, the 2 million Rwandans cramped in camps in Zaire and Tanzania have nothing to return to, nothing to look forward to. Agricultural markets have been destroyed, local-level food production and the coffee economy have been shattered, and urban employment and social programs have been erased. The reconstruction of Rwanda will require an alternative economic program implemented by a genuinely democratic government based on interethnic solidarity and free from donor interference. Such a program presupposes erasing the external debt together with an *unconditional* infusion of international aid. It also requires lifting the straightjacket of budgetary austerity imposed by the IMF, mobilizing domestic resources, and providing for a secure and stable productive base for the rural people.

Note

1. The system of export quotas of the International Coffee Organization (ICO) was lifted in the aftermath of the Florida meetings in July 1989. The freight-on-board price in Mombassa declined from $1.31 a pound in May 1989 to $0.60 in December (*Marchés Tropicaux*, May 18, 1990: 1369; June 29, 1990: 1860).

8

The Horn of Africa: Security in the New World Order

Mohamed A. Mohamed Salih

The security perspective adopted in this chapter transcends the orthodox security approach by questioning the notion that nation-states can maintain regional peace and hence global tranquillity on the basis of multilateral institutions dependent on the use of military coercion. On the contrary, it is argued that a concept of security grounded on interstate relations often overlooks the fact that the state itself can be a source of citizen insecurity. Furthermore, as an object of state actions, citizen security has often been sacrificed in order to maintain an element of security based on militarism. The problem with orthodox security is that nation-states are treated as the dominant actors in international relations in a manner analogous to the states' dominance in managing their domestic affairs. There is a compelling need for the state to act as a provider of citizen security, rather than being a source of citizen insecurity.

In this chapter, human security is used to broaden the debate from the threat, use, and control of military force to encompass nonconventional concerns such as ecology, human rights, and social capital, which if not properly addressed would pose similar threats to human survival. This broadening of the concept is politically informed by contemporary developments in international relations, particularly the approach that takes issue with the state as the main provider of security. Krause and Williams's (1997: 43) argument that "security is synonymous with citizenship" is highly relevant to this chapter. Despite this argument's diverse theoretical strands, in Krause and Williams's words (1997: 44), "one set of challenges has been united by a common desire to treat the object of security not as the sovereign state, but as the individual: security is a condition that individuals enjoy, and they are given primacy both in the definition of threats and of who (or what) is to be secured. In this regard, citizen security or insecurity can be undermined or enhanced by the state (Buzan, 1983), and one of the main objectives of the evolving critical security studies is to shift the focus from the state's military security to open the state for critical scrutiny (Krause and Williams, 1997). This possibility does not preclude the importance of also scrutinizing the global processes that, through interstate relations and superpower hegemony, jeopardize citizen security.

Hence from the evolving critical security studies perspective, the foundational ethos of the new world order renders conventional concepts and definitions of an international security based on the nation-state futile. Thomas and Wilkin (1997) refer to this idea of security as part of the neoliberal hegemony that constructs notions of security built on a misconceived understanding of global security. The ethos of neoliberal hegemony has been outlined by Axford (1995: 182), in a different context, as follows: (1) With the end of the Cold War, bipolarity (Eastern and Western blocs) has given way to unipolarity, that is, the emergence of the United States and its Western allies as the only globally recognized superpower. (2) There are prospects for lasting peace in the new world order, and these are enhanced by revitalized multilateral bodies like the United Nations, with U.S.-led coalitions. (3) The geoeconomic dimension of the new world order is such that market liberalism and democracy should be expanded to the rest of the world through the growing interconnectedness and interdependence of the world economy.

An increased global interdependence has been portrayed as a contributor to a reduced role for the state in the face of neohegemonic stability exercised either by global economic power or U.S.-led UN interventions. For instance, Keohane and Nye (1996: 58) argue that "the traditional orientation towards military and security affairs implies that the crucial problems of foreign policy are imposed on states by the actions or threats of other states. . . . Yet as the complexity of actors and issues in world politics increases, the utility of force declines and the line between domestic policy and foreign policy becomes blurred." But when applied to the Horn of Africa, the theory of hegemonic stability (Keohane, 1996) and an increased interdependence in the new world order have produced neither the desired political stability nor a decrease in the utility of force, even now when the dividing line between domestic and external politics (within and outside the subregion) is diminishing. This anomaly has been addressed by Keohane and Nye (1996: 62) in the following terms: "One would expect traditional theories to fail to explain international regime change in situations of complex interdependence. But, for a situation that approximates realist conditions, traditional theories should be appropriate." What is significant in this debate is whether the attributes of the new world order are relevant to the Horn of Africa and whether the "institution of sovereignty retains the state's power as a constitutive feature of social reality" (Axford, 1995: 131). To what extent does the liberal and the realist conviction of the state as a maximizer of power or a major player in the global power game hold ground?

In the context of the Horn of Africa it must be asked whether states that have been made to fail have reason to celebrate the new world order. Have these states reached the promised land, in which they are able to rid themselves of the effects of bipolar politics? One may argue that in the new world order, the states of the Horn of Africa should prosper as a result of reduced expenditure on arms and the reorientation of the subregion's national economies from militarization to human security attainment. On the contrary, the new world order has ushered in the genesis of a geopolitics in which new forms of hegemonic instability emanate from the remains of the old world order. Moreover, the political and economic challenges of the new world order are voiced in relation to concerns about potential unipolar hegemony (Harvey, 1995), downsizing, and exclusion (Brecher and Costello, 1994); the erosion of state capacity to influence transnational economic and political processes that often intervene with its sovereignty (Hirst and Thompson, 1996); and transnational corporations' command over domestic policies. These questions raise issues pertaining to the security of states, and the consequences of this for the security of citizens. Before turning to that, however, let us examine the promises and challenges of the new world order in the context of the Horn of Africa.

Prelude to the New World Order

During the Cold War, the states of the Horn of Africa were the scene of superpower rivalry between the Soviet Union and the United States, supported by the Eastern and Western blocs, respectively. Ethiopia, for instance, fell under Soviet influence at the end of the imperial regime in 1974 and remained so until the defeat of the Mengistu regime by the Ethiopian Peoples Revolutionary Democratic Forces (EPRDF) in 1991. From 1956 to 1969, Sudan was under the influence of the United States and the Western bloc countries, particularly Britain, its former colonial power. The May 1969 military coup d'état brought Sudan under the influence of the Soviet Union, but from 1977 to 1989 Sudan changed its ideological orientation and returned to the influence of the United States and its Western allies. The Siad Barre military coup of October 1969 had created socialist Somalia under the influence of the Soviet Union. Following the Somali defeat in the war against Ethiopia (1978), Somalia reverted to U.S. influence, which continued until the collapse of the Somali state in 1991.

Unlike other countries in the Horn of Africa, Djibouti retained a strong French military presence under the Djibouti-French Cooperation Summit. Although Djibouti has not featured prominently in the politics of the Horn of Africa, its political instability exhibits patterns similar to the rest of the subregion. Today Djibouti has some 350,000 inhabitants, 35 percent of whom are Afar and 65 percent Somali. This distribution is markedly different from that in 1977, when Djibouti gained independence from France: at that time there were almost equal numbers of Somali and Afar. Since 1981, however, Djibouti has been plagued by political rivalry between the two nationalities, a situation directly affected by its geographical position and ethnic makeup. The Afar insurgency in the northern part of the country has been influenced by historical ties with the Eritrean and Ethiopian Afar, whereas the present population imbalance is a direct result of the civil war in Somalia and Djibouti's proximity to the northern border of the Republic of Somalia (now the northern border of the Republic of Somaliland) and the Ethiopian-Somali.

The Horn of Africa represents a reverse of the theory of hegemonic stability (Keohane, 1996), in which superpower hegemony deepens rather than lessens political stability. During the Cold War, external hegemony was militated by the continued dependence of these countries on the former colonial powers. Ethiopia was independent at the onset of the Cold War, but Sudan, Somalia, and Djibouti, which gained their independence in 1956, 1967, and 1977, respectively, were still under the influence of their former colonial powers (Britain in the case of Sudan and Somalia and France in the case of Djibouti). All three countries are largely dependent on external development and military aid. Furthermore, these are conflict-ridden countries whose recent history is peppered with inter- and intrastate wars, such as the civil war in southern Sudan (1955 to date) and the Eritrean war of independence (1962–1991). There were also internal conflicts between the Ethiopian state and several liberation fronts, among which were the Oromo Liberation Front (OLF), Tigray People's Liberation Front (TPLF), Western Somali Liberation Front (WSLF), and Afar Liberation Front (ALF). The protracted Somali-Ethiopian war (1978–1988) gave rise to the development of organized Somali liberation fronts such as the Somali National Movement (SNM), the United Somali Congress (USC), and the Somali Salvation Democratic Front (SSDF). Ironically, it was these very liberation fronts that heralded the collapse of the Siad Barre regime and whose internal conflicts contributed significantly to the total collapse of the Somali state in 1991.

The artificiality of the borders erected by the colonial powers and the coexistence of similar nationalities across the borders of the countries of the Horn of Africa (Oromo, Somali, Nuer, Beni Amir, Afar, and many more) only magnifies the difficulty of dealing with these conflicts as national conflicts. Insurgency and national liberation movements were supported by rival states to discredit their opponents, depending on their ideological orientation (capitalist or socialist). An exception was the war between Somalia and Ethiopia (1978), in which both were initially supported by the Soviet Union. However, when the Soviet Union chose to support Ethiopia, Somalia switched its allegiance to the United States, a situation that persisted until the collapse of the Somali state in 1991. Similarly, Sudan supported the Eritrea liberation fronts (Eritrea Liberation Front [ELF] and Eritrea Peoples Liberation Front [EPLF]) and several other Ethiopia-based liberation fronts against the Ethiopian government; the Mengistu regime of Ethiopia supported the south-based Sudan People's Liberation Army (SPLA) and its socialist-oriented political wing, the Sudan People's Liberation Movement (SPLM), in the war against northern Sudanese hegemony (Mohamed Salih, 1991; Harbeson, 1995b).

The persistence of internal and interstate conflicts increased the dependence of the countries of the Horn of Africa on the superpowers, which exerted tremendous political leverage over them. Clapham (1996) observes, "The search for outside resources to maintain domestic power structures was central to the foreign policies of the great majority of the African states." In the Horn of Africa case, he argues, "Where the conventions of territoriality never fully applied, internal ethnic or religious divisions were still harder to insulate from the structure of regional or global alliances. . . . Domestic and regional policies were no more than parts of the same equation" (Clapham, 1996: 65–66). Consequently, political instability has been exacerbated by the extent to which some of the Horn countries were able to play one superpower against the other depending, at times, on internal political factors. As indicated, neither the alliances between the countries of the Horn of Africa nor those between them and the superpowers were permanent, with the exception of Djibouti (still under French patronage), which has remained firmly under Western influence. It is also important that during the countdown to the collapse of the Eastern bloc and the Soviet Union, Ethiopia was the only country in the Horn of Africa that was still within the orbit of the Soviet Union. By the onset of unipolarity, virtually all the countries of the Horn of Africa were strong advocates of the ethos of neoliberalism and market economy principles with the exception of Sudan, which advocates a Muslim fundamentalist system of government.

In the following sections I argue that the end of bipolarity has not contributed to the creation of a regional context conducive either to traditional state-centric security or to a human-centered security in the Horn of Africa. This is reflected in citizen insecurity resulting from state actions, including human rights abuses; the absence of democratic experience; and general political discontent. These have contributed to the continuation of civil wars in most countries of the Horn of Africa. The end of bipolarity has produced new forms of polarization (ethnic, religious, economic) that have engulfed state and civil society in protracted acts of violence threatening the security of both citizen and the state.

Unipolarity: Squandering the Peace Dividend

In common with most other regions contested by the superpowers during the Cold War, the countries of the Horn of Africa have been experiencing political turmoil of alarming proportions. The decline of bipolarity has not reduced the intensity of the civil wars in Djibouti, Sudan, and Somalia. Most conflicts have in fact taken on new magnitudes and dimensions. The civil war in Sudan, for instance, not only continued but was further complicated by the split of the SPLA in 1991 into Garang and Machar factions and several other splinter groups. Despite several cease-fires between the Sudan government and the SPLA and SPLM factions, the situation of the refugees and internally displaced peoples continued to pose serious human security issues, including famine, food shortages, malnutrition, disease, and human rights abuses by the warring factions.

Although the post–Cold War order has contributed to the collapse of the Siad Barre regime in Somalia and the Mengistu regime in Ethiopia, the reactions of the two countries to the post–Cold War order differed considerably. The Somali civil war continued amid frustrations and mistrust between the south and the north, the Somali National Movement (SNM) proclaiming the independence of the self-declared Republic of Somaliland in the north. Even in Somaliland, however, there have been sporadic conflicts among the various power contenders (Mohamed Salih and Wohlgemuth, 1994). The collapse of the Somali state and Somaliland's declaration of independence have, in a sense, restrained Somali nationalism and its quest for the creation of Greater Somalia, that is, the unitary state of the Somali people in Somalia proper (north and south), northern Kenya, western Ethiopia, and Djibouti. Both Somaliland and Somalia have introduced elements of Islamic shari'a laws, although they have not declared themselves Islamic states. Ethiopia, keen to prevent Islamic fundamentalist groups from operating near its fragile borders with Somalia, has used artillery and air bombardment to destroy the bases of the Islamic groups inside Somalia.

The silent civil war between the government of Djibouti and the Afar opposition continued, and the Republic of Somalia ceased to exist amid a brutal civil war between the warring factions. Ethiopia is still largely peaceful after Eritrea's independence in 1993 but continues to face strong opposition from the Oromo Liberation Front and its claims for an Oromo state (Oromyia). Fears of worsening Sudano-Ethiopian relations surfaced following an attempt by Sudan-based Muslim extremists to assassinate President Hussni Mubarak of Egypt, in Addis Ababa in 1994. This was sufficient cause for the Ethiopian government to reopen the offices of the Sudan People's Liberation Front (SPLA) and allow Sudan opposition groups and liberation movements, including the SPLA-SPLM, to operate from Ethiopia. The presence of large numbers of Somali refugees represents a further element of political instability, as does the emergence of more than thirteen Somali political organizations with various demands ranging from independence to federalism or regional autonomy. The Ogaden Liberation Front and Western Somali Liberation Front are still active, using hostile and at times military confrontations to solve outstanding political issues.

Three years after independence, Eritrea was at loggerheads with the Sudan government, accusing it of supporting the Eritrean Islamic Jihad, a militant Islamic group that calls for the introduction of Islamic shari'a laws and the Islamization of the Eritrean state. As a result, Eritrea became the center for the Sudanese northern-based opposition outside Sudan. Since 1994, Eritrea had offered military support to the Sudan National Democratic Alliance (NDA), a coalition of political parties that oppose the National Islamic Front (NIF) government of Sudan. The government of Eritrea handed over the Sudan embassy in Asmara to the Sudanese opposition forces (see Medhanie, 1994, for more details).

In January 1997, the Sudan government accused Ethiopia and Eritrea of supporting the rebel offensives in eastern (Kassala Province) and southeastern (Blue Nile Province) Sudan. With battles between the Sudan armed forces and the Sudanese opposition forces in progress at the time of writing, it seems clear that the relationship between Sudan, Ethiopia, and Eritrea has, to a large extent, retained its Cold War pattern. Ethiopia and Eritrea support the Sudan opposition and liberation movements, and in retaliation the Sudan government supports the Ethiopian and Eritrean opposition.

The Eritrea-Djibouti nexus has also played a different role in the post–Cold War Order. The Djibouti government shifted its position from harboring the Afar Liberation Front (ALF) against the Mengistu regime, fearful of a potential alliance among the Djibouti Afar, Eritrean Afar, and Ethiopian Afar. The collapse of the Somali state and the declaration of independence by the Republic of Somaliland means that Djibouti is less threatened by the territorial claims of the Republic of Somalia over Djibouti as part of Greater Somalia. In spite of internal political instability, Djibouti remains the headquarters of the Intergovernmental Authority on Drought and Development (IGADD), which was established in 1986 by Djibouti, Ethiopia, Kenya, Somalia, Sudan, and Uganda and was joined by Eritrea after its independence in 1993. IGADD was originally conceived by its drought-prone founding member states as a way of coordinating measures to combat the effects of drought and desertification. Recently the U.S. administration has been increasingly in favor of using IGADD to find a solution to the southern Sudan civil war and Sudan's complex problems with Eritrea. This in a sense gives Djibouti a political weight that some countries, such as Kenya, consider inappropriate to its size and economic potential.

In short, the post–Cold War order heightened the expectations of the peoples of the Horn of Africa for peace and prosperity. However, most civil wars continued, new problems emerged, and others resurfaced under new forms and structures. The current situation negates the orthodox realist and liberal security positions, as the states of the Horn of Africa neither are in control of the direction of their domestic affairs nor have the necessary powers to influence the structure of the international relations into which they have been locked. The states of the Horn of Africa have continued to deteriorate and can hardly be called power maximizers. Worst of all they have not been able to yield any tangible benefits from the prosperity promised by the new world order. The greatest disappointment to the peoples of the Horn is that the new world order has not produced development, security, or political stability. In the midst of failed states that cannot even practice the minimal requirements of sovereignty, they were subjected and hence further compromised by heavy-handed, ill-thought-out multilateral interventions that have in some instances aggravated rather than improved the situation.

Questioning the Military Ethos of Neomultilateralism

In terms of the effects of ill-considered humanitarian interventions, the U.S.-led UN intervention in Somalia was the epitome of all that could go wrong. Following the collapse of the autocratic regime of Siad Barre in Somalia, the country fell into the hands of the main rebel forces, the south-based United Somali Congress (USC) and the north-based Somali National Movement (SNM). The civil war regained momentum, particularly with the withdrawal of SNM to its northern power base (at Hargesa, the capital of the self-declared Somaliland) and the internal power struggle and split of the USC into the factions of Mohamed Farah Aideed and Ali Mahdi. In December 1992, famine and the deterioration of the security situation contributed to the deaths of an estimated 250,000 people. When the ensuing fighting between the Somali factions prevented the delivery of relief food, a U.S.-led UN intervention force code-named Operation Restore Hope was authorized by the U.S. administration. The UN version of this operation was the United Nations Intervention Force (UNIF), which after stiff resistance in Mogadishu became the United Nations Operations in Somalia (UNOSOM I and UNOSOM II). According to Lyons and Samatar (1995: 33–34), "The US mission to the United Nations argued that Somalia provided the opportunity to increase UN credibility in peace keeping in the post–cold war era, a policy advocated by Bush as part of his New World Order."

Many positive and negative evaluations of the humanitarian intervention in Somalia have already been published. Omar and de Waal (1994) highlighted human rights abuses by the UN intervention forces; Prendergast (1995) reported on the failure of the UN intervention forces to reach out to the Somali peoples; Okafor (1996) described the intervention as an oppression by the United Nations against an African people; Malanczuk (1993) questioned the legitimacy of the use of force by the United Nations; and Williams (1995) focused on the moral dilemmas surrounding the UN intervention and gave detailed accounts of the reasons surrounding the UN failure to fulfill its mandate.

The case of the U.S.-led UN intervention in Somalia stands as testimony to the failure of neomultilateralism, under the new world order, to live up to its expectations. According to Prendergast (1995), the UN troops left Somalia with more to be done than when they had arrived. In "Toward a Taxonomy of Failed States," Jean-Germain (1996: 469) argues that the new world order has enhanced the decay of Somalia and other states such as Rwanda, Liberia, and Haiti. These negative aspects of neomultilateralism expose one of the foundations of the new world order, leading some to argue that it is founded on the supremacy of a system of global governance dominated by the United States and what it calls its Western allies (i.e., those countries that emerged victorious from World War II). This distinctive post–World War II sentiment has been reinforced by the arrogance exhibited by victorious states the world over, including those who heralded the collapse of the Eastern bloc and the emergence of unipolarity.

Operation Lifeline Sudan was conceived in 1989 amid SPLA-SPLM advances against Sudan government forces in the south. The capture of almost two-thirds of the south by the SPLA-SPLM also meant that large numbers of southern Sudanese (estimated at the time to total some 1.6 million) were displaced with no sources of food or shelter. The collapse of the government defenses in the war zone, and even in some of the northern provinces bordering the south, created a desperate situation (see Deng, 1995). The elected prime minister, Sadiq El Mahdi, agreed to allow relief aid to both sides in the civil war in what was termed by USAID-Sudan a neutral relief program. Operation Lifeline Sudan was based in Nairobi and involved USAID-led UN institutions (UNICEF, ICRC, and the World Food Program [WFP]) and a consortium of Western nongovernmental organizations. According to Burr and Collins (1995: 176), the conditions for Operation Lifeline Sudan stipulated:

> The Sudan Government should grant the donors the most favourite dollar exchange rate, ensure rapid customs clearance of relief commodities, issue visas and travel permits promptly, and allow participants to operate relief flights within Sudan and across international boundaries. Finally, Private Voluntary Organizations (PVOs or NGOs) operating in the field would be granted licences to use radios. To ensure that the government abide by its agreement, the donors wanted to have a High Ministerial Committee established. It would review complaints and resolve problems—especially with regard to military cooperation and to operations involving the Sudan Railways Cooperation and the River Transport Authority. Eventually, Sadiq, the Prime Minister, agreed to its creation and was named chair with the Relief and Rehabilitation Commission (RRC) as the committee's secretariat.

In a report commissioned by UNICEF (Mohamed Salih, 1989b), I wrote that in agreeing to Operation Lifeline Sudan (OLS) conditions, the Sudan government had, out of desperation, ceded a substantial part of its sovereignty to the U.S.-led UN operations in southern Sudan. Since OLS was originally intended to operate in war-torn and drought-affected regions, it could be inferred that not only the south but the sovereignty of the whole of Sudan had been greatly compromised. This interference with sovereignty would have been justified if it had been merely for humanitarian purposes. However, Duffield (1993) and Duffield and Prendergast (1994) claim that such interventions in the Horn of Africa have created a parallel economy that is administered by NGOs and that, contrary to intentions, is to the benefit of merchants and military officers.

Operation Lifeline Sudan thus represented a blessing in disguise for Sudan's northern-dominated economy, which had suffered considerably from the civil war. In this particular case, humanitarian intervention reinforced the Sudan economy and supported its war effort by obtaining badly needed foreign exchange to finance the purchase of weapons and ammunition. The fact that many lives have been saved by relief food may not, in the final analysis, justify the loss of life by the ammunition that was made available by renting out Sudanese cargo planes and transport to Operation Lifeline Sudan. Reports by NGOs have shown that the Sudan government often commandeered private trucks for the war effort, making their owners genuine stakeholders in the continuity of war.

Humanitarian intervention has also been justified under the pretext of protecting human rights: sadly, however, there have been reports of UN forces committing human rights abuses against civilians in Somalia (Omar and de Waal, 1994). In Sudan, Operation Lifeline Sudan has not contributed to any improvement in the human rights situation either inside or outside the war zone. In fact, reports on Sudan (Africa Watch, 1990; Amnesty International, 1995; and Merheb, 1995) reveal an unprecedented increase in human rights violations in the war zone, both by government and rebel forces. The greatest failure of Operation Lifeline Sudan was its lax attitude toward human rights violations in southern Sudan while it carried out its mandate of feeding the hungry.

With these points in mind, one cannot help but agree with Okafor (1996: 225) in concluding that the failure of UN interventions such as those in Sudan and Somalia can be explained by (1) the structural exclusion and selective application of international law and the involvement of the United Nations in oppression; (2) the resultant undermining of the legitimacy of the global system of governance, reduction in the state's voluntary compliance with international normative requirements; and (3) impairment of the UN's ability to cultivate local support. The total situation ineluctably results in the perpetuation or multiplication of human misery and oppression.

At least three main conclusions can be drawn from humanitarian interventions in Somalia and Sudan. First, multilateral institutions can neither replace the functions of the state nor reconstruct the state institutions they have directly or indirectly participated in destroying. Second, multilateral institutions often tend to operate in isolation from the recipient communities, therefore creating externally driven quasi-state institutions (such as military or security protection forces, social welfare institutions, public works, and so on). Such externally driven institutions often undermine the state's normative rules without offering an alternative with which the populace can identify. Third, most multilateral institutions are undemocratic; thus they do not offer an example of democratic governance to the subjects of the intervention, whom they are attempting to rescue from the tyranny of military dictators or authoritarian regimes. Although humanitarian intervention may save lives in the short run, the long-term consequences may include new forms of hegemony and dependence.

Market Liberalism and Democracy at Odds

Market liberalism without a human face has always thwarted people's efforts to democratize the state. All the surviving countries of the Horn of Africa (Djibouti, Eritrea, Ethiopia, and Sudan—the latter having been politically isolated or economically restrained) are undergoing some form of economic policy reforms. Unlike the first phase of structural adjustment, which was implemented in close collaboration between the African states and the World Bank and IMF, the second phase calls for a reduction in the scope of state activities (World Bank, 1994a). This is the result of the

World Bank and IMF's conclusion that Africa needs "good governance" to develop. In other words, the World Bank and IMF blame "bad and corrupt governance" for the failure of the first phase of economic policy reforms, in which the African states were partners. This is a ridiculous charge when one considers the conditionality regime attached to structural adjustment programs and the direct involvement of the World Bank and IMF in their conception and implementation. These reforms took the shape of both official and informal policy windows: structural adjustment programs to be officially implemented by the state and externally driven political reforms that were entrusted to Western NGOs, whose role was to influence civil society's struggle for human and democratic rights.

In the Horn of Africa, the promised transition from military rule and one-party states to democracy during the post–Cold War order has been haunted by political instability. With all its internal troubles, Ethiopia seems to be the only country in the Horn of Africa that has some democratic credentials to show. In Sudan, the post–Cold War order witnessed the reverse process: a transition from multiparty democracy to military rule with a strong Islamic fundamentalist position vis-à-vis U.S. policies in the Horn of Africa. The rise of Islamic fundamentalism in Sudan may be attributable to the misery created by the structural adjustment programs, which weakened the Sudanese state and reduced its resolve to act as guardian of the public good. Also, the conditions imposed by Operation Lifeline Sudan humiliated the Sudanese armed forces, which sent several ultimatums to Sadiq El Mahdi, the elected prime minister, demanding that he consider a peaceful solution to the southern Sudan conflict (Mohamed Salih, 1989a). This proved to be a dangerous liaison: with the support of the National Islamic Front (NIF), the Sudanese army felt it had the justification it needed to seize power in June 1989.

Eritrea was first ruled by an assembly (formed in 1991) composed of the Central Committee of the Eritrea Peoples Liberation Front (EPLF), which led the independence struggle; thirty members of provincial assemblies; and thirty members selected by the EPLF Central Committee. In April 1994, the Constitutional Commission of Eritrea (CCE) was established and in June 1996 the first draft of the new constitution was approved by the Eritrean parliament. Since independence, opposition has consisted mainly of Muslim groupings—Islamic Jihad, a Muslim fundamentalist organization, and a splinter group called the Assembly of Islamic Call for Reformation. There is also the Eritrean Liberation Front–Revolutionary, a splinter group from the lowland-based Eritrean Liberation Front that started the Eritrean war of liberation against Ethiopia in 1962.

The Eritrean opposition claims that the EPLF is nondemocratic and monopolizes power and that the new constitution is not set up for multiparty democracy. In an interview in the Arabic daily *Al Sharq al-Awsat*,

July 26, 1996, President Afewerki of Eritrea is quoted as saying: "We do not want any absolute or childish democracy, and neither do we advocate European or US-style democracy which would not be suitable for our society, because these were established in circumstances different from what we have gone through. . . . We now need a political climate which will guarantee stability and the reconstruction processes." This statement has been widely interpreted by the opposition forces to imply that Eritrea will not opt for a multiparty democracy, although the draft constitution contains an article on the freedom to organize, thereby making it possible to form political parties. It is difficult at present to predict the outcome of Eritrea's internal political instability and its conflict with the Sudan Islamic government; time will tell whether the two countries will slide back into hostilities similar to those perpetuated by Cold War politics. The Sudan-Eritrea situation is further complicated by the 110,000 Eritrean refugees who live in Sudan, some of whom are active in the opposition to the Eritrean government; the military opposition to Sudan operates from Eritrea. The fear is that these intra- and interstate conflicts may harden EPLF's attitudes toward the opposition and thus thwart any hopes for a democratic system informed by Eritrea's culture and history.

The polity and economy of Djibouti, as we have seen, are still largely influenced by France. The Djibouti-Franco Cooperation Committee has been very active in defining the French role and in bringing the government and the opposition to the negotiating table. Although many had thought that the French element would enhance Djibouti's security and lessen its internal conflict, this expectation faded following the 1986 military skirmishes between the government and the Isaq-based Democratic Front for the Liberation of Djibouti (FDLD) and the Djibouti National Movement for the Restoration of Democracy (MNDID) and with the formation in 1991 of the Front for the Restoration of Unity and Democracy (FRUD), which consists of three militant Afar groups.

Although this is not the place to discuss the pros and cons of structural adjustment policies, the point here is that they have weakened the state's ability to undertake political repair and to attend to the development of social capital. Jean-Germain (1996: 469) laments that "the Structural Adjustment Policies' insistence on reducing the state has missed the point entirely because on the contrary implementing such programmes requires states that can negotiate with the donors' aid conditionalities and have the necessary social capital to implement these policies in the face of widespread resistance. The entropy of failed states is such that they can deliver neither." Even more disturbing, the human rights situation has improved only slightly or, in some states, not at all. As we will see in the following section, as far as the Horn of Africa is concerned, the deterioration of human security is one of the major drawbacks of the new world order.

Coping with Insecurity

The states and peoples of the Horn of Africa have duly been compelled to choose between total collapse through civil wars or political survival with an uncertain future. Both choices have been detrimental to human security and have at times augmented insecurity. One cannot therefore assume that the security of citizens has been enhanced as a result of the new world order or its misconceived global security designs. In fact, security has either worsened or remained at pre–Cold War levels. The states of the Horn of Africa have been engulfed in perpetual civil war and famine, to the detriment of or causing the total collapse of some states such as Somalia. At the same time, failed states increase the propensity for conflict and social unrest, so that the interplay between state insecurity and citizen insecurity has increased during the post–Cold War era. In essence, global security as conceived by the new world order has not trickled down to the impoverished peoples of the Horn of Africa.

The manifestations of human insecurity in the new world order can be attested to by examining a number of parameters that show whether the states of the Horn of Africa are better prepared to provide an enabling environment and social safety nets for their citizens, including the satisfaction of their basic needs. Four points should be made clear from the outset: (1) all countries of the Horn of Africa are producers of primary products and are predominantly agrarian (65–85 percent of the population is engaged in agriculture or pastoralism); (2) like other underdeveloped regions, the Horn of Africa's agricultural policies have an inherent bias toward cash-crop production, to the detriment of food security (Mohamed Salih, 1994a); (3) the states of the Horn of Africa are still largely dependent on rudimentary technology and have the lowest per hectare production rates in the world; (4) invariably, the industrial sector is small (2 to 6 percent of the GDP at most) and overly dependent on imports of capital, technology, and raw materials. If the new world order is to bring desirable changes to the lives of the people of the Horn of Africa, the starting point in cementing the ethos of neomultilateralism, market liberalism, democracy, peace, and prosperity is to address these issues. This process requires a shift from the neopolitics of containment of dissident voices, because of imagined threats posed by invisible enemies, to the acceptance of a diversity of problem-solving scenarios.

Economically, the countries of the Horn of Africa have not done well even at the macroeconomic indicator level, on which the new global order tends to congratulate itself: (1) In 1994, per capita income either declined (Sudan and Somalia) or stagnated (Ethiopia, Djibouti, and Eritrea). (2) Ethiopia is the only country with improved GDP growth rate (from −10 in 1990 to +9.1 in 1993 and +1.8 in 1994); all other countries are experiencing negative growth rates. (3) The 1990–1994 data show that reserves in months of import were stagnant, ranging from 0.4 months in Sudan to 1.8 months in Djibouti and 3.4 months in Eritrea to 5.9 months in Ethiopia. (4) Ethiopia is the only country that receives direct foreign investment (US$100 million in 1994); the rest are still dependent on dwindling official development assistance (ODA) (World Bank, 1996c).

As to the association between state security and the critical security of citizens, the socioeconomic indicators (World Bank, 1996c) of the countries of the Horn of Africa reveal an alarming tendency that ranges between stagnation and decline. From World Bank data, the following picture emerges:

- Between 1989 and 1995, life expectancy at birth remained very low, even by standards of the South: 47 years in Djibouti, 48.2 years in Eritrea, 48 years in Ethiopia, 47.2 years in Somalia, and 51 years in Sudan.
- Primary school enrollment (23–53 percent) and secondary school enrollment (11–14 percent) remain low, with a considerable decrease in Somalia and Sudan relative to the pre–civil war situation. There is a slight improvement in Eritrea as a result of postwar rehabilitation, but a slight decrease in Ethiopia despite a relatively high growth rate during 1995–1997.
- The availability of medicine and health facilities aside, the number of doctors, nurses, and midwives has decreased rather than increased in countries such as Sudan, Somalia, and to some extent Djibouti.
- The only glimmer of hope is the increase in food production in Ethiopia; food self-sufficiency increased there from 65 percent to 86 percent in 1996. Other countries continue the trend of high food imports (Sudan, Eritrea, Djibouti, and Somalia), although some claim that these are food items used by the urban elite.

In extremely underdeveloped countries, a reduced role for the state in managing public risks and opportunities contributes to a reduced responsibility for the redistributional mechanisms necessary for replenishing the social capital on which the state depends. A debilitated state that fails in its functions (as guardian of the public good, as protector of peace and order, and as sovereign over its territory) invites social conflicts and political instability (Buzan, 1983; Mohamed Salih, 1989b). A decline of state control over sovereignty also contributes to the decline of the state's capacity to influence national events. It derails its agenda from development to the bare maintenance of peace and order, often by using extra-jurisdiction rules, including the abuse of human rights and even engagement in civil wars, as has been described earlier. Both situations, as in the case of the Horn of Africa, induce insecurity at state and citizen levels.

Many commentators hasten to hail citizens' struggles to fend for themselves as testimony to the irrelevance of the state. In my view such irresponsible commentaries miss the point in two regards: (1) People's political activities outside the state have reflected the need to resist externally imposed policies under first, hegemonic stability during the Cold War and second, neoliberal hegemony during the new world order. (2) People have learned through bitter lessons that they have to overtake the state and hence transform it into an institution that serves their securities and where their own visions of security become paramount. Had people thought the state irrelevant, they would not have struggled to capture and control it.

Instead of leaving the reader with the impression that the peoples of the Horn of Africa are helpless in coping with insecurity, and by way of summing up this section, I argue that like in other parts of the world (as has been recently shown in the British and French elections), people are resisting neoliberal hegemony. There are impressive democratic movements and liberation fronts across the Horn of Africa with strong people-centered political and social welfare organizations. There is also an impressive proliferation of advocacy groups for indigenous peoples, women against violence, and human rights groups, environmental movements, small-scale enterprises, and so on. Cheru (1997: 153) describes people's struggles against the state institutions as "the silent revolution and the weapon of the weak." There is also the process of postwar rehabilitation in Ethiopia and Eritrea and the reconstruction of civil society in the areas liberated by the SPLA-SPLM in southern Sudan. However, this silent revolution is not against legitimate, accountable, responsible, and democratic states that care for the security of their citizens. The resistance is against authoritarian states that have been kept in power for too long to serve global designs largely determined by the Cold War and that used the people and the states of the Horn of Africa as a "gap filler" in externally driven security designs.

Conclusion

The new world order has brought about a shift from external military hegemony to a global conformity that has failed to induce significant changes in the Horn of Africa's regional political dynamics or to improve the mutual security of states and citizens. By and large, discourse has prevailed that has drawn on a dominant discourse that justifies and hence reinforces the making of new enemy images. Moreover, invisible barriers at the national or the regional level are manifested in real struggles and wars fought by the dispossessed, the displaced, the hungry, and the victims of human rights abuses. As far as human security is concerned, the post–Cold War order has produced meager changes in the lives of the moral majority, which bore the brunt of the Cold War's injustices.

In the Horn of Africa, the so-called global unipolarity has been transformed into regional bipolarity represented by secular states (Djibouti, Eritrea, and Ethiopia) and Islamic-oriented states (Somalia, Somaliland, and Sudan). This bipolarity attracts limited global interest because of the region's insignificant economic contribution to, and political power in, the new world order. In contrast, the secular states have, in many ways, been used by external forces to contain the Islamicist states, leading to a conflict situation similar to that of the old world order.

In short, it will take more to come to terms with the politics of the new world order than for the peripheral states of the Horn to preach the ethos of neomultilateralism and market liberalism. It will require a vision divorced from the reminiscences of the old world order and from the invisible barriers that it has erected in the psyche of those entrusted with the politics of the post–Cold War order. If that world order is to succeed, it has to be based on human rather than orthodox notions of security, for the new world order has arrived through people's struggles and not through military conquest.

9

Security and State-Society Crises in Sierra Leone and Liberia

Max Sesay

Located on the west coast of Africa, Sierra Leone and Liberia are among the world's poorest states. Despite the fact that they share geographical boundaries, the two states have differences that are quite apparent even at first glance. They include, among others, differences in colonial experience or its lack thereof, differences in constitutional development, and differences in demographic profile. Nevertheless, beneath these differences lie a range of striking historical, cultural, political, and economic commonalities. Both societies are replete with contrasts, dichotomies, and inequalities that, broadly speaking, fit into a "centre-periphery" analysis (Clapham, 1976).

There is the historic significance of the dichotomy between the coastal regions, represented by the two capital cities of Freetown and Monrovia, and the interior, or hinterland. Rural/urban differences have thus always been sensitive issues in the political development of both states. There has been tension between settler communities of African descendants from Europe and the Americas, who either came to dominate these societies or enjoyed more privileged positions, and the indigenous Africans. Largely because the allocation of resources also occurred along center-periphery lines, political competition was predominantly for control of the center. The development of similarly exploitative clientelistic political systems in societies with disparate communities was as much the product of internal regional variations as the need of political elites to develop a network of dependable supporters to ensure regime survival. This relationship between political patrons and their clients assumed a class form in which the political elites remained dominant and more privileged. Furthermore, local

145

reactions to the dominant economic position of the Lebanese, at least in the case of Sierra Leone, should be understood both in class and racial terms.

From the above, it is evident that both Liberia and Sierra Leone are inherently tension-laden societies exhibiting a basic lack of equality in the allocation of power, resources, and privilege among sections of society with conflicting interests. The challenge has always been that of bridging the gap between urban-coastal and rural-interior areas or inhabitants, between political elites and their clients, between "foreign" and indigenous business, and between men and women. The level of political stability and of the effectiveness and legitimacy of the state has thus historically been largely determined by the manner of interaction between various diametrically opposed interests and the success of political elites at either truly mobilizing the various sections of society for national development or else manipulating the divisions and inequalities. Sierra Leone and Liberia provide complex but illustrative examples of factors that can contribute to the collapse of state-society relations and thus impact directly on human security.

The similarities between Liberia and Sierra Leone are reflected not only in the historic ties between the two countries but also in their more recent experiences. Both states fit into Zartman's broadly defined category of "collapsed states," otherwise known as "soft states," "failed states," or "nonsovereign states" (Zartman, 1995). This vocabulary refers to the multiple debilitating crises that plague many contemporary African states (see Mazrui, Chossudovsky, this volume). Like many African states, Liberia and Sierra Leone possess juridical statehood, no doubt, but they lack in the 1990s most of the attributes usually associated with the empirical essence of statehood in Europe and North America. State capacity is generally weak and state authority rarely extends beyond the capital city. Both states have been successfully challenged and crippled not only by the economic and political activities of individuals or groups of individuals but also by insurrectionist forces. In both cases, the irrelevance of the state is manifest in its lack of mobilizational capacity and lack of involvement of the bulk of its citizenry in the overall governance of society (Riley, 1997a). At the international level, politics has been fundamentally about obtaining resources to ensure regime survival at home (Clapham, 1996).

In recent times, Sierra Leone and Liberia have been riddled by a crisis of governance resulting from weak or poor leaderships and the inability of the state in both societies to function effectively. By the early 1980s, there was already reference to the "politics of failure" as distinctly characterizing state governance in both societies (Clapham, 1982). The preoccupation of political elites with wealth accumulation for personal purposes, the skewed nature of development, and the economic and fiscal crises gradually but effectively eroded state capacity and destroyed state institutions. This process produced, and was accelerated by, civil war in both countries. The result has been the almost terminal disintegration of these states (see Mazrui and Wilkin, this volume).

It can reasonably be suggested that to fully understand recent developments in Sierra Leone and Liberia, one necessarily has to focus on the social processes at work and assess the relationship between globalization and internal crises in both states. Thus there is a concern with state-society relations at the local, regional, and global levels, where the structures of capitalism and an interstate system are codetermining of world order (see Wilkin, this volume).

Both Sierra Leone and Liberia now have to contend with a multiplicity of problems that have left them more susceptible to external leverage than ever before and, in several respects, mirror developments in other parts of sub-Saharan Africa. The heightened political and economic vulnerabilities of the two states have given rise to a set of circumstances in which security concerns must be understood not in traditional realist terms but rather in ways that will generate appropriate responses and solutions to the problems. The collapse of the state in Sierra Leone and Liberia has come about not as a result of any obvious external military threat but is rather due to a complex interaction of political and social forces at the national and subnational levels and insecurity in the global economic system. To fully understand this process, there is a need to examine the dynamics and unravel the levels, extent, and consequences of the polarization that has occurred and continues to occur in both states. The significance of issues of justice, class, race, gender, and community should be illuminated and understood against the backdrop of the social, political, and economic crises that have afflicted Sierra Leone and Liberia both in the past and in recent times.

Problems of Human Security:
State Power and the Crisis of Governance

Even though Liberia and Sierra Leone differ in terms of the historical development of the state, both are good examples of countries whose developments have been retarded by the pathological effects of "neo-patrimonialism" (Sandbrook, 1985). In each case, the state by far outstripped any other formal organizations both in size and resources. Its dominant role in the economic and social life of both countries transformed it into an authoritarian, coercive machine with huge potential for patronage. This, together with its capacity to enrich through the privatization of public resources, explains why the intense competition between various groups for control of the state in both countries is an end in itself (see Wilkin, this volume).

State-Society Relations in Liberia

The modern Liberian state arose from coastal settlements established by the American Colonization Society (ACS) in 1822 around the area of the capital, Monrovia. In 1847, these settlements, housing an amalgam of repatriated Africans from Europe and the Americas as well as Africans liberated from slave ships (the "Congos"), became an independent state. By the early twentieth century, this state had incorporated its hinterland through conquest. Composing less than 2 percent of the population, these Americo-Liberians, as they came to be known, governed Liberia consistently until 1980, when their rule was brutally terminated by a coup d'état. This coup, led by the almost untutored Samuel Doe, a master sergeant in the Armed Forces of Liberia (AFL), represented a massive change in the configuration of Liberian politics and society. It transferred the reins of power for the first time to someone with no Americo-Liberian connection. Doe hailed from the poorly educated Krahn, an ethnic group that composed only 4 percent of the population.

An intricate clientelistic system had conferred relative stability to the Liberian polity for a century and a half. Similarly, it had provided the circumstances for a deep well of resentment that erupted in 1980 and thereafter transformed Liberia into an anarchic society. The crisis and eventual collapse of the Liberian state should thus be seen as the product of a long process of search for justice in society: the need to replace an old order that typified exclusionary politics with a new inclusive and, perhaps, democratic one (Dolo, 1996).

It is no exaggeration that governance through the prewar Liberian state was, for the most part, carried out by and for the coastally based settlers to the exclusion of the majority population, which lived in the interior. Indigenous Liberians were accorded, more or less, second class status by their exclusion from the mainstream of society. They lacked the vote, could not hold central and local government positions, and lacked any say in the decisionmaking process. The hierarchical political structures established after the conquest of the interior were personned by Americo-Liberians. Appointment to office, both at local and central government levels, was the prerogative of the chief executive, and officeholders came largely from the Americo-Liberian community. The balkanization or amalgamation of the interior into chiefdoms was done on the basis of political expediency and not local requirements. Communal land was expropriated and used either as estates by absentee landlords from the coast or for exploitation by foreign companies. Above all, forced unpaid labor drawn from the local communities was used to work the expropriated lands (Lowenkopf, 1976).

Despite the rancor bound to be whipped up by this institutionalized exploitation, the Americo-Liberians succeeded in maintaining their dominance.

This occurred mainly through an extension of the patronage system to the interior and the gradual reform of the system. The political elite from the coast was not completely remote; members of the elite came into frequent contact with interior people through their estates, which came to serve as retreats and channels for the distribution of patronage. The co-optation and eventual integration of interior inhabitants into the political system came through the implementation of two policies by Liberia's best known president, William Tubman (1947–1971). The pacification of the interior was achieved through a policy of unification that accorded equal treatment to the coastal settlements and the interior. This policy opened up the system for interior participation in central administration and politics. Hinterland citizens could now send representatives to the legislature as well as hold local government jobs.

The "open door" policy, which sought to encourage foreign investment in Liberia, led to unprecedented economic growth, although not development (Clower et al., 1966). Foreign capital provided enormous state revenues that served as the lubricant for the smooth running of such a clientelistic machine. But the longevity of the Americo-Liberian hegemony was, finally, due to the personal leadership style of Tubman. His folksy style, his wide network of personal contacts and informants, and his astuteness in appointing to offices only close and trusted people formed the bedrock on which the system rested.

However, it was clear by the time Tubman's vice president, William Tolbert, succeeded him as president in 1971 that the hegemony of the Americo-Liberian oligarchy had run its full course. A lethal combination of internal and external factors brought this rickety machinery to a halt: Tolbert's lack of his predecessor's astuteness and personal touch, the economic decline of the 1970s (see below), and the growth in numbers of well-educated and politically articulate people from the interior who sought to transform the system. Tolbert's attempt to carry out overdue political and social reforms, in response to unprecedented opposition, nevertheless deviated from the political logic and requirements of Tubman's legacy. In the end, the system came under severe strain and broke down. The spark was an increase in the price of rice, the staple food, in April 1979. This led to widespread demonstrations and violence that rocked the foundations of the political establishment and led to a massacre by security forces ordered to suppress the demonstrations. The government's unpopularity in the aftermath of these events led to a bloody military coup d'état a year later, in which Tolbert was assassinated.

Even though Doe promised to transform Liberian society, his emergence to power accelerated the disintegration of the Liberian state. By the end of the Doe era in 1989, state machinery had literally ceased to function. His rule was characterized by massive human rights violations, a steep economic decline partly due to corruption and mismanagement, political drift, and the elimination of real and imagined enemies. The regime's brutality was markedly represented by the hasty executions of alleged coup plotters; the televised execution in 1980 of former government ministers on a Monrovia beach; and the government's ferocious response to a failed coup in 1985, led by former head of the Liberian army Thomas Quiwonkpa. Lacking a political base and propelled by an advanced form of paranoia, Doe resorted to governing through tribalism. The bureaucracy, the army, security forces, and public services became permeated with his Krahn tribesmen. This intensified the divisions in Liberian society, and when Doe tried to hold on to power by falsifying the election results of 1985, Liberia was put on a dangerous precipice. Doe also plundered state coffers for his own purposes and for distribution to his clients. But continued economic decline and external pressure meant that resources for patronage were in very short supply. By December 1989, an insurrection to topple him from power degenerated into a civil war that effectively undermined what remained of the prewar state (Liebenow, 1987; Sawyer, 1992).

State-Society Relations in Sierra Leone

The state of Sierra Leone has also collapsed but through a more complex interaction of forces. The modern Sierra Leone state emerged from the formal integration in 1961 of British-established coastal settlements of repatriated Africans from England, Nova Scotia, and the Caribbean of Africans from the immediate hinterland. The coastal settlements, established around present-day Freetown in 1787, were governed directly as a British colony beginning in 1808; the hinterland remained relatively independent until 1896, when it became a British protectorate and was governed indirectly through traditional institutions.

By the time of independence in 1961, Sierra Leonean society was polarized along several lines. The first was that between the more Westernized, better educated, and more coherent settler community in Freetown (the Krio, variant of Creoles) and the less educated and disparate communities of the interior. The tension between the two categories of people was more prominent in the last days of British colonial rule but persisted into the postcolonial period. By virtue of their education, the Krio, who made up less than 2 percent of the population, held a disproportionate number of jobs in the central administration and the professions. This advantage was a serious source of conflict between them and the majority population from the interior. However, unlike their counterparts in Liberia, the Krio failed to gain control of the state because the British introduced universal adult suffrage in the 1950s, thereby instituting majority rule.

Sierra Leone society also came to be polarized along ethnoregional lines: between the north (made up of the Temne, Limba, Susu, and other ethnic groups) and the south (made up mostly of the Mende but with a number of smaller groups). In the context of the tense electoral competition for state control, this division became the most prominent and enduring after independence. The two political parties that have dominated post-independence Sierra Leone politics are regionally based: the Sierra Leone People's Party (SLPP) has traditionally been southern based; the All People's Congress (APC) drew most of its support from the north.

There was, furthermore, the tension generated by the presence of the Lebanese community. Lebanese migration to Sierra Leone dated back to the 1880s. By the time of independence, the Lebanese had come to dominate all sectors of the Sierra Leone economy. But Lebanese economic success, due partly to a deliberate British colonial policy that favored them and partly to their hard work, has always been viewed unfavorably by the rest of Sierra Leone society. As such, the Lebanese have been the object of enormous local resentment and sometimes abuse and attack (Van der Laan, 1975). Excluded from any form of politics, the Lebanese nevertheless became economic powerhouses, providing political elites with the spoils they badly needed for distribution as patronage. Since the 1970s, the Lebanese have wielded considerable informal influence in state matters; political leaders can attack them, but only at their peril.

Even at the local level, there was conflict and tension between the local hereditary rulers (paramount chiefs), who had considerable prestige and wealth, and their subjects. Thus there are crosscutting, interwoven and complex sources of conflict—between coastal settlers and interior inhabitants; between the north and south; between the major ethnic groupings; between regionally based political parties; between classes (politicians and workers, chiefs and their subjects, and educated and uneducated); and between the Lebanese "settlers" and indigenous Sierra Leoneans—that always have had the potential for creating instability in the Sierra Leone polity. Thus some scholars are correct in arguing that it is inaccurate to see conflict in Sierra Leone society as occurring simply along ethnic lines (Mukonoweshuro, 1990).

Unlike with Liberia, Sierra Leone's social fragmentation and the development of its export-dependent economic base (see below) can be traced to the period of British colonial rule (Sesay, 1993). The British deliberately chose administrative arrangements, leaders, and organizations through which they could direct resources. To ensure "tranquil rule on the cheap" (Migdal, 1988: 121), the British governed through traditional institutions, notably paramount chiefs. Despite their inefficiency and authoritarian and extortionate tendencies, the chiefs became the channels for social development. Governance through chiefs superseded old forms of social control and survival strategies and enhanced the power of chiefs to the extent that they sometimes posed a threat even to the stability of

British colonial rule. The chiefs now also came into direct conflict with the educated elite, who sought to play a more prominent role in the society. In the end, British colonial rule had a great impact on the nature of post-colonial social relationships (Kilson, 1965).

The postcolonial Sierra Leone polity is predicated on kleptocracy, patronage, and preferment (Luke and Riley, 1989: 136) and generally characterized by a personalized form of governance. Political parties are loose alliances based on factional loyalties rather than ideological orientation. The essence of politics has been the desire to hold political office, which guarantees both legal and illicit wealth. A succession of rulers have weakened state institutions and used access to resources as a weapon against political opponents. The need for regime survival has fostered a need for cronies and strongmen, some of whom have become so powerful as to be able to engage, undermine, and often cripple the state. Their influence has affected the initiation, implementation, and success of almost every government policy (Reno, 1995a). In this sense, Sierra Leone typifies countries characterized by a strong society and a weak state (Sesay, 1995). The postcolonial Serria Leone polity thus has had only fragile stability. The chiefs' mobilizational resources have made it hard for postcolonial rulers to attempt any reform of the system.

However, most of the features of Sierra Leone politics and society today can be attributed to the political culture instituted by the regime of Siaka Stevens and his APC Party. By the end of Stevens's seventeen-year rule in 1985, Sierra Leone had been transformed into a country aptly described as a "land of waving palms" (Riley, 1983), as it had reached almost terminal economic decline. Stevens was a master of manipulatory politics and took no chances with time and luck. In the end, he established an inefficient, unaccountable, and repressive political system that has had lasting consequences for Sierra Leone society.

Stevens's APC party, which had poor beginnings as an opposition party in the 1960s, eventually dominated the center of politics through a monopoly of all the means of coercion. These were effectively used against disloyal members of the party, the military, the police, the opposition, and other noncompliant state functionaries (Riley and Parfitt, 1987). But patronage became Stevens's most effective political weapon. By the end of his rule and despite lacking a regional base, Stevens had a carefully woven web of very useful loyalties; he had successfully detribalized his position and had eliminated nearly all forms of opposition. Despite this, Stevens failed to construct either a legitimate, effective, or durable political system with any mobilizational capacity. The paradox, however, was that he achieved political stability (even if a fragile one) in the midst of economic decline and state degeneration (Ly, 1980). Physical violence for regime survival was resorted to with unprecedented insensitivity and ruthlessness. As Clapham (1982: 88) observed, Stevens had "a clear grasp of the basic features of Sierra Leonean political organisation, and (had) few inhibitions about the means he was prepared to use to stay in power."

The net result of Stevens's political strategy was the destruction of state institutions, economic stagnation, political immobilism, and, because state resources were distributed only in accordance with the requirements of his clientelistic system, lopsided development. When he and his supporters also plundered state coffers with impunity, Stevens successfully instituted a kleptocratic system. IMF and World Bank economic reform measures, which included cabinet downsizing and the enhanced administrative capacity of central agencies, were deliberately not implemented because they defied the logic of Stevens's established political networks (Parfitt and Riley, 1989: 132; Reno, 1993).

Thus when Joseph Momoh, Stevens's hand-picked successor in 1985, professed to introduce a new order through "constructive nationalism," few doubted that he risked alienating the old guard. The two major challenges that Momoh faced were first, the need to break away from the stranglehold of the enormously unpopular Lebanese traders and their political supporters in order to establish his authority. Second, because he lacked viable financial options, Momoh had to do something to attract sources of financial support outside the circles of Stevens's legacy. To this end, Momoh favored economic reform. This approach provided him with access to foreign official and private capital, and with this capital came safer political partners and the means to repay debt and combat the subversive tendencies of Stevens's cronies by establishing his own system of patronage. Momoh's state-building strategy had the potential to ensure the revitalization of the decaying state machinery and an efficient government by rendering the inherited patrimonial networks and institutions redundant (Reno, 1993; Sesay, 1995).

But his strategy failed. Creditors pressed for regular debt repayment. The old guard resisted and economic decline continued and led to the collapse of a number of important state institutions—including the army and security forces, which by early 1991 were waging a counteroffensive against invading rebels from Liberia. In April 1992, Momoh was almost effortlessly ousted by a handful of youthful soldiers of the Sierra Leone Army (SLA), who were led by Captain Valentine Strasser. The advent of military rule, with continued economic decline and destructive rebel activity, further undermined the remaining capacity of the institutional state to govern (Reno, 1996).

Economic Decline and State Crisis—
Generating Insecurity

By the late 1980s and early 1990s in West Africa, the interaction between internal and external forces had produced two classical losers in the increasingly competitive global system. The collapse of markets for the exports of both countries led to serious fiscal crises in the 1980s. These crises in turn led to checkered experiences with external donors and international financial institutions (IFIs), which have wielded enormous leverage by intervening in the economic management of both countries (see Chossudovsky, this volume).

Like most other African states, Sierra Leone and Liberia have long been influenced by the processes of globalization. Colonization and capitalist expansion incorporated both states into the global economy in a manner that defined their roles as exporters of raw materials to markets in North America, Europe, and Japan, on the one hand, and importers of manufactured goods from the same sources, on the other. This heavy dependence on extremely volatile and uncertain external markets was crucial in undermining developmental objectives and political support.

By the time of independence in 1961, Sierra Leone had come to rely on the export of a narrow range of commodities. These included both agricultural commodities (cocoa, coffee, and palm oil) and minerals (diamonds, iron ore up to the early 1980s, bauxite, and rutile). Unlike with agricultural products, the exploitation of mineral resources was carried out by multinational corporations from the West, which possessed the capital, technology, and knowledge required. Until 1970, diamond mining in Sierra Leone, which dates back to 1932, was carried out by the Sierra Leone Selection Trust, a wholly owned subsidiary of Consolidated African Selection Trust (CAST). The Sierra Leone Development Company (DELCO), which mined iron ore, was also a wholly owned subsidiary of a British company, African and Eastern Trading Corporation (Zack-Williams, 1995). Rutile, the source of titanium dioxide, has been exploited since 1972 by Sierra Rutile, a subsidiary of the American-owned Nord Resources Corporation of Dayton, Ohio. The mining of bauxite has always been the monopoly of the Sierra Leone Ore and Metal Company (SIEROMCO), owned by Swiss Aluminium Industries (or Alusuisse).

Like Sierra Leone, Liberia has played the role of a rentier state for most of its history, having depended heavily on income from the foreign exploitation of its natural resources and from maritime services (mostly through flags of convenience). Although Liberia has been politically independent since 1847 and never experienced European colonization, it was nevertheless not immune from the effects of capitalist expansion across the globe. Liberia was host to Firestone, the largest rubber plantation in the world, which commenced operations as early as 1926 and for decades acted as the major source of foreign exchange for the country. After World War II, Tubman was so impressed with the financial benefits and economic growth generated by the activities of Firestone that he embarked on his open door policy, which encouraged foreign investment in iron ore. Two major companies became involved in exploiting iron ore: DELIMCO (German Liberian Mining Company), a German-Italian company with Liberian government participation, and LAMCO (Liberian-American Swedish Mineral Company), an American-Swedish company in which the Liberian government also had shares. Both companies had their parent organizations in Europe and North America (Clower et al., 1966). Later, foreign exploitation of Liberian resources extended to timber. Although this area later became heavily contested by both foreign and local companies, the two major participants were U.S.-based: the Maryland Logging Company (MLC) and the Maryland Wood Processing Industry (MWPI).

In both Sierra Leone and Liberia, therefore, the processes of global capital accumulation have long been crucial in the organization of both economies and hence in determining the security of their state-society relations in the global economic system. Both societies are characterized by enclave economies that are oriented toward the outside. To a large extent, the pace and nature of the development process in these countries became heavily dependent on the activities of foreign companies and the nature of external markets. The two societies thus became vulnerable on a number of fronts, in particular to price fluctuations for exports. By the 1970s, the scope of effective state influence in Sierra Leone and Liberia was reduced to the mere production of minerals, rubber, and timber.

Liberia and Sierra Leone are two states characterized by a heavy dependence on direct taxation for official revenue. Part of the explanation for the fiscal crisis since the 1970s is thus connected with the poor performance of this sector. As both the volumes and value of exports fell, revenue derived from direct taxes correspondingly declined. Even though maritime services continued to yield steady income to the government of Liberia, this was never enough to avert the looming financial crisis. By the end of the 1970s, therefore, both states were in the grip of a severe fiscal crisis. It was this financial crisis that intensified the need in both countries for increased external borrowing and, consequently, debt accumulation. This debt, and the need to ensure repayment, set in motion a process that has left Liberia and Sierra Leone incapable of insulating themselves from external leverage for policy change at home.

Debt Accumulation and External Intervention

Against this background, it is reasonable to suggest that another way in which globalization has affected Sierra Leone and Liberia is the increased external indebtedness of both states. This led to the gradual and later dramatic involvement of creditors and donors in the determination of both the content and direction of their economic policies. The debts of both states have grown steadily over the years, leading to their classification as debt-distressed countries and, because of poor repayment records, blacklisting by the IMF by the late 1980s.

Liberia and Insecurity

Liberia has a long history of external borrowing, especially from the United States and Britain. It was the desperate search for finance in the interwar period of 1918–1939 that led to the granting of a concession to Firestone in 1926 in return for $5 million to cover the country's public debts.

Tubman's open door policy was largely informed by the need to alleviate the financial crisis and improve the revenue base of the government. Together with the Investment Code of 1966, with its generous tax incentives, the open door policy attracted substantial foreign investment to Liberia. Foreign companies soon became not only dependable sources of revenue for the government through taxes and royalties but also sources from which the government borrowed substantially.

Plans by the government to redress the fiscal crisis in the 1970s were dealt a heavy blow by oil price shocks. Part of the rationale for the four-year development plan adopted in 1974 was to diversify the production base of the economy as a way out of the structural crisis in the medium and long term. But as the plan required a capital outlay of $712 million, the government had to resort to further external borrowing to raise most of the amount. The 10 percent interest rates were certainly very high, especially considering that some of the debts had a short grace period. But even more contentious was the decision of the government to spend 26 percent of the plan budget on hosting the annual summit meetings of the OAU in 1979 (Pereira-Lunghu, 1995).

As the 1980s set in, the Liberian state was being plagued by multiple financial crises: the drying up of foreign investment, dwindling export earnings, increased indebtedness, and a high debt-service ratio. Even the government's recourse to increased timber exploitation, which had overtaken iron ore and rubber as the major source of government income by 1979, did nothing to abate the situation. The collapse of fiscal discipline with the advent of military rule following Doe's seizure of power in 1980 further worsened matters. Between 1980 and 1988, the economy registered a negative annual growth rate of 2.8 percent despite an estimated $500 million in aid from the United States in the same period. Capital flight resulting from political instability combined with a decline in economic activity and lack of fiscal discipline to produce a crisis of confidence in the Liberian economy in the 1980s.

By 1988, it was clear that Liberia was unable to service its public debts, which stood at $1,427 million (external) and $507 million (internal). The efforts by the IMF and World Bank to ensure prudence and restore confidence to the Liberian economy came to nothing. By this time, even the United States, Liberia's greatest benefactor, was becoming gravely concerned. The seventeen-person U.S. team of Operational Expert (Opex), provided on Liberia's request in 1987 to help deal with the financial crisis, pulled out in 1988 when it became clear that the Doe regime was unable and unwilling to ensure probity in the financial management of the country. When the U.S. government also pulled out, the U.S. Agency for International Development (USAID) closed its offices, in March 1989.

Prior to that, in 1988, both the IMF and World Bank had suspended their operations in, and blacklisted, Liberia. This effectively denied Liberia access to external loans and other sources of funding. The government's printing of fiat money in response to the serious liquidity crisis that set in in the late 1980s accelerated the inflationary pressures on the economy. By 1989, the Liberian state had imploded; only a spark was now needed to set ablaze what was, by all definitions, a desperate and volatile situation (Jarret, 1996).

Sierra Leone and Insecurity

Sierra Leone developed along a similar economic trajectory. Economic performance in the 1980s was disastrous, reflected in declining state revenues and negative GDP growth rates (from an average 1.5 percent in the 1970s). As with Liberia, Sierra Leone's imports, especially of oil and rice, were increasing at a time when export revenue and external sources of funding were drying up. This necessitated public borrowing to finance the deficits. As public debt grew (from $68.5 million in 1971 to $1.2 billion in 1992), so did the debt-service ratio, which averaged 22 percent in the early 1980s and continued to rise throughout that decade. Most of Sierra Leone's debts were incurred from official sources, many in the early 1980s in the form of short-term suppliers' credits contracted on terms that continued to be unfavorable with increased indebtedness (Parfitt and Riley, 1989).

Since 1979, in order to recover loans, the IMF and World Bank have ensured an almost permanent participation in the country's economic management. A series of controversial structural adjustment programs, intended to reform the perceived distortions in the Sierra Leone economy, were agreed on. These involved the devaluation of the local currency (the leone); the provision of incentives to increase the production of agricultural exports; the desubsidization of most essential items, including fuel and rice, the staple food; the privatization of loss-making government agencies and parastatals; and recognition of the need to reduce the influence of certain powerful groups, especially the role of the Lebanese, in the economic administration of the country (Weeks, 1992).

As in the case of Liberia, however, the commitment of political leaders to economic reform was only superficial. There was a clear determination on the parts of Stevens and Momoh to avoid the implementation of any measure that could potentially undermine the fragile political base of their regimes or produce unpalatable consequences (such as student disturbances, anarchic scenes, and possibly a military coup d'état). In response, the IMF had suspended programs and withdrawn credit. Again like Liberia, Sierra Leone was blacklisted by the IMF in 1988. Relations between external creditors and the Sierra Leone government in the 1980s were thus mostly turbulent; accusations of inflexibility and incompetence were often traded. But as with Liberia, the effects of the partial implementation of economic reforms could be compared only to those of economic decline. As noted, the economic reforms implemented by Momoh and Strasser and intended to bolster their positions led to neither economic recovery nor the strengthening of state institutions.

Civil War and State Collapse

By the end of the 1980s, both Liberia and Sierra Leone were reeling from the combined effects of authoritarianism, economic decline, fiscal mismanagement, and corrupt and incompetent leaderships. This situation propelled both states along the path of political violence. In Liberia, the autocratic Doe resorted to brutal tactics in the hope of ensuring the survival of the nonliberal and noncompetitive political system over which he presided. In Sierra Leone, Momoh embarked on rather cosmetic political reforms and reintroduced multiparty politics in 1991. But these measures were widely interpreted as a political ploy because although he needed external financial support, few believed Momoh could genuinely tolerate political and economic rationalization.

As the economic crisis deepened and political leaders became reclusive or deceptive, the state became increasingly irrelevant. The governments could neither provide jobs, pay salaries on time, nor provide such basic services as health and education. Thus they lost control over the most vital sectors of society, including the security and armed forces. Rulers resorted to governance through cronyism or reliance on tribesmen. The state became increasingly coercive as political insecurity heightened.

State influence and authority now barely extended beyond the capital. The collapse of the formal education system outside Monrovia and Freetown and the retrenchment of workers from the public services as demanded by external donors produced a pool of hungry and desperate urban and rural youth with no source of livelihood, no confidence in the system, and no hope for the future. Excluded from the system, this category of people became the most vulnerable in society and prone to the temptation of pursuing unconventional methods to achieve social objectives (Richards, 1995). In both cases, the situation was compounded by pressure from creditors to ensure regular debt repayment as well as both good government and good governance.

By the end of 1989, the situation finally exploded in Liberia when only a few hundred rebel fighters of the National Patriotic Front of Liberia (NPFL), led by Charles Taylor, invaded from northeastern Liberia. Taylor was a fugitive who, as head of the General Services Agency in charge of government procurement under Doe, had fled Liberia in 1983 to escape trial and possible imprisonment for alleged embezzlement of state funds. Taylor recruited unemployed and semieducated rural youth from Nimba County, a region of Liberia alienated by Doe's brutal suppression of the 1985 coup. The Armed Forces of Liberia (AFL), whose lack of discipline and professionalism was a miniature reflection of the institutional disarray in Liberian society, proved incapable of repelling the rebels and fled instead to defend the capital.

With the comprehensive destruction of physical infrastructure built over a century and a half of history, the collapse of what was already an embattled economy, the reduction of the writ of the official government to the capital, and the collapse of almost every state institution, the government of Liberia ceased to function after 1990 and with it the state. Rebel forces denied the government in Monrovia any access to rural assets, effectively undermining what remained of the fiscal basis of the prewar state.

In its place, rebel leader Taylor, with over 90 percent control of Liberia, established a predatory regime that obeyed the logic of its predecessors. He "privatized" these rural resources and walked away from both the internal and external obligations of the prewar state (Reno, 1995b). The violence, conducted largely along ethnic lines, destroyed any sense of community that was left in Liberian society. As a society, Liberia is now more polarized and vulnerable. With over half of the prewar population of 2.5 million internally displaced, over 700,000 seeking refuge in other countries, over 150,000 killed, and 10 percent of the 60,000 former combatants child soldiers, the collective psyche of the Liberian nation will remain scarred for a long time to come (Ellis, 1995; Jarret, 1996; Sesay, 1996).

Apart from provoking an unprecedented regional intervention, the Liberian civil war precipitated state collapse in Sierra Leone. The war spilled over to Sierra Leone in March 1991, when rebels of the Revolutionary United Front (RUF), led by Corporal Foday Sankoh and initially backed by Taylor, invaded eastern Sierra Leone from Liberia. The RUF initially consisted of a hard core of fighters not exceeding twenty, some of them Burkinabe mercenaries (Riley and Sesay, 1995). Sankoh was a photographer and a signals and radio technician in the SLA who was imprisoned and later dismissed from service for his alleged role in a coup attempt in 1971. Like Taylor, Sankoh later recruited—sometimes voluntarily but often through mindless violence—from a reserve pool of rural youth with no education, employment, or hope for the future.

But the formal army's lack of discipline and weapons with which to fight meant that it was fighting a losing battle. Those who were later recruited from the urban unemployed and uneducated and hastily trained to fight the rebels resorted to diamond mining, looting, and the displacement of the civilians they were meant to protect. Led by Strasser, poorly armed and disaffected soldiers of the SLA seized power in April 1992 when Momoh's government failed to pay army salaries on time. However, Strasser and his respective military and civilian successors, General Maada Bio and Ahmed Tejan Kabba, tried but failed to eliminate the rebels. In May 1997, the army again intervened only fifteen months into the life of the democratically elected government of Tejan Kabba (Richards, 1996; Reno, 1997; Riley, 1997b).

Prior to the events of May 1997, rebel activity in Sierra Leone had, meanwhile, displaced half the country's 4.4 million population and led to about 10,000 deaths; about a quarter of the population had become refugees in other countries. All the export sectors of the economy had been ground to a halt, and state revenues were severely curtailed. As in Liberia, most state institutions, including the formal army, had collapsed; state authority hardly extended beyond Freetown. The final collapse of the state, however, came with the events of May 25, 1997, when unprecedented violence broke out in the capital. There was widespread looting of banks, shops, and UN and expatriate offices. This outbreak led to the closure of educational institutions and foreign missions and to a Nigerian-led regional air and sea blockade of Freetown in an attempt to force the military to restore power to constitutional authority. With virtually no one in control in Freetown, the Sierra Leone state has literally ceased to function.

Conclusion—Obstacles to Critical Security in Sierra Leone and Liberia

This study of Sierra Leone and Liberia demonstrates the inadequacy of traditional notions of security in explaining the manner in which states function in the international system. In both cases, there was no obvious military threat from outside and yet both countries now belong to a group of collapsed states in contemporary Africa. Both historically and at present, the sources of threat to the state in Sierra Leone and Liberia can be identified as both internal and external.

From within, the major source of threat was the inability of political functionaries to establish valid, representative, inclusive, and accountable political systems. Concerned with self-aggrandizement and regime survival, weak and incompetent political elites and their supporters employed exploitative, suppressive, and highly divisive methods of governance that heightened the tensions in these very disparate communities. Whatever political stability was achieved, this was bound to be fragile and susceptible to internal shocks arising from the explosion of pent-up frustrations and stresses.

From outside, both states suffered from severe vulnerability to fluctuating external markets and price shocks for their exports, particularly because of the nature (raw materials) and the narrow range (a few agricultural and mineral products) of these exports. Internal development was thus made highly dependent on uncertain sources of income (see Tickner, Chossudovsky, this volume). This uncertainty of income from exports and the resultant economic decline had two major effects. First, they led to increased external borrowing and indebtedness and the corollary susceptibility to leverage from external creditors on the lookout for opportunities to spread their political and economic ideologies. Second, they eroded the fiscal basis of the state and undermined political leaders, some of whom already had weak political bases. The unwillingness of political leaders to pay short-run political costs impelled them to employ brutal tactics in order to stay in power.

The impact of the lethal combination of both sources of insecurity precipitated the crumbling of the Sierra Leone and Liberian states. By the early 1990s, almost all vital state institutions were either in disarray or had collapsed. Crippled and bankrupted by the incompetence, corruption, and mismanagement of the political elites, the Sierra Leone and Liberian states succumbed quite easily to internal insurrection. The collapse of military authority led to the inability of the formal armies to defend the state against comparatively fewer and unprofessional rebel fighters with very light weapons. In either case, there was no external military threat but rather threat from volatile forces within. This fact, together with the dominance of multinational corporations and international financial institutions in both economies, suggests that an alternative to the traditional understanding of security is needed. Such an approach must draw out the complexities of the causes of human insecurity and suffering in a world order where global economic restructuring has acted to undermine already fragile social orders—albeit differentially across the globe.

10

African Security:
The Erosion of the State
and the Decline of Race as a
Basis for Human Relations

Ali Mazrui

Two great streams of global change, the rise and decline of the state and the rise and decline of race as a basis of human relations, have helped to construct our orthodox ideas of security (see Thomas and Wilkin, this volume). The demise of the nation-state and race as integral to human security are changing these orthodox views.

The foundations of the African colonial state can be traced back to the Berlin Conference convened by Otto von Bismarck in 1884–1885, which helped to set the stage for the partition of Africa. The erosion of the state in Africa has ranged from pressure for total collapse in countries like Somalia and Rwanda to forces of political decentralization, as in KwaZulu, Ethiopia, and southern Sudan. The United Nations and its agencies are increasingly engaged with this painful process of state erosion either as peacemakers or peacekeepers or as caregivers for refugees. Elsewhere in the world the UN's credibility is severely in question, but in Africa the United Nations is helping to deal with some of the most severe consequences of Otto von Bismarck and his legacy. Meanwhile Africans themselves are seeking to be more effective as continental actors in tandem with the efforts of this world body. The next section, "From Bismarck to Boutros-Ghali," deals with the decline of the state and security in Africa through the time of the sixth Secretary-General of the world body.[1]

The second grand theme is the rise and decline of race as a mover of history. Here too I could have chosen a period of about a century and discussed race from the beginning of social Darwinism to the ideology of apartheid. But Western racism affected Africa and its critical security much earlier than did Western colonialism. I have therefore decided to address the issue of race partly from a cultural perspective—from Shakespeare's Othello to the predicament of O. J. Simpson.

From Bismarck to Boutros-Ghali: From Orthodox to Critical Security in Africa

Why would one choose the period from Bismarck to Boutros-Ghali to consider the issue of states, societies, and security in Africa? To some degree, the link gives us a century of relations between the West and the African world. Prince Otto von Bismarck was in power in Germany in the 1880s, busy reinventing the state. By the 1990s Africa had experienced a century of Western colonization, emerged from the old-style colonial state, and produced the first African secretary-general of the United Nations.

Otto von Bismarck was perhaps the most influential statesman of the Western world in his day. Boutros Boutros-Ghali is arguably one of the most influential statesmen of the world in his own day a century later. The black world as a whole was profoundly affected in the great transition from the age of Bismarck to the era of Boutros-Ghali.

Since this chapter is partly about the rise and decline of the state and orthodox notions of security and secure societies, it is worth remembering that Bismarck reinvented the state in Europe. He was a pioneer of the welfare state and one of the architects of the socially engaged system of governance. The satisfaction of human needs is a key theme in the evolving debate on critical security studies, and somewhat ironically, Bismarck is an important figure in the emergence of the responsibility of state institutions for this task (see Guest, this volume).

One of the great paradoxes about Otto von Bismarck was that he united the Germans and helped to divide Africa. He helped to unite the Germans partly through war and partly through welfare: by territorial unification and through social welfare policies that pacified large sections of the population during a period of social unrest. He divided Africa partly through his role in the 1884–1885 Berlin conference, which worked out the rules to guide Europeans in their scramble for Africa, and partly by being among those colonialists scrambling for territory.

Bismarck was responsible for introducing state insurance in his country: for sickness in 1883, for accident in 1884, and for old age in 1889. He united Germans through social healing in this manner. It has been suggested that "these measures of state socialism appear now as precursors of the modern welfare state. . . . Despite this policy, Bismarck was opposed to any regulation of working hours or working conditions" (Lutz, 1980:

224–225). It has also been argued: "The tragedy of Bismarck's career was that he himself created in united Germany that monarcho-military power which first overthrew him and then in the fateful years of 1914–1918 destroyed his empire" (Lutz, 1980: 224).

But before Bismarck was overthrown in Germany, he had carved out his place in African history with monumental consequences for the emergence of the African state and security relations. In 1884, Bismarck quarreled with Britain and within the course of a single year obtained the Cameroons, South-West Africa (now Namibia), East Africa (Tanganyika, Rwanda, and Burundi), and part of New Guinea. In 1889, Bismarck declared, "I am not a colonial man." But he brought Germany closer to a colonial role than any other modern figure with the exception of Adolf Hitler.

The Berlin conference closed in 1885. In 1945 the United Nations was born. In 1960 more than fifteen newly independent African states became members. By 1995 the United Nations was knee-deep in some of the problems of those states—including salvage operations for collapsed states. Again, this is a central theme for human security—what causes the collapse of states and societies? (See Sesay and Chossudovsky, this volume.)

Regional Integration and African Security

Some regard Cambodia as a UN triumph in peacemaking; many regard Somalia as a failure of both the United Nations and the United States. Many would accuse the United Nations of criminal negligence over Rwanda in 1994. More could have been done to reduce, if not avert, the catastrophe (Touval, 1994: 44–57; see also Chossudovsky, this volume). Yet the collapse was part of the wider decline of the state in Africa.

Is the UN underutilizing preventive diplomacy in pursuit of peace? Is the UN too cautious in pursing peace enforcement? Is the UN doing enough to avert the impending catastrophe in Burundi?

All of these are difficult questions to answer. They merely illustrate that although we have indeed averted a world war in the second half of the twentieth century, we have multiplied regional, local, and ethnic wars— and escalated their human cost (Rosenau, 1992). The human cost of the Cold War and its orthodox security themes of militarism, the national interest, and the balance of power—and terror—are only part of the range of issues and themes that human security advocates are now turning their attention to.

Should regions like Africa look for alternative peacekeeping arrangements? The UN wants to keep the peace once somebody else has made it. Who is to make peace in Africa? Who is to enforce it? If the state is in decline, where are the transitional arrangements for Pax Africana? Most crucially, how do ideas of human security impinge on these outcomes?

Some African countries will simply need to be temporarily controlled by other African countries. Inevitably, some dysfunctional countries would need to submit to trusteeship and even tutelage for a while, as Zanzibar did when it was annexed by Tanganyika in 1964 to form Tanzania.

Although the world body bears the name the United Nations, some of its members are among the most fragmented and insecure states and societies in human history (Weiss, Forsythe, and Coate, 1994). In Africa the UN is a peacekeeper but not often a peacemaker—and certainly not a peace enforcer. Africa needs alternative solutions.

Regional integration is one solution in some cases. Should Tanzania, Burundi, and Rwanda be persuaded to form one federation? Certainly if Burundi and Rwanda had been united into a large state, where the balance between Tutsi and Hutu would have been part of more diverse population, the savagery of 1994 could possibly have been averted (Goose and Smith, 1995: 2–6). If Hutu and Tutsi became part of the United Republic of Tanzania, they might well discover what they have in common—and unite politically against other Tanzanians.

This is a safer solution than uniting Rwanda and Burundi with Uganda. The latter would simply destabilize Uganda by seriously altering the ethnic balance between the Baganda and the ethnic compatriots of Ankole, and any residual balance between north and south in Uganda. But even a federation of Rwanda, Burundi, and Tanzania would need to be financed by the international community. Incentives would be needed, especially to persuade Tanzania. The security of state-society relations in Africa is vastly more complex, of course, than colonialism and imperialism ever allowed for. The future security of African state-societies requires a social and political structure that reflects rather than denies this fact.

If recolonization or self-colonization is the path that lies ahead for Africa, there must be a continental authority to ensure that such an order does not merely mask base aims of exploitation. Collective responsibility should have the effect of ensuring moral restraint (Mazrui, 1994; Pfaff, 1995: 2–6). If the UN does not want to enforce peace, can Africa create a machinery for Pax Africana? Can the UN become the mechanism for redressing state-society relations in Africa? Can it yet become the mechanism for the transition to a world order concerned with attaining human security for all peoples? What I have in mind is a proposal that would set in place a regional organization that would have the authority and resources needed to help bring about and orchestrate such a restructuring of African state-society relations. In effect, this would help the continent in its move toward attaining the goals of human security.

The state in Africa may be in decline and in crisis, but the wider international system is still state-based. What I propose as one longer-term solution to problems exposed by today's crises is the establishment of an

African security council composed of five pivotal regional states that would oversee the continent. This council would have a pan-African emergency force, an army for intervention and peacekeeping, at its disposal. And there would also be an African high commissioner for refugees linked to the UN's High Commission. Africa accounts for one-tenth of the world's population, but it sometimes accounts for nearly one-half of the world's refugees and displaced persons. It is time Africa took a leading role in organizing the relief of its own refugees.

Temporarily, should pan-Africanism mold itself in the image of the UN? An African security council formed over the coming decades would be anchored in the north by Egypt and the south by South Africa. Although it is currently experiencing troubling times, Nigeria would be the pivotal state in west Africa. Its size and resources could give it the equivalent weight of India in South Asia if it can find political stability. In east Africa, the pivotal country is still in doubt. Ethiopia, among the most fragile of the largest African states today, is the most likely anchor because of its size. Although Kenya is more stable, it is far smaller.

In central Africa, the presumed regional power of the future—Zaire—is currently itself in need of trusteeship. If Zaire can avoid collapse into chaos in the near future, it will be one of the major actors in Africa in the twenty-first century. Zaire has the population and resources to play a major role. In the next century it will even surpass France as the largest French-speaking nation in the world.

As permanent members of an African security council, these five states would coordinate among each other and with the UN. Regional integration is the order of the day in Europe, in North America, in East Asia, and even, tentatively of course, in the Middle East. If Africa, too, does not follow this path, the lack of stability and economic growth will push the entire continent further into the desperate margins of global society. In tandem with the efforts of the UN to establish a peaceful world order, Africans need an African peace enforced by Africans, from Angola to Algeria. Africans need to be collectively responsible for the fate of Africa in the postcolonial age if security is to be achieved.

These are no doubt frightening ideas for proud peoples who spilled so much blood and spent so much political will freeing themselves from the onslaught of European powers unleashed by Otto von Bismarck. To be sure, self-colonization, if Africa can manage it, is better than resurrecting Bismarck and reestablishing colonization by outsiders. Better still would be self-conquest. But that implies an African capacity for self-control and self-discipline rarely seen since before the curse of Otto von Bismarck—colonialism. Such discipline will have to be found in the twenty-first century if Africa is to undertake successful social engineering and build resilient and solid foundations for the poststate age of the future.

The African Condition and the State of the World: Achieving Security

The end of the Cold War has diminished Africa's influence in the United Nations (Kouassi, 1993: 829–904). But the same post–Cold War era has contributed to the expansion of the UN's role in Africa. African leverage on the UN has declined; the UN's leverage on Africa has expanded (Swatuk, 1995: 103–117). Let us take each of these propositions in turn.

With the end of the Cold War Africa has lost a major constituency for Third World causes in the United Nations—the old socialist bloc. On most issues of concern for Africa, the members of the old Warsaw Pact could be relied on to vote with those forces in Africa that were eager for change. East European socialists were often allies of Africa in world affairs. The collapse of official communism in Eastern Europe, and the disintegration of the USSR and the dismantling of the Warsaw Pact, have produced an Eastern Europe far more likely to listen to the wishes of Washington, D.C., than to the yearnings of the Third World (Brzezinski, 1995: 26–42). Africa's voting base in the United Nations has shrunk dramatically. The state has declined in power in the former Warsaw Pact also, and Africa is among the losers.

The disintegration of the USSR and Yugoslavia, and the split of Czechoslovakia into two separate countries, have also been part of the decline of the state. The result is more than fifteen additional non-African members to the total membership of the United Nations. Thus Africa has lost not only its socialist allies but also its status as one-third of the total membership of the United Nations. Its percentage in the voting statistics of the world body has shrunk further—with additional damage to its self-confidence. After all, Africa's main strength had been in its number of votes.

The end of the Cold War has also weakened Africa in the United Nations by undermining the old checks and balances of the former two superpowers. Small countries are no longer in the envious position of playing one imperial power against another. Competitive imperialism is better than monopolistic imperialism precisely because big-power rivalry of the kind characterized by the Cold War was sometimes to the advantage of weak regions like Africa.

The end of the Cold War has shaken the self-confidence of those African countries and leaders that once thought that there were alternatives to capitalism in the quest for development. Suddenly many of these leaders and countries see themselves as being so vulnerable to Western economic power that they have given up trying to have an independent foreign policy. Even former radical leaders in countries like Tanzania, Ghana, and Zimbabwe and the African Nation Congress of South Africa have permitted themselves to mellow and acquiesce in the face of Western triumphalism after the Cold War. The old African warriors of self-reliance have become the new implementers of Western-sponsored policies of structural adjustment (see Chossudovsky and Guest, this volume). The wider economic fears of African leaders at home make them cautious collaborators at the United Nations. Africa is enfeebled by the consequences of the end of the Cold War. As the state declines worldwide, Africa is marginalized further.

And yet just when Africa is losing influence in the United Nations, the world body is increasing its influence in Africa. One reason is the political collapse of a number of African states and societies—especially Somalia, Rwanda, and Liberia, in order of degree of UN involvement.

A related factor is the aftermath of the messy withdrawal of Portugal from its African colonies—leaving behind a civil war in Angola and conceding independence without preceding multiparty elections in Mozambique. The mess has cost hundreds of thousands of lives since the late 1970s. The United Nations inherited part of the mess. Fortunately the UN has made real progress toward a solution in Mozambique and even in Angola, though progress in the latter is more modest.

A third factor behind increasing UN involvement in Africa is that the world body has had its first African secretary-general, Boutros Boutros-Ghali. At first sight one would have thought that Boutros-Ghali's role would reduce the enfeeblement of Africa in the United Nations, and to some extent this has been the case.

But Boutros-Ghali has also viewed Africa as being in special need of UN intervention. His own convictions on this matter were one of the factors behind the nature of the UN intervention in Somalia (Ruggie, 1993: 26–31). With the best intentions, Boutros Boutros-Ghali has felt that it is more important that the United Nations exercise more power in Africa than that Africa exercise more influence in the United Nations. Quite understandably, the secretary-general has felt that Africa needed UN help more than the UN needed Africa's help.

But perhaps that is where we and Boutros Boutros-Ghali should stop and pause. The UN's role as a peacekeeper may stand or fall according to whether it can make a success of its African responsibilities. The problems of state and society in Africa are already horrendous and are likely to get worse. Even mere peacekeeping (as distinct from peace enforcing) has many risks (Durch, 1993). As the African state fragments, political violence is often let loose (see Mohamed Salih, Sesay, and Chossudovsky, this volume). Often highly militarized states and societies have collapsed into civil war.

The United Nations should not undertake any new direct peacekeeping role outside of Africa before the year 2010. Until then the UN should use Africa as its only school for learning the dynamics of ethnicity and human security in world affairs. But the UN should keep the option of persuading some of its members to assume responsibilities on its behalf elsewhere.

Why should the UN focus on Africa? The security of the African continent depends on the UN assuming this mantle. First, the UN can make a much bigger difference in Africa than elsewhere. Even the so-called failed enterprises in Somalia probably saved more lives than the UN's so-called success in Cambodia. Certainly the United Nations and the United States together in Somalia may have saved more people from starvation than have UN missions in Cyprus, Lebanon, Croatia, and elsewhere combined (Crocker, 1995: 2–8). The stakes in terms of human lives of conflicts in Africa can be very high. During 1994 the Angolan civil war sometimes caused as many as 1,000 deaths a week. Helping to end such a war has a much bigger human return for UN efforts than have some of its peacekeeping efforts elsewhere.

Second, peacekeeping within a country is almost the lowest denominator in governance, and governance in some African countries is at this rudimentary stage. Thus in Africa both the UN and African governments could be jointly learning the skills and ethics of governance. The accountability and responsibility of governing institutions is a prerequisite for the possibility of secure societies.

Third, during the next fifteen years of Afrocentric peacekeeping the UN and the OAU could explore ways of institutionalizing self-policing by African states themselves—including the creation of a pan-African rmergency force and an African security council with the five pivotal states mentioned previously. Autonomy and self-governance are critical aspects of any transition to secure societies.

Fourth, the UN may also have to learn in Africa about a future world with a reduced role for the state. Some African countries are in retreat from the state—Somalia, Rwanda, Liberia (not by design), and Ethiopia (by design). Somalia is back to a kind of prestate condition; Western Europe through regional integration may be moving toward a poststate condition. The UN may have to adjust itself to a poststate age, conceivably in the late twenty-first century. The UN can be educated about prestatehood and poststatehood partly by engagement in Africa (Grunwald, 1995: 82). The attainment of secure societies is dependent in part on the nature of the political institutions that emerge in the wake of the fragmenting of states in Africa. What ideas of democracy will they embody, if any?

There has been another great stream of global change apart from the rise and decline of the state: the rise and decline of race as a historical force. The impact of this racial force on the fortunes of the African people is even older than the impact of the colonial state. We shall approach this second global stream from a cultural perspective.

From Shakespeare's Othello to O. J. Simpson: The Roots of Racism and Human Insecurity in the World Order

Othello, the Moor of Venice, was written by William Shakespeare at a time when color-based racism in Europe was in the process of being born. The tragedy of O. J. Simpson and Nicole Brown, in contrast, took place at a time when overt color-based racism was in decline. The two tragedies together—Othello and Desdemona and O. J. Simpson and Nicole Brown— bracket the golden age of overt racial prejudice in Western history.

Racism has been one of the main threats to the possibility of establishing secure societies. Its modern roots are heavily entwined within the expansion of European empires. Racism and the construction of the alien "other" that serves to help unite the nation-state against potential enemies is a recurring theme of the modern world order.

Shakespeare's life covered the period April 1564–April 1616. When Shakespeare was writing, religious prejudice was still significantly stronger than color prejudice. That is why *The Merchant of Venice* is more anti-Semitic than *Othello* is antiblack. Although Shakespeare gives him great egalitarian lines, Shylock in *The Merchant of Venice* is ultimately an unsympathetic figure—and his demands for his pound of flesh pander to some of the most persistent Western stereotypes about so-called Semitic avarice.

Othello is about a white woman Desdemona, falling in love with a black man, Othello, who marries her. There are a number of racist references to his making love to her, precursors to an issue that was later at the heart of Western racism—cross-color sexuality. And yet Shakespeare is on the side of the lovers. The most racist character in the play, and the absolute villain, is Iago, a white man.

Before long the new evil of racism was firmly married to an ancient evil called slavery in the most racist system of slavery in history, the trans-Atlantic slave trade. Othello's racial compatriots in Africa entered a long period of hardship and humiliation—and O. J. Simpson's ancestors were deeply affected by the traumatic disruptions of enslavement.

By the time O. J. Simpson ascended to national prominence in the America of the twentieth century, a fundamental change was under way. The color-based racism being born when *Othello* was staged in London and that had led to rationales for enslavement and colonization had diminished to the point that a black man could become a millionaire hero of racially mixed sports. Further, O. J. Simpson could marry a white woman without violating antimiscegenation laws—in effect in some American states until 1969. A more direct, military analogy to Othello is Colin Powell, whose poverty-stricken parents came from Jamaica; he helped win wars for white-led America and rose to become chairman of the U.S. Joint Chiefs of Staff. Desdemona was a senator's daughter; Colin Powell as Othello would probably have become a senator himself.

Young Nicole Brown and young Desdemona may have been attracted to their husbands partly because of racial and class contrasts. Certainly there was some element of hero worship. Othello was the great military hero of the battlefield; O. J. Simpson was the great sporting hero of the football field. And both Othello and Simpson had a physical presence that was almost larger than life. The similarities between warfare and competitive sports have intrigued sociologists. Moreover, both war and competitive sports such as football and boxing have been preeminently masculine.

Somewhere between Othello and O. J. Simpson lies Paul Robeson, the astonishingly versatile African American who dazzled the world early in the first half of the twentieth century. On Broadway in 1943 Paul Robeson played the part of Othello, and the production lasted longer than any other Shakespeare play (nearly 300 performances). His second New York production of *Othello* was staged soon after World War II. He saw the play as a tragedy of the outsider—citing the analogy of a black American soldier trying to court a Japanese woman in Japan. Othello was not only dark-skinned, he was also not of Venetian society, a stranger in Venice. Paul Robeson preferred the paradigm of the outsider rather than the paradigm of race. He became increasingly convinced that the most enduring and most lasting divide in society is not race but class. For radically different reasons, O. J. Simpson had also become a class-oriented citizen rather than a race-oriented citizen. By the time he married Nicole Brown, O. J. Simpson was marrying "below his station." Othello, in contrast, was to some extent marrying within his class. As a general, he was almost in the same class as a senator's daughter but for his status as an outsider.

The Africanization of O. J. Simpson is a consequence of the double-murder trial. Some are born African, some become African, and some have Africanization thrust upon them. It might even be true that some are born black, some become black, and some have blackness thrust upon them. It took a monumental tragedy for O. J. Simpson to combine class identity with a racial identity.

In southern Africa there is, of course, an immense corpus of literature addressing the problem of apartheid and the sociocultural pathologies of racism and McCarthyism. In South Africa itself this literature includes new Desdemonas—as in Peter Abraham's *Path of Thunder*. A colored man, Larry Swartz, and an Afrikaner woman, Sarie Villiers, fall in love. All the absurdities of apartheid are exposed in this Othello-and-Desdemona affair. As one of Peter Abraham's characters says, "The tragedy is not in Swartz and this girl. The tragedy is in the land and in our time. You must be a native or a half-caste or a Jew or an Arab or an Englishman or Chinaman or a Greek: that is the tragedy. You cannot become a human being. . . . For that reason Swartz and this girl who have now become human beings will suffer."

On October 24, 1818, the following announcement was made at the Cape of Good Hope:

ENGLISH THEATRICALS: Under the sanction of His Excellency, The Governor. . . . This Evening the amateur company will perform the Tragedy of Othello with the musical farce of The Poor Soldier.

These were the lighter moments of the European colonization of Africa. But for that very reason they were the most pregnant with meaning. The white man was now in Africa—not merely with his ship anchored in the harbor, not merely with his guns, not merely with his technology of production, but also with his culture and his art.

The play was given in Dutch for the first time on May 28, 1836—*Othello, of De Jaloersche Zwar* (Othello, or the Jealous Black) (Rosenthal, 1964: 210). The play continued to be quite popular against the background of "illicit" interracial intimacy in South Africa. Dutch-speaking South Africans had been among the most vociferous opponents of racially mixed marriages and mixed sex; and yet the great majority of the Cape colored population of South Africa (people of mixed origin) is Afrikaans-speaking. Many include some Afrikaner ancestry in their genealogy.

The nearness of tragedy to comedy is sometimes emphasized in situations of anxiety. Even in the nineteenth century, South Africa was in such a situation. *Othello* was sometimes produced as a comedy with white men taking the part of both Othello and Desdemona. One production made the most of "Desdemona's little endearments towards her black 'hobby.'" That production, apparently hilarious, was given again a few days later.

On December 30, 1854, Gustavus V. Brook, from the Theatre Royal of Liverpool, arrived at the Cape and announced he would stage *Othello*. Sometimes alterations were made to spare combined Calvinist and Victorian sensibilities, but on balance *Othello* continued to be to white South Africans "a play better understood here than any other of Shakespeare's works. Its hero (a colored man) who had wooed and won a white lady, ships, bay soldiers, a castle and a governor, being all-familiar in the colonist's ear" (Rosenthal, 1964: 212–213).

The literary historian Eric Rosenthal has shown that by the end of the nineteenth century, few towns in South Africa had not witnessed at least an amateur performance of Shakespeare. And because of the real racial predicament, the most popular play was *Othello*.

Were the laws to prevent the marriage of an Othello to a Desdemona really wrong? After all, *Othello* was a tragedy. The black man murdered his devoted white wife. And yet *Othello* is not really a tragedy of racial incompatibility but a tragedy of subversion and hate. The evil factor in

Othello is the force that seeks to separate black from white by constantly seeking to cultivate occupational and sexual insecuritites in human beings otherwise destined to live together. Racism, then, is a key factor in the undermining of secure societies and one that has served to offer legitimacy to imperialism and colonialism, both of which have crucially shaped and stunted the history of modern Africa.

Shakespeare's Iago was the philosophy of apartheid incarnate. The question was whether this philosophy would in the end drive the blacks of South Africa to rise against the whites. Both sides were united in their love for the land. Yet unless the pernicious Iago of hate in their midst was exorcised in time, one patriot from either side might one day be forced to lament (act 5, scene 2, lines 341–344) :

> When you shall these unlucky deeds relate,
> Speak of me as I am, nothing extenuate.
> Nor set down aught in malice: then must you speak
> Of one that loved not wisely, but too well.

In terms of South Africa the play could be seen as an allegory of contradictions. The blacks were falling in love with white culture but not with white people. The whites loved Africa, the land, but not Africa, the people. Subversive white racism called Iago could have made blacks rise against whites—and then self-destruct, like Othello. Has South Africa's Othello been rescued in time?

Conclusion

If in the days of Shakespeare's *Othello* the religious divide was more important than the racial divide (as illustrated by *The Merchant of Venice*), is the class divide becoming more important in the days of O. J. Simpson and Colin Powell? When religious prejudice declined after Shakespeare, color prejudice intensified. Now that color prejudice is in decline, is it being replaced by class struggle or by a resurrection of religious prejudice? (See Wilkin, this volume.) New anti-Jewish plays like *The Merchant of Venice* are unlikely in mainstream Western civilization. But Muslim equivalents of Shylocks are already being invented. *The Merchant of Venice* may be a thing of the past, but the thief of Baghdad is back as a revised Western stereotype of Muslim villainy. Not the noble Moor but the terrorist Arab is the new image.

Have we come full circle? Are we now seeing race prejudice decline and religious prejudice rise—after centuries of the reverse? Or are both race and religion giving way to two entirely different confrontations— class struggle (rich, black O. J.; poor, white Nicole) and the war of the sexes (which gender is abusing which)?

The full answer lies in the womb of the twenty-first century. But I am convinced that the theatrical tragedy of Othello and Desdemona at the end of the sixteenth century and the real-life tragedy of O. J. Simpson and Nicole Brown toward the end of the twentieth bracket the golden age of color-conscious racism in Western civilization. Othello and Desdemona were at the beginning of color-conscious Western racism; O. J. Simpson and Nicole were caught up in the contradictions of its decline.

There are still many racial battles to be fought, many struggles against religious bigotry to be engaged. But when all is said and done, racial conflict will be overwhelmed by the gender redefinitions of the future. The only cliché that continues to make powerful sense is the proposition that the struggle continues. As Desdemona reminded us in act 3, scene 4, "Men's natures wrangle with inferior things, Though great ones are their object. Tis even so. For let our finger ache, and it endues Our healthful members even to a sense of pain." Yes, even today racism scars contemporary social and political life. Racism, anti-Semitism, and chauvinism have been rising in the 1990s in Bismarck's old country, the newly reunited Germany, and in Shakespeare's land, "that sceptred isle, demiparadise." History is playing out its contradictions.

Bismarck helped to set the stage of the West's penetration of Africa. The Conference of Berlin of 1884–1885 helped to define the rules of annexation. O. J. Simpson's land, the United States, was as ambivalent as Germany regarding colonial ambitions. Both countries were colonially peripheral but became capitalistically central. They built relatively small territorial empires, but against the background of considerable domestic development. And both touched the destiny of the black world: the United States was a major factor in the history of slavery, and Germany was a major factor in the history of imperialism at different stages.

It is ironic that the last colony to celebrate independence in Africa was among the first of Bismarck's colonies—Namibia, or South-West Africa. Once a German colony following the Conference of Berlin, it became a mandate of the League of Nations after World War I and was administered by South Africa for more than sixty years. Equally ironic is the fact that partly under UN auspices, the United States under Reagan and Bush helped facilitate Namibia's independence. O. J. Simpson's country helped liberate Bismarck's last surviving black dependency.

What is the connecting link between the erosion of the state and the decline of race? Central is the continuing expansion and globalization of capitalism (see Chossudovsky, Tickner, and Thomas, this volume). As has been pointed out repeatedly, capitalism has been eroding the exclusivity of state sovereignty. The global marketplace is dictating its own terms to governments and to the nation-state. Phenomena like the European Union are, in addition, illustrations of the enlargement of political scale within which individual nations lose control over movement of labor, goods, services, and capital in relation to their neighbors. Is the European Union a potential state writ large? Or is it a poststate formation? The evidence would seem to favor the latter scenario. Capitalism is a major cause behind this decline of the state.

Political apartheid in South Africa was killed as much by the logic of capitalism as by the forces of African nationalism and struggle. Overt compartmentalized racial discrimination was inimical to market forces. In time, among the greatest opponents of apartheid were the great capitalistic and pro-market forces in the country. Racism had become an antiquated chain restraining the pursuit of profit and the maximization of returns. So the decline of racism was also, in part, a response to the logic of global capitalism.

But as capitalism was weakening states, societies, and racism, it was inadvertently releasing other cultural forces as the twentieth century approached its close. Consciousness of class and relative deprivation had begun to take new forms, potentially transformative (see Wilkin, this volume). There was a new consciousness of ancestry, ethnicity, and tribal origins—ranging from the ethnic convulsions in Bosnia to the demands for political decentralization for KwaZulu and the Kenya coast region. The new Ethiopian constitution seeks to devolve power to ethnocultural regions. The right-wing militias in the United States represent a special kind of tribalism. The erosion of the state and society and the decline of race have helped to give a new lease on life to primordial forces of religion—ranging from Islamic militancy in Iran and Algeria to Hindu militancy in India and from right-wing Christian movements in the United States to the Buddhist faction in the Sri Lankan civil war (Mazrui, 1993).

The question now is whether capitalism has inadvertently released forces that will in time check its own seemingly relentless expansion. Capitalism may have succeeded in cutting race and racism down to size. But in so doing capitalism has released once again the ancient forces of ethnicity, ancestry, tribalism, religion, and cultural nationalism. Are these the human forces that will one day arrest the once relentless expansion of capitalism? Are these the human forces that will one day cut down to size capitalism itself? The question is wide open—and South Africa might well be one of the global laboratories of such momentous social changes.

Note

1. For inspiration regarding the title and thrust of this theme, I am indebted to Negus say Ayele from Ethiopia and to feedback on my earlier paper "The German Factor in the Black Experience: From the Berlin Conference to the Berlin Wall," keynote address at the international symposium "Cross-Currents: African Americans, Africa and Germany in the Modern World," held at the Pennsylvania State University, University Park, Pennsylvania, September 30–October 1, 1994.

PART 3
Conclusion

11

Furthering the Debate on Human Security

Caroline Thomas

Human security describes a condition of existence in which the basic material needs of human beings are met and in which human dignity, including meaningful participation in the life of the community, can be realized. Neither the market nor the state has attended adequately or consistently to the human security of Africans. Indeed, the unpredictability of the former has compounded all the uncertainties of the latter. Faced with this crisis, African people have been pursuing human security through their own efforts. They have been continuing their traditional pursuit of coping strategies to alleviate their basic human insecurity.

We have seen how peasants in the Senegal valley formed self-help groups to deal with the adverse consequences of structural adjustment in the 1980s, such as the closure of previously mentioned parastatals so vital for credit. Such groups acted as springboards for political activism with women taking advantage of the gap in traditional authority structures that had opened up as a result of development to play a leading role. In 1992 some of them appealed to the Senegalese government to work with them to solve difficulties central to their human security: land allocation, the release of an artificial flood, and health problems resulting from the dam. Sadly, two years later they had still not received a reply from their own government.

The example from the Senegal basin is but one of many. Other examples exist across the continent of microcommunities at the village level collectively providing for local needs such as sanitation and health care. The Green Belt movement in Kenya involves over 2,000 local groups in tree-planting activities. These local expressions of community-based action are important illustrations of indigenous democracy at work.

The international community has been pressing a conception of civil and political rights that are by implication supportive of the private sector, but the emphasis on Western-style democratic reform has given the illusion of empowering people while resigning them to economic marginalization. However, alongside Western-style democratization, there are many examples of spontaneous protest in Africa and of developing political activism. This is important in the quest for a stronger sense of community in Africa, and more secure state-society relations. Referring to indigenous (rather than externally generated) challenges to authoritarian rule in Africa, especially since 1990, Michael Barratt Brown (1995: 343–344) remarks:

> These are part of a long and continuing struggle in Africa for democratic policies and systems. They did not emerge suddenly in 1990 as a response to the collapse of authoritarian movements in eastern Europe. They came out of movements of peasant protest, women's demands, trade union organization and the radicalization of students and intellectuals over many years. . . . They were triggered by events much nearer home, by the collapse of African commodity prices in world markets and the increasing burden of foreign debt affecting so many African countries. . . . Pressure for ending single party rule in African countries has come partly from below—from students, organized workers, women, religious groups and disaffected professionals, occasionally linking up with peasant protest. But it has also come from above, from an excluded elite, particularly under regimes where one man and his gang have operated the principle of "winner takes all."

Action, Not Words:
The International Financial Institutions

IMF and World Bank policies have, over the past few decades, contributed to increased income gaps globally and within states. They have therefore directly undermined human security. The dangers of this have been recognized by World Bank president James Wolfensohn, who at the 1997 annual general meetings of the bank and the IMF warned that further economic and social polarization would decrease the chance for global peace and stability. Michel Camdessus, the managing director of the IMF, also called for developed countries to recognize their responsibility to "help minimise the social and cultural costs of integration into the global economy" (*Guardian,* September 24, 1997: 21).

Modifications in the thinking of the leadership of these institutions are clear in the previous comments. Changes are also apparent in some reports. In 1996, World Bank and UNDP data seemed to suggest that countries with smaller gaps between the top and bottom of society had performed better in the 1980s and 1990s, and the UNDP argued that there is a positive correlation between economic growth and income equality (UNDP, 1996: 53–54). The World Bank argued that what mattered was the nature of equality, in particular the ownership of assets such as land and education (World Bank, 1996a: 47). We have yet to see major changes in policy. Wolfensen and Camdessus are speaking the right language, but action speaks louder than words. Support for different policies would lend weight to their words.

IMF–World Bank support for the complete cancellation of African debts, debts often accumulated by leaders unaccountable to their citizens, would be a step in the right direction. Most sub-Saharan African countries continue to carry a debt burden in the mid-1990s of over 60 percent of annual GNP. These countries are also for the most part among the least developed in the world, exhibiting very low GNP per capita. In terms of the human development index, they do not do well either. The Ugandan Debt Network, critical of African governments' lack of support for its international campaign to cancel debt, recently argued: "The external debt will only be repaid by sacrificng the health and eduction of poor people. . . . This means that poor people will remain in debt bondage for much of their lifetime" (Uganda Debt Network, 1998). The Highly Indebted Poor Countries (HIPC) debt-relief strategy is linked to the IMF and its extended structural adjustment facility programs. Tying debt relief to six years of "on track" IMF structural adjustment is inappropriate.

Cancellation of debt needs to be accompanied by a better understanding by the IMF and World Bank and other financial institutions of the links between the workings of the global economy and the human security of the citizens of Africa. This improved understanding can be put to good use in terms of the development of more sensitive policies. The case study of Rwanda shows in stark relief how powerless the producers of primary commodities are in the face of unstable commodity prices. It shows also how inappropriate economic policies, in particular shock economic liberalization therapy drawn up by the IMF without regard to the specific sociopolitical context, can precipitate or fuel an appalling tragedy. The polarization of social forces places further strain on already fragile societies.

The global structure of trade, which contributes to human insecurity in Africa, needs to be transformed. Reform is not enough, but it would be a start. In the early 1970s there were calls in the UN for measures such as the index linking of the price of commodities to the price of manufactured goods. These have been shelved. Africa will be marginalized further within the liberalizing global trading structure without such measures, yet that structure itself militates against such measures. There has to be fair trade—not free trade—for African human security.

An Alternative Agenda

A consideration of the impact of globalization on human security raises a new research agenda. We need to map the human security experiences of social groups within a global framework. A starting point would be to map material poverty and inequality globally, not simply in terms of northern and southern states. Of course, the statist categorization remains significant, not least because there is an indisputable concentration of poverty in the geographic South. But a simple territorial categorization masks the global social distribution of inequality and in a sense hides the transnational dimension of human security. A concern with human security requires us to understand entitlement and distribution within states and how this relates to and reflects the global construction of entitlement and distribution. But the new style of mapping needs to go further than a head count; it must disaggregate to reveal disparities in terms of gender, race, class, urban/rural, and other relevant categories. For example, some analysts have already pointed to the feminization of poverty.

Human security requires a different development, different in terms of its aims, methods, and results. The global mapping of inequality across a range of possible indicators such as wealth, income, land, mortality, education, will lend support to the urgency of this endeavor. Clearly something has gone wrong with development to date. There is something odd about a situation where we can put people on the moon but have not been able to devise workable methods for developing access to clean water or adequate food for hundreds of millions of people. The gap in global income distribution between the world's richest and poorest 20 percent of the population has increased dramatically. Perhaps the gap in itself would not be such a cause for concern if all the basic material needs of the global population were met, but they are not. Moreover, human security requires not simply material needs satisfaction but attendance to nonmaterial aspects as well.

There is a question as to whether the neoliberal policies currently in vogue in the international financial institutions, and accepted and implemented by governments, can attend to human security. Following the argument of Wilkin, there is an important contradiction at work here: the increasing inequality generated by these policies "denies those without the necessary social, economic and political power control over or consumption of the very products that capitalism is able to generate" (Wilkin, 1997: 19). There is the *appearance,* rather than the reality, of individual freedom and empowerment. For many, the benefits of neoliberalism are not obvious.

Development must empower people to make choices within their own community, giving them more control over their lives, and not leave them to the whims of the market. Michael Barratt Brown (1995: 345) refers to a development project checklist developed by Ben Wisner. Is the project oriented toward the needs of the people involved in it? Is the focus on a disadvantaged group, such as women, and will the project shift power in their favor? Will new alliances form through the project? Does the project make use of local human and material resources, and is it sustainable? Is the external finance limited so that people do not become dependent on it? Also required in Africa is the development of an education system that reaches everyone.

To help facilitate this type of development and thus promote both aspects of human security, international financial institutions must devise policies in tune with the specific social, economic, political, and environmental reality and in cooperation with the people who will have to live with those policies. Policies must be owned by the users—both in government and at the grassroots level. Attention must be paid to local knowledge, for development that is instituted in ignorance of this is doomed to failure. From the limited data available, it is clear that attention to the specific locality under study is extremely important as there is much variation.

Human security is indivisible; it must not be pursued by one group at the expense of another. As a central pillar of human security, development must be oriented toward the human security of everyone. Thus it must diminish, rather than increase, gaps—whether between North and South, black and white, rich and poor, male and female, or urban and rural.

Acronyms

ACFODE	Action for Development
ACS	American Colonization Society
AEC	African Economic Community
AFL	Armed Forces of Liberia
ALF	Afar Liberation Front
AMU	Arab Maghreb Union
APC	All People's Congress
AWEPON	African Women's Economic Policy Network
BP	British Petroleum
CAST	Consolidated African Selection Trust
CBO	community-based organization
CCE	Constitutional Commission of Eritrea
CEAO	Economic Community of West Africa
CEEWA	Council for Economic Empowerment of Women in Africa
CFD	Caisse Française de Développement
COMESA	Common Market for Eastern and Southern Africa
DAWN	Development Alternatives with Women for a New Era
DELCO	Sierra Leone Development Company
DELIMCO	German Liberian Mining Company
DENIVA	Development Network of Indigenous Voluntary Associations
ECOWAS	Economic Community of West African States
EIB	European Investment Bank
ELF	Eritrea Liberation Front
EPLF	Eritrea Peoples Liberation Front
EPRDF	Ethiopian Peoples Revolutionary Democratic Forces
EPZ	export processing zone
EU	European Union

FAO	Food and Agriculture Organization
FDLD	Democratic Front for the Liberation of Djibouti
FIS	National Islamic Front
FRUD	Front for the Restoration of Unity and Democracy
G7	Group of 7
GATT	General Agreement on Tariffs and Trade
GFA	globalization from above
GFB	globalization from below
HIPC	Highly Indebted Poor Countries
ICA	International Coffee Agreement
ICO	International Coffee Organization
ICRC	International Committee of the Red Cross
IDA	Institute of Development Anthropology
IDA	International Development Association
IFI	international financial institution
IGADD	Intergovernmental Authority on Drought and Development
IMF	International Monetary Fund
IR	international relations
IRED	Innovations et Réseaux pour le Développement
LAMCO	Liberian-American Swedish Mineral Company
MIFERMA	Société des Mines de Fer de Mauritanie
MLC	Maryland Logging Company
MNC	multinational corporation
MNDID	Djibouti National Movement for the Restoration of Democracy
MOSOP	Movement for the Survival of the Ogoni People
MWPI	Maryland Wood Processing Industry
NDA	National Democratic Alliance
NGO	nongovernmental organization
NIEO	new international economic order
NIF	National Islamic Front
NOVIB	Netherlands Organization for International Development Cooperation
NPFL	National Patriotic Front of Liberia
NRM	National Revolutionary Movement
OAU	Organization of African Unity
ODA	official development assistance
OECD	Organization of Economic Cooperation and Development
OLF	Oromo Liberation Front
OLS	Operation Lifeline Sudan
OMVS	Organisation pour le Mise en Valeur du Fleuve Sénégal

OPEC	Organization of Petroleum Exporting Countries
Opex	Operational Expert
PAMSCAD	Program of Actions to Mitigate the Social Costs of Adjustment
PAPSCA	Program for the Alleviation of Poverty and the Social Costs of Adjustment
POW	prisoner of war
PVO	private voluntary organization
RRC	Relief and Rehabilitation Commission
RSA	Republic of South Africa
RUF	Revolutionary United Front
SADC	Southern African Development Community
SAED	Société d'Aménagement et d'Exploitation des Terres du Delta de Fleuve Sénégal et des vallées du Fleuve Sénégal et de la Falème
SAP	structural adjustment program
SIEROMCO	Sierra Leone Ore and Metal Company
SLA	Sierra Leone Army
SLPP	Sierra Leone People's Party
SNM	Somali National Movement
SONADER	Société Nationale de Développement Rural (Mauritanie)
SPLA	Sudan People's Liberation Army
SPLM	Sudan People's Liberation Movement
SSDF	Somali Salvation Democratic Front
TNC	transnational corporation
TPLF	Tigray People's Liberation Front
UMOA	West African Monetary Union
UNCTAD	United Nations Conference on Trade and Development
UNCLDC	United Nations Conference on the Least Developed Countries
UNDP	United Nations Development Program
UNECA	United Nations Economic Commission for Africa
UNICEF	United Nations Children's Fund
UNIDO	United Nations International Development Organization
UNIF	United Nations Intervention Force
UNOSOM	United Nations Operations in Somalia
UNPO	Unrepresented Nations and Peoples Organizations
USAID	U.S. Agency for International Development
USC	United Somali Congress
VDO	voluntary development organizations
WFP	World Food Program
WSLF	Western Somali Liberation Front
WTO	World Trade Organization

References

Acharya, A. (1997) "The Periphery as the Core: The Third World and Security Studies," in K. Krause and C. M. Williams (eds.) *Critical Security Studies: Concepts and Cases.* London: University College of London Press.

Adams, A. (1977) *Le Long Voyage des Gens du Fleuve Sénégal.* Paris: François Maspero.

Adams, A. (1985) *La Terre et les Gens du Fleuve.* Paris: l'Harmattan.

Africa Confidential (1989) 30, 19 (September 22).

Africa Watch (1990) *Denying the Honour of Living: Sudan, a Human Rights Disaster.* New York: Africa Watch.

Ajomo, M. A., and Adewale, O. (eds.) (1993) *African Economic Community Treaty: Issues, Problems, and Prospects.* Lagos: Nigerian Institute of Advanced Legal Studies.

Ake, C. (1996) *Democracy and Development in Africa.* Washington, D.C.: Brookings Institution.

Allen, C. (1978) "Sierra Leone," in J. Dunn (ed.) *West African States: Failure and Promise.* Cambridge: Cambridge University Press.

Al Sharq al-Awsat (1996) July 27 (daily newspaper in Arabic).

Aly, A. H. M. (1994) *Economic Cooperation in Africa: In Search of Direction.* Boulder: Lynne Rienner.

Amin, S. (1997) *Capitalism in the Age of Globalization.* London: Zed Books.

Amnesty International (1995) *Sudan: The Tears of Orphans.* London: Amnesty International.

An-Na'im, A. A., and Deng, F. (eds.) (1990) *Human Rights in Africa: Cross-Cultural Perspectives.* Washington, D.C.: Brookings Institution.

Anderson, P. (1992) *English Questions.* London: Verso.

Ashley, R. K. (1986) "The Poverty of Neo-Realism," in R. O. Keohane (ed.) *Neoliberalism and Its Critics.* New York: Columbia University Press.

Axford, B. (1995) *The Global System: Economics, Politics, and Culture.* Cambridge: Polity Press.

Azarya, V. A. (1988) "Re-Ordering State-Society Relations: Incorporation and Disengagement," in D. Rothchild and N. Chazan (eds.) *The Precarious Balance: State and Society in Africa.* Boulder: Westview.

Baldwin, D. A. (ed.) (1993a) *Neorealism and Neoliberalism: The Contemporary Debate.* New York: Columbia University Press.

Baldwin, D. A. (1993b) "Neoliberalism, Neorealism, and World Politics," in D. A. Baldwin (ed.) *Neorealism and Neoliberalism: The Contemporary Debate.* New York: Columbia University Press.

Barge, A. (1979) *La Politique Française de Coopération en Afrique: Le Cas du Sénégal*. Dakar: Nouvelles Éditions Africaines.

Barnet, R. J., and Muller, R. (1974) *The Global Reach*. New York: Simon and Schuster.

Barratt Brown, M. (1995) *Africa's Choices: After Thirty Years of the World Bank*. London: Penguin.

Barratt Brown, M., and Tiffen, P. (1992) *Short-Changed: Africa and World Trade*. London: Pluto Press.

Bayart, J. F. (1993a) *Jeune Afrique* (April 15–21).

Bayart, J. F. (1993b) *The State in Africa: The Politics of the Belly*. London: Longman.

Baylis, J., and Smith, S. (eds.) (1997) *The Globalization of World Politics*. Oxford: Oxford University Press.

Belvaude, C. (1989) *La Mauritanie*. Paris: Karthala.

Bergsten, C. F. (1996) "Globalizing Free Trade," *Foreign Affairs* 75, 3 (May–June): 105–120.

Best, G. (1995) "Justice, International Relations, and Human Rights," *International Affairs* 71, 4.

Bhaskar, R. (1979) *The Possibility of Naturalism*. Brighton: Harvester Wheatsheaf.

Bird, G., and Killick, T. (1995) *The Bretton Woods Institutions: A Commonwealth Perspective*. London: Commonwealth Secretariat.

Bird, J., et al. (eds.) (1993) *Mapping the Future: Local Cultures, Global Change*. London: Routledge.

Blakett, P. M. S. (1962) "Steps Towards Disarmament," *Scientific American* (April).

Block, F. (1987) *Revising State Theory*. Philadelphia: Temple University Press.

Boele, R. (1995) *Ogoni: Report of the UNPO Mission to Investigate the Situation of the Ogoni of Nigeria February 17–26*. The Hague: Unrepresented Nations and Peoples Organization.

Booth, K. (1991) "Security and Emancipation," *Review of International Studies* 17, 4.

Booth, K. (1994) "Strategy," in A. J. R. Groom and M. Light (eds.) *Contemporary International Relations: A Guide to Theory*. London: Pinter.

Booth, K. and Smith, S. (eds.) (1995) *International Relations Theory Today*. Cambridge: Polity Press.

Booth, K., and Vale, P. (1997) "Critical Security Studies and Regional Insecurity: The Case of Southern Africa," in K. Krause and C. M. Williams (eds.) *Critical Security Studies: Concepts and Cases*. London: University College of London Press.

Booth, K., Smith, S., and Zalewski, M. (eds.) (1996) *International Theory: Positivism and Beyond*. Cambridge: Cambridge University Press.

Boutillier, J-L., and Schmitz, J. (1987) "Gestion Traditionelle des Terres et Transition vers l'Irrigation," *Cahier Science Humaine* 23, 3–4: 533–554.

Boutillier, J. L., et al. (1962) *La Moyenne Vállée du Sénégal: Etude Socio-Economique*. Paris: Presses Universitaires de France.

Bradshaw, Y. W., and Wallace, M. (1996) *Global Inequalities*. London: Pine Forge Press.

Braidotti, R., et al. (1994) *Women, the Environment, and Sustainable Development: Towards a Theoretical Synthesis*. London: Zed Books.

Brandt Commission (1980) *Brandt Commission Report—North-South: A Programme for Survival*. London: Pan Books.

Brecher, J., and Costello, T. (1994) *Global Village or Global Pillage?* Boston: South End Press.

Brecher, J., et al. (1993) *Global Visions*. Boston: South End Press.

Brittain, V., and Elliott, L. (1977) "Dollar-a-Day Losers in the Global Economy," *Guardian* (June 12).

Broad, R., and Cavanagh, J. (1995–1996) "Don't Forget the Impoverished South," *Foreign Policy* (Winter): 18–35.

Brown, C. (1992) *International Relations Theory: New Normative Approaches*. New York: Columbia University Press.

Brown, M. (1995) *Africa's Choices*. London: Penguin.

Brown, M. (1996) "Aid Moves from the Messianic to the Managerial," *World Today* (June): 157–159.

Brzezinski, Z. (1995) "A Plan for Europe," *Foreign Affairs* 74, 1 (Jan.–Feb.).

Burr, J. M., and Collins, R. O. (1995) *Requiem for the Sudan*. Boulder: Westview Press.

Butterfield, H., and Wight, M. (eds.) (1966) *Diplomatic Investigations*. London: Allen and Unwin.

Buzan, B. (1983) *People, States, and Fear: The National Security Problem in International Relations*. Brighton: Harvester Wheatsheaf.

Buzan, B. (1991a) "The Idea of the State and National Security," in R. Little and M. Smith (eds.) *Perspectives on World Politics*. London: Routledge.

Buzan, B. (1991b) *People, States, and Fear: An Agenda for International Security Studies in the Post–Cold War Era*, 2nd edition. Brighton: Harvester Wheatsheaf; and Boulder: Lynne Rienner.

Buzan, B., Jones, C., and Little, R. (1993) *The Logic of Anarchy: Neorealism to Structural Realism*. New York: Columbia University Press.

Bygrave, M. (1997) "A Lion for Africa," *Guardian Weekend* (Feb. 15): 22–26.

Callaghy, T. M. (1988) "The State and Development of Capitalism in Africa," in D. Rothchild and N. Chazan (eds.) *The Precarious Balance: State and Society in Africa*. Boulder: Westview.

Callaghy, T. M. (1995) "Africa and the World Political-Economy," in J. W. Harbeson and D. Rothchild (eds.) *Africa in World Politics*. Boulder: Westview.

Cartwright, J. (1970) *Politics in Sierra Leone, 1947–67*. Toronto: University of Toronto Press.

Cartwright, J. (1978) *Political Leadership in Sierra Leone*. London: Croom Helm.

Charney, C. (1987) "The Contemporary African State: A 'Ruling Class,'" *Review of African Political Economy* 38 (April): 66–77.

Cheru, F. (1989) *The Silent Revolution in Africa: Debt, Development, and Democracy*. London: Zed Books.

Cheru, F. (1997) "The Silent Revolution and the Weapons of the Weak: Transformation and Innovation from Below," in S. Gill and J. H. Mittelman (eds.) *Innovation and Transformation in International Studies*. Cambridge: Cambridge University Press.

Chipman, J. (1989) *French Power in Africa*. Oxford: Blackwell.

Chomsky, N. (1992) *Deterring Democracy*. London: Verso.

Chomsky, N. (1993) *Year 501: The Conquest Continues*. London: Verso.

Chomsky, N. (1994) *World Orders: Old and New*. London: Pluto Press.

Chomsky, N. (1996a) *Class War*. London: Pluto Press.

Chomsky, N. (1996b) *Powers and Prospects*. London: Pluto Press.

Chossudovsky, M. (1994a) "Global Impoverishment and the IMF–World Bank Economic Medicine," *Third World Resurgence* 49 (September): 17–21.

Chossudovsky, M. (1994b) "IMF–World Bank Policies and the Rwandan Holocaust," *Third World Resurgence* 52 (December): 27–31.

Chossudovsky, M. (1997) *The Globalization of Poverty: Impacts of IMF and World Bank Reforms*. London: Zed Books.

Clapham, C. (1976) *Liberia and Sierra Leone: An Essay in Comparative Politics.* Cambridge: Cambridge University Press.

Clapham, C. (1978) "Liberia," in J. Dunn (ed.) *West African States: Failure and Promise.* Cambridge: Cambridge University Press.

Clapham, C. (1982) "The Politics of Failure: Clientelism, Political Instability, and National Integration in Liberia and Sierra Leone," in C. Clapham (ed.) *Private Patronage and Public Power: Political Clientelism in the Modern State.* London: Frances Pinter Publishers.

Clapham, C. (1993) "Democratisation in Africa: Obstacles and Prospects," *Third World Quarterly* 14, 3: 423–439.

Clapham, C. (1996) *Africa and the International System: The Politics of State Survival.* Cambridge: Cambridge University Press.

Clower, R. W., Dalton, G., Harwitz, M. and Walters, A. A. (eds.) (1966) *Growth Without Development: An Economic Survey of Liberia.* Evanston: Northwestern University Press.

Conac, G., Savonnet-Guyot, C., and Conac, F. (1985) *Les Politiques de l'eau en Afrique: Développement Agricole et Participation Paysanne.* Paris: Économica.

Cox, R. W. (1987) *Production, Power, and World Order.* New York: Columbia University Press.

Cox, R. W. (1994) "Global Restructuring: Making Sense of the Changing International Political Economy," in R. Stubbs and G. Underhill (eds.) *Political Economy and the Changing Global Order.* London: Macmillan.

Cox, R. W. (1997) *The New Realism.* Basingstoke: Macmillan.

Crocker, C. (1995) "The Lessons of Somalia," *Foreign Affairs* 74, 3 (May–June).

Crousse, B., Mathieu, P., and Seck, S. M. (eds.) (1991) *La Vallée du Fleuve Sénégal.* Paris: Karthala.

Dahl, R. A. (1985) *A Preface to Economic Democracy.* Los Angeles: University of California Press.

Davidson, B. (1992) *The Black Man's Burden: Africa and the Curse of the Nation-State.* London: Currey.

Deng, F. M. (1995) *War of Visions: Conflict of Identities in the Sudan.* Washington, D.C.: Brookings Institution.

Deng, F. M. (1996) "Anatomy of Conflict in Africa," in L. Van de Goor et al. (eds.) *Between Development and Destruction: An Enquiry into the Causes of Conflict in Post-Colonial States.* Basingstoke, U.K.: Macmillan.

Diemer, G., Fall, B., and Huiberg, H. P. (1991) "Promoting a Smallholder—Centred Approach to Irrigation: Lessons from Village Irrigation Schemes in the Senegal Valley," *Irrigation Management Network Paper—ODI London* 6 (October).

Dolo, E. (1996) *Democracy Versus Dictatorship: The Quest for Freedom and Justice in Africa's Oldest Republic, Liberia.* Washington, D.C.: University Press of America.

Domhoff, W. (1970) "Who Makes American Foreign Policy?" in D. Horowitz (ed.) *Corporations and the Cold War.* Boston: New England Free Press.

Duffield, M. (1993) "NGOs Disaster Relief Transfer in the Horn: Political Survival in a Permanent Emergency," *Development and Change* 24, 1.

Duffield, M., and Prendergast, J. (1994) "Sovereignty and Intervention After the Cold War: Lessons from the Emergency Relief Desk," *Middle East Report* 24, 2–3 (March–June): 187–188.

Dumont, R. (1988 [1966]) *False Start in Africa.* London: Earthscan.

Dunne, T. (1997) "Realism," in J. Baylis, and S. Smith (eds.) *The Globalization of World Politics.* Oxford: Oxford University Press.

Dunning, J. H. (1993) *The Globalization of Business*. London: Routledge.

Durch, W. (ed.) (1993) *The Evolution of UN Peacekeeping: Case-Studies and Comparative Analysis*. New York: St. Martin's Press.

Eakins, D. (1970) "Business Planners and America's Post-War Expansion," in D. Horowitz (ed.) *Corporations and the Cold War*. Boston: New England Free Press.

Economist (1997) "Editorial: Emerging Africa" (June 14): 15–16.

Economist Intelligence Unit (1994) *Country Profile, Rwanda Burundi 1993/94*. London: EIU.

Edgell, S. (1993) *Class*. London: Routledge.

Edgley, A. (1995) "Chomsky and the State," *Politics* 15, 3: 153–159.

El-Ayouty, Y. (ed.) (1994) *The Organization of African Unity After Thirty Years*. Westport: Praeger.

Elliott, L. (1997a) "Africa's Turn at the Top Table," *Guardian* (June 20).

Elliott, L. (1997b) "World Warned of Poverty Time Bomb," *Guardian* (September 24): 21.

Elliott, L., and Brittain, V. (1997) "Seven Richest Could End Want," *Guardian* (June 12).

Elliott Berg Associates (1990) *Adjustment Postponed: Economic Policy Reform in Senegal in the 1980s*. Report prepared for USAID/Dakar, October. Daker: USAID.

Ellis, S. (1995) "Liberia 1989–1994: A Study of Ethnic and Spiritual Violence," *African Affairs* 94, 375: 165–197.

Elson, D. (1991) "Structural Adjustment: Its Effects on Women," in T. Wallace (ed.) *Changing Perceptions: Writings on Gender and Development*. Oxford: Oxfam.

Enloe, C. (1989) *Bananas, Beaches, and Bases: Making Feminist Sense of International Politics*. Berkeley: University of California Press.

Etzioni, A. (1995) *Communitarian Thinking: No Persons, Virtues, Institutionism, and Communities*. Charlottesville: University of Virginia.

Falk, R. (1971) *This Endangered Planet*. New York: Random House.

Falk, R. (1975) *A Study of Future Worlds*. New York: Free Press.

Falk, R. (1995) *On Humane Governance*. Cambridge: Polity Press.

Falk, R., et al. (eds.) (1991) *The United Nations and a Just World Order*. Boulder: Westview.

Fearon, J. (1988) "International Financial Institutions and Economic Reform in Sub-Saharan" *Journal of Modern African Studies* 26, 1: 113–137.

Featherstone, M., et al. (eds.) (1995) *Global Modernities*. London: Sage.

Finer, S. (1975) "State and Nation-Building in Europe: The Role of the Military," in C. Tilly (ed.) *The Formation of National States in Western Europe*. Princeton: Princeton University Press.

Friedman, J. (1994) *Cultural Identity and Global Process*. London: Sage.

Fukuyama, F. (1989) "The End of History?" *National Interest* (Summer): 3–18.

Furedi, F. (1994) *The New Ideology of Imperialism*. London: Pluto Press.

Gamble, A., and Payne, A. (1996) "Conclusion: The New Regionalism," in A. Gamble and A. Payne (eds.) *Regionalism and World Order*. Basingstoke: Macmillan.

Gardiner, L. (1970) "New Deal, New Frontiers, and the Cold War," in D. Horowitz (ed.) *Corporations and the Cold War*. Boston: New England Free Press.

George, S. (1998) *A Fate Worse Than Debt*. London: Penguin.

Gerberding, W. (1966) *U.S. Foreign Policy—Perspectives and Analyses*. New York: McGraw Hill.

Gervais, M. (1993) "Étude de la Pratique des Ajustments au Niger et au Rwanda," *Labour, Capital, and Society* 26, 1.

Gib, Sir Alexander, and Partners (1978) *Global Evaluation of the Regional Development Programme.* Dakar: OMVS, July.

Gib, Sir Alexander, and Partners (1987) *Final Report Concerning the Creation of a Management Agency for the Common Works.* Dakar: OMVS, August.

Giddens, A. (1991) *Modernity and Self-Identity: Self and Society in the Late Modern Age.* Cambridge: Polity Press.

Gill, S. (1990) *American Hegemony and the Trilateral Commission.* Cambridge: Cambridge University Press.

Gill, S. (1995) "Globalisation, Market Civilisation, and Disciplinary Neoliberalism," *Millennium* 24, 3: 399–423.

Gill, S., and Law, D. (1990) *Global Political Economy: Perspectives, Problems, and Policies.* Brighton: Harvester Wheatsheaf.

Gillies, D. (1996) "Human Rights, Democracy, and Good Governance: Stretching the World Bank's Policy Frontiers," in J. M. Griesgraber and B. G. Gunter (eds.) *The World Bank.* London: Pluto Press.

Goose, S., and Smith, F. (1995) "Arming Genocide in Rwanda," *Foreign Affairs* 74, 1 (Jan.–Feb.).

Gordon, A. (1996) *Transforming Capitalism and Patriarchy: Gender and Development in Africa.* Boulder: Lynne Rienner.

Griffiths, M. (1992) *Realism, Idealism, and International Politics: A Reinterpretation.* London: Routledge.

Groom, A. J. R., and Light, M. (1994) *Contemporary International Relations: A Guide to Theory.* London: Pinter.

Gros, Jean-Germain (1996) "Towards a Taxonomy of Failed States in the New World Order," *Third World Quarterly* 17, 3.

Grunwald, H. (1995) "When Peacekeeping Doesn't Work," *Time* 26, 145 (June 26).

Guichaoua, A. (1987) *Les Paysans et l'Investissement-Travail au Burundi et au Rwanda.* Geneva: Bureau International du Travail.

Guichaoua, A. (1989) *Destins Paysans et Politiques Agraires en Afrique Centrale.* Paris: l'Harmattan.

Hall, S. (1991) "The Local and the Global: Globalization and Ethnicity," in A. D. King (ed.) *Culture, Globalization, and the World-System.* London: Macmillan.

Halliday, F. (1995) "International Relations and Its Discontents," *International Affairs* 71, 4.

Hamalengwa, M., et al. (comps.) (1988) *The International Law of Human Rights in Africa: Basic Documents and Annotated Bibliography.* Dordrecht: Nijhoff.

Hamilton, M., and Hirszowicz, M. (1993) *Class and Inequality.* Hemel Hempstead: Harvester Wheatsheaf.

Hamza, A. (1973) "The State in Post-Colonial Societies: Pakistan and Bangladesh," in K. P. Gough and H. P. Sharma (eds.) *Imperialism and Revolution in South Asia.* New York: Penguin.

Harbeson, J. W. (1995a) "Africa in World Politics," in J. W. Harbeson and D. Rothchild (eds.) *Africa in World Politics: Post–Cold War Challenges.* Boulder: Westview.

Harbeson, J. W. (1995b) "Post–Cold War Politics in the Horn of Africa: The Quest for Political Identity Intensified," in J. W. Harbeson and D. Rothchild (eds.) *Africa in World Politics: Post–Cold War Challenges.* Boulder: Westview Press.

Harbeson, J. W., and Rothchild, D. (eds.) (1995) *Africa in World Politics: Post–Cold War Challenges.* Boulder: Westview.

Harding, S. (1986) *The Science Question in Feminism.* Ithaca: Cornell University Press.

Harrington, M. (1992) "What Exactly Is Wrong with the Liberal State as an Agent of Change?" in V. S. Peterson (ed.) *Gendered States: Feminist (Re)Visions of International Relations Theory.* Boulder: Lynne Rienner.

Harris, N. (1986) *The End of the Third World.* London: Penguin.

Harrison, F. (1991) "Women in Jamaica's Urban Informal Economy: Insights from a Kingston Slum," in C. Mohanty, A. Russo, and L. Torres (eds.) *Third World Women and the Politics of Feminism.* Indianapolis: Indiana University Press.

Harvey, R. (1995) *The Return of the Strong: The Drift to Global Disorder.* London: Macmillan.

Hayes, C. J. H. (1966 [1926]) *Essays on Nationalism.* New York: Russell & Russell.

Hayter, T. (1971) *Aid as Imperialism.* London: Penguin.

Hayter, T. (1992) *The Creation of World Poverty.* London: Pluto Press.

Hayward, F. (1984) "Political Leadership, Power, and the State: Generalisations from the Case of Sierra Leone," *African Studies Review* 27: 19–39.

Hayward, F., and Kandeh, J. D. (1987) "Perspectives on Twenty-Five Years of Elections in Sierra Leone," in F. Hayward (ed.) *Elections in Independent Africa.* Boulder: Westview.

Held, D. (1995) "Cosmopolitan Democracy and the Global Order: Reflection on the 200th Anniversary of Kant's 'Perpetual Peace,'" *Alternatives* 20, 4.

Helleiner, E. (1994) "From Bretton Woods to Global Finance," in R. Stubbs and G. Underhill (eds.) *Political Economy and the Changing Global Order.* London: Macmillan.

Hettne, B., and Inotai, A. (1994) *The New Regionalism: Implications for Global Development and International Security.* Helsinki: UNU/WIDER.

Hine, R. C. (1992) "Regionalism and the Integration of the World Economy," *Journal of Common Market Studies* 30.

Hirst, P., and Thompson, G. (1996) *Globalization in Question: The International Economy and the Possibilities of Governance.* Cambridge: Polity Press.

Hobsbawm, E. J. (1992) *Nations and Nationalism Since 1780: Programme, Myth, Reality,* 2nd edition. Cambridge: Cambridge University Press.

Holcomb, B., and Rothenberg, T. (1993) "Women's Work and the Urban Household Economy in Developing Countries," in M. Turshen and B. Holcomb (eds.) *Women's Lives and Public Policy.* Westport, Conn.: Greenwood Press.

Hoogevelt, A. (1997) *Globalization and the Postcolonial World.* London: Macmillan.

Horowitz, D. (1971) *From Yalta to Vietnam.* London: Penguin.

Horowitz, D. (ed.) (1970) *Corporations and the Cold War.* Boston: New England Free Press.

Hulme, D., and Moseley, P. (1996) *Finance Against Poverty: Volume 1.* London: Routledge.

Huntington, S. P. (1968) *Political Order in Changing Societies.* New Haven: Yale University Press.

Huntington, S. (1993) "The Clash of Civilizations," *Foreign Affairs* 72, 3 (Summer): 22–50.

Hurrell, A., and Woods, N. (1995) "Globalisation and Inequality," *Millennium* 24, 3: 447–470.

Hymer, S. H. (1979) *The Multinational Corporation.* Cambridge: Cambridge University Press.

IDA (1990) *Suivi des Activités du Bassin du Fleuve Sénégal: Phase I, Rapport Définitif.* Dakar and Binghampton, N.Y.: IDA, November.

Imam, A. (1992) "Democratisation Processes in Africa," *Review of African Political Economy* 54 (July): 102–105.

Jackson, R. H. (1990) *Quasi-States: Sovereignty, International Relations, and the Third World.* Cambridge: Cambridge University Press.

Jackson, R. H., and Rosberg, C. G. (1982) "Why Africa's Weak States Persist: The Empirical and the Juridical in Statehood." *World Politics* 35, 1: 1–24.

Jackson, R. H., and Rosberg, C. G. (1986) "Sovereignty and Underdevelopment: Juridical Statehood in the African Crisis," *Journal of Modern African Studies* 24, 1: 1–31.

Jarret, M. (1996) "Civil War in Liberia: A Manipulation of Chaos?" Master's dissertation, University of London.

Jarvis, A. (1989) "Societies, States, and GeoPolitics: Challenges from Historical Sociology," *Review of International Studies* 15: 281–293.

Jean-Germaine, G. (1996) "Toward a Taxonomy of Failed States in the New World Order," *Third World Quarterly* 17, 3.

Jonah, J. O. C. (1994) "The OAU: Peace Keeping and Conflict Resolution," in Y. El-Ayouty (ed.) *The Organization of African Unity After Thirty Years.* Westport, Conn.: Praeger.

Kaplan, R. (1994) "The Coming Anarchy?" *Atlantic Monthly* (February): 44–76.

Kasfir, N. (1984) *State and Class in Africa.* London: Frank Cass.

Katznelson, I. (1981) *City Trenches: Urban Politics and the Patterning of Class in the US.* Chicago: Chicago University Press.

Katznelson, I., and Zoldberg, I. (1986) *Working-Class Formation: C19 Formations in Western Europe and the US.* Princeton: Princeton University Press.

Keller, J. (1995) "Remaking the Ethiopian State," in I. W. Zartman (ed.) *Collapsed States: The Disintegration and Restoration of Legitimate Authority.* Boulder: Lynne Rienner.

Kende, I. (1971) "Twenty Five Years of Local Wars," *Journal of Peace Research* 8: 5–22.

Kende, I. (1978) "Wars of Ten Years 1967–1976," *Journal of Peace and Research* 15, 3.

Kennan, G. F. (1966) "Our Duty to Ourselves," in G. Stourzh, et al. (eds.) *Readings in American Democracy.* New York: Oxford University Press.

Keohane, R. O. (1996) "The Theory of Hegemonic Stability and Changes in the International Economic Regimes 1967–1977," in C. R. Goddard, J. T Passé-Smith, and J. O. Conklin (eds.) *International Political Economy: State-Market Relations in the Changing Global Order.* Boulder: Lynne Rienner.

Keohane, R. O. (ed.) (1986) *Neorealism and Its Critics.* New York: Columbia University Press.

Keohane, R. O., and Nye, J. (1996) "Realism and Complex Interdependence," in C. R. Goddard, J. T. Passé-Smith, and J. O. Conklin (eds.) *International Political Economy: State-Market Relations in the Changing Global Order.* Boulder: Lynne Rienner.

Khadiagala, G. M. (1995) "State Collapse and Reconstruction in Uganda," in I. W. Zartman (ed.) *Collapsed States: The Disintegration and Restoration of Legitimate Authority.* Boulder: Lynne Rienner.

Kidron, M., and Segal, R. (1987) *The New State of the World Atlas.* London: Pan Books.

Kilson, M. (1965) *Political Change in a West African State: A Study of the Modernisation Process in Colonial Sierra Leone.* New York: Atheneum.

King, A. D. (ed.) (1991) *Culture, Globalization, and the World-System*. London: Macmillan.

Knight, D. (1994) *A Burning Hunger*. London: Panos.

Kofman, E., and Youngs, G. (eds.) (1996) *Globalization: Theory and Practice*. London: Pinter.

Kokole, O. H. (1996) "Ethnic Conflicts Versus Development in Africa: Causes and Remedies," in L. Van de Goor, et al. (eds.) *Between Development and Destruction: An Enquiry into the Causes of Conflict in Post-Colonial States*. Baskingstoke, U.K.: Macmillan.

Kolko, G. (1969) *The Roots of American Foreign Policy*. Boston: Beacon.

Kothari, R. (1993) "The Yawning Vacuum: A World Without Alternatives—Anarchy: Gender and Development," *Alternatives* 18: 119–139.

Kouassi, E. K. (1993) "Africa and the United Nations Since 1945," in Ali A. Mazrui (ed.) *Africa Since 1935,* vol. 3 of *General History of Africa*. London: Heinemann; and Berkeley: University of California Press.

Krause, J. (1996) "Gender Inequalities and Feminist Politics in Global Perspective," in E. Kofman and G. Youngs (eds.) *Globalization: Theory and Practice*. London: Pinter.

Krause, K., and Williams, M. C. (eds.) (1997) *Critical Security Studies: Concepts and Cases*. London: UCL Press.

Krauthammer, C. (1991) "The Unipolar Moment," *Foreign Affairs* 70, 1.

Leanne, S. (1994) "African-American Initiatives Against Minority Rule in South Africa: A Politicized Diaspora in World Politics." Doctoral dissertation, University of Oxford.

Lee, J. M. (1969) *African Armies and Civil Order*. London: Chatto and Windus.

Leftwich (1994) "Governance, the State, and the Politics of Development," *Development and Change* 25: 363–386.

Leys, C. (1996) *The Rise and Fall of Development Theory*. Indiana: Indiana University Press.

Liebenow, J. G. (1987) *Liberia: The Quest for Democracy*. Bloomington: Indiana University Press.

Lim, L. (1990) "Women's Work in Export Factories: The Politics of a Cause," in I. Tinker (ed.) *Persistent Inequalities: Women and World Development*. Oxford: Oxford University Press.

Linklater, A. (1995) "Realism and Neo-Realism: Primary Differences," in K. Booth and S. Smith (eds.) *International Relations Theory Today*. Cambridge: Polity Press.

Lipschutz, R. D. (ed.) (1995) *On Security*. New York: Columbia University Press.

Little, R., and Smith, M. (eds.) (1991) *Perspectives on World Politics*. London: Routledge.

Lovering, J. (1987) "Militarism, Capitalism, and the Nation-State: Towards a Realist Synthesis," *Environment and Planning D: Society and Space* 5, 283–302.

Lowenkopf, M. (1976) *Politics in Liberia* (Stanford, Calif.: Hoover Institution Press.

Luke, D. (1988) "Continuity in Sierra Leone: From Stevens to Momoh," *Third World Quarterly* 10, 1: 67–78.

Luke, D., and Riley, S. (1989) "The Politics of Economic Decline in Sierra Leone," *Journal of Modern African Studies* 27, 1: 133–141.

Luke, D., and Riley, S. (1991) "Economic Decline and the New Refom Agenda in Africa: The Case of Sierra Leone," *IDPM Discussion Paper 28*. Manchester: University of Manchester.

Lutz, R. H. (1980) *Collier's Encyclopedia*. New York: Macmillan Education Corporation and P. F. Collier, vol. 4 of 24 vols.

Ly, F. (1980) "Sierra Leone: The Paradox of Economic Decline and Political Stability," *Monthly Review* 32 (June): 10–26.

Lyons, T., and Samatar, A. (1995) *Somalia: State Collapse, Multilateral Intervention, and Strategies for Political Reconstruction*. Washington, D.C.: Brookings Institution.

Malanczuk, P. (1993) *Humanitarian Intervention and the Legitimacy of the Use of Force*. Inaugural lecture, University of Amsterdam, January 22. Het Spinhuis: University of Amsterdam.

Mann, M. (1995) "Sources of Variation in Working Class Movements in C20 Europe," *New Left Review* 212: 14–54.

Manor, J. (1995) "Democratic Decentralization in Africa and Asia," *IDS Bulletin* (April 26).

Marchand, M. (1996) "Reconceptualising 'Gender and Development'" in an Era of Globalisation," *Millennium* 25, 3: 577–603.

Marchand, M., and Parpart, J. (eds.) (1995) *Feminism/Postmodernism/Development*. London: Routledge.

Mazrui, A. (1993) "Global Apartheid? Race and Religion in the New World Order," in G. Lundestad and O. A. Westad (eds.) *Beyond the Cold War: New Dimensions in International Relations*. Stockholm: Scandinavian University Press.

Mazrui, A. (1994) "Decaying Parts of Africa Need Benign Colonization," *International Herald Tribune* (August 4).

Medhanie, T. (1994) "Eritrea and Neighbours in the New World Order," *Bremen Afrika Studien* 15.

Mendlovitz, S. (ed.) (1975) *On the Creation of a Just World Order*. New York: Free Press.

Merheb, N. (1995) "Sudan," in P. Baehr, et al. (eds.) *Human Rights in Developing Countries Yearbook*. The Hague: Kluwer Law International and Nordic Human Rights Publications.

Mies, M. (1986) *Patriarchy and Accumulation on a World Scale: Women in the International Division of Labour*. London: Zed Books.

Migdal, J. (1988) *Strong Societies and Weak States: State-Society Relations and State Capabilities in the Third World*. Princeton, N.J.: Princeton University Press.

Miller, R. P. (1985) *Peasant Autonomy and Irrigation: Innovation in the Senegal River Basin*. Ithaca: Cornell University.

Mills, C. W. (1978) *The Power Elite*. Oxford: Oxford University Press.

Mistry, P. S. (1996) *Regional Integration Arrangements in Economic Development: Panacea or Pitfall?* The Hague: Fondad.

Mittelman, J. (1997) "The Dynamics of Globalization," in J. Mittelman (ed.) *Globalization: Critical Reflections*. Boulder: Lynne Rienner.

Moghadam, V. (1994) "Economic Restructuring, Identity Politics, and Gender: Parallels and Contrasts in Eastern Europe and the Middle East." Conference paper, IPSA, Berlin.

Mohamed Salih, M. A. (1989a) "New Wine in Old Bottles: Tribal Militias and the Sudanese State," in *Review of African Political Economy* 45-46.

Mohamed Salih, M. A. (1989b) *The Impact of War on Women and Children in Southern Sudan*. Nairobi: UNICEF, Inter-Africa Group.

Mohamed Salih, M. A. (1991) *The Current Situation in the Horn of Africa*. Proceedings of the African Forum, November 22. Uppsala: Scandinavian Institute of African Studies.

Mohamed Salih, M. A. (1994a) *Inducing Food Insecurity: Perspectives on Food Policies in Eastern and Southern Africa.* Uppsala: Scandinavian Institute of African Studies.

Mohamed Salih, M. A. (1994b) "The Ideology of the Dinka and the Sudan People's Liberation Movement," in K. Fukui and J. Markakis (eds.) *Ethnicity and Conflict in the Horn of Africa.* Athens: Ohio University Press.

Mohamed Salih, M. A., and Wohlgemuth, L. (eds.) (1994) *Management of the Crisis in Somalia.* Uppsala: Scandinavian Institute of African Studies.

Mohanty, C., Russo, A., and Torres, L. (eds.) (1991) *Third World Women and the Politics of Feminism.* Indianapolis: Indiana University Press.

Moore, B. (1966) *The Social Origins of Dictatorship and Democracy.* London: Penguin.

Moore, B. (1978) *Injustice: The Social Bases of Obedience and Revolt.* London: Macmillan.

Morgenthau, H. J. (1960) *Politics Among Nations.* New York: Knopf.

Mukonoweshuro, E. G. (1990) "Ethnicity, Class, and Clientelism in Sierra Leone: A Methodological Critique," *Plural Societies* 20, 2: 65–91.

Murphy, C., and Rojas de Ferro, C. (1995) "The Power of Representation in International Political Economy," *Review of International Political Economy* 2, 1: 63–69.

Nahimana, F. (1993) *Le Rwanda, Emergence d'un État.* Paris: l'Harmattan.

Naldi, G. J. (ed.) (1992) *Documents of the Organization of African Unity.* London: Mansell.

Ndegwa, S. N. (1996) *The Two Faces of Civil Society: NGOs and Politics in Africa.* West Hartford: Kumarian.

'Nyong'o, P. A. (1992) "Democratisation Processes in Africa," *Review of African Political Economy* 54 (July): 97–102.

OECD (1996) "OECD Employment Outlook," SG/COM/PUN (96)65. Paris: OECD, July 9.

Ohmae, K. (1991) *The Borderless World: Power and Strategy in the Interlinked Economy.* New York: Harper Perennial.

Okafor, O. C. (1996) "Between Normative Idealism and National Interest: The Process of US/UN Interventions in African Civil Strife," *Scandinavian Journal of Development Alternatives* 15, 3–4.

Omar, R., and de Waal, A. (1994) "Somalia: Human Rights Abuse by the United Nations," in OMVS, *Les Objectives et les Grandes Lignes de la Stratégie de Développement Intégré du Bassin du Fleuve Sénégal.* Dakar: OMVS, May.

Onimode, B. (1988) *A Political-Economy of the African Crisis.* London: Zed Books.

Onimode, B. (1992) *A Future for Africa: Beyond the Politics of Adjustment.* London: Earthscan.

Ould-Mey, M. (1994) "Global Adjustment: Implications for Peripheral States," *Third World Quarterly* 15, 2: 319–336.

Panitch, L. (1997) "Rethinking the Role of the State," in J. Mittelman (ed.) *Globalization: Critical Reflections.* Boulder: Lynne Rienner.

Parfitt, T. W., and Riley, S. (1989) *The African Debt Crisis.* London: Routledge.

Pasha, M. K. (1996) "Security as Hegemony," *Alternatives* 21, 3 (July–Sept.): 283–302.

Pereira-Lunghu, J. (1995) "Trends in Government Deficits in the Liberian Economy from 1912–1990: Implications for Fiscal Policy in Post–Civil War Liberia," *Liberia Studies Journal* 20, 2: 207–231.

Peterson, V. S., and Runyan, A. (1993) *Global Gender Issues.* Boulder: Westview.

Pfaff, W. (1995) "A New Colonialism? Europe Must Go Back into Africa," *Foreign Affairs* 74, 1 (Jan–Feb).

Phillips, P. D., and Wallerstein, I. (1985) "National and World Identities and the Interstate System," *Millennium* 14.

Prendergast, J. (1995) "When the Troops Go Home: Somalia After the Intervention," *Review of African Political Economy* 64.

Prunier, G. (1995) *The Rwandan Crisis: History of a Genocide 1959–1994.* London: C. Hurst.

Pye-Smith, C., and Feyerabend, P. (1994) *The Wealth of Communities.* London: Earthscan.

Raghavan, C. (1990). *Recolonisation: GATT, the Uruguay Round, and the Third World.* Penang: Third World Network.

Rawls, J. (1978) *A Theory of Justice.* Boston: Harvard University Press.

Ray, A. K. (1989a) "Insecurity and Instability in the Third World," in J. Bandopadhyaya, et al. (eds.) *Dimension of Strategy: Some Indian Perspectives.* Calcutta: Jadavpur University Press.

Ray, A. K. (1989b) "The International Political System and the Developing World: A View from the Periphery," in C. Thomas and P. Saravanamuttu (eds.) *Conflict and Consensus in South/North Security.* Cambridge: Cambridge University Press.

Ray, A. K. (1996) *The Global System: A Historical View from the Periphery,* VRF series no. 272. Tokyo: Institute of Developing Economies.

Reis, H. (1970) *Kant's Political Writings.* Cambridge: Cambridge University Press.

Reno, W. (1993) "Economic Reform and the Strange Case of Liberalisation in Sierra Leone," *Governance* 6, 1: 23–42.

Reno, W. (1995a) *Corruption and State Politics in Sierra Leone.* Cambridge: Cambridge University Press.

Reno, W. (1995b) "Reinvention of an African Patrimonial State: Charles Taylor's Liberia," *Third World Quarterly* 16, 1: 109–120.

Reno, W. (1996) "Ironies of Post–Cold War Structural Adjustment in Sierra Leone," *Review of African Political Economy* 67: 7–18.

Reno, W. (1997) "Privatising War in Sierra Leone," *Current History* (May): 227–230.

République Rwandaise, Ministère des Finances et de l'Économie (1987) *L'Économie Rwandaise, 25 Ans d'Efforts (1962–1987).* Kigali: Government of Rwanda.

Richards, P. (1995) "Rebellion in Liberia and Sierra Leone: A Crisis of Youth," in O. Furley (ed.) *Conflict in Africa.* London: I. B. Tauris Publishers.

Richards, P. (1996) *Fighting for the Rainforest: War, Youth, and Resources in Sierra Leone.* London: James Currey.

Richardson, J. (1997) "Contending Liberalisms: Past and Present," *European Journal of International Relations* 3, 1: 5–33.

Riley, S. (1983) "'The Land of Waving Palms': Corruption Enquiries, Political Economy, and Politics in Sierra Leone," in M. Clarke (ed.) *Corruption: Causes, Consequences, and Control.* London: Frances Pinter.

Riley, S. (1997a) "The Coming Anarchy? State Collapse and Social Reconstruction in Contemporary Africa." Paper presented at the India International Centre, 9 April.

Riley, S. (1997b) "Sierra Leone: The Militariat Strikes Again," *Review of African Political Economy* 72: 287–292.

Riley, S., and Parfitt, T. W. (1987) "Party or Masquerade? The All Peoples Congress of Sierra Leone," *Journal of Commonwealth and Comparative Politics* 25, 2: 161–179.

Riley, S. P., and Parfitt, T. W. (1994) "Economic Adjustment and Democratization in Africa," in J. Walton and D. Seddon (eds.) *Free Markets and Food Riots: The Politics of Global Adjustment*. Oxford: Blackwell.

Riley, S., and Sesay, M. A. (1995) "Sierra Leone: The Coming Anarchy?" *Review of African Political Economy* 63: 121–126.

Robertson, R. (1995) "Globalization: Time-Space and Homogeneity-Heterogeneity," in M. Featherstone et al. (eds.) *Global Modernities*. London: Sage.

Rosenau, J. (1980) *The Scientific Study of Foreign Policies*. London: Pinter.

Rosenau, J. (1992) *The United Nations in a Turbulent World*. Boulder: Lynne Rienner.

Rosenthal, E. (1964) "Early Shakespeare Productions in South Africa," *English Studies in Africa* 7, 2 (Sept.).

Rothchild, D. (1995) "The U.S. and Conflict Management in Africa," in J. W. Harbeson and D. Rothchild (eds.) *Africa in World Politics: Post–Cold War Challenges*. Boulder: Westview.

Rothchild, D., and Chazan, N. (1988) *The Precarious Balance: State and Society in Africa*. Boulder: Westview.

Ruggie, J. G. (1993) "Wandering the Void: Charting the UN's New Strategic Role," *Foreign Affairs* 72, 5 (Nov.–Dec.).

Ruggie, J. G. (1994) "At Home Abroad, Abroad at Home: International Liberalisation and Domestic Stability in the New World Economy," *Millennium* 24, 3: 507–526.

Rumiya, J. (1992) *Le Rwanda sous le Régime du Mandat Belge (1916–1931)*. Paris: l'Harmattan.

Safa, H. (1986) "Runaway Shops and Female Employment: The Search for Cheap Labor," in E. Leacock and H. Safa (eds.) *Women's Work: Development and the Division of Labor by Gender*. South Hadley, Mass.: Bergin and Garvey.

Sandbrook, R. (1985) *The Politics of Africa's Economic Stagnation*. Cambridge: Cambridge University Press.

Sassen, S. (1996) "The Spatial Organization of Information Industries: Implications for the Role of the State," in J. Mittelman (ed.) *Globalization*. Boulder: Lynne Rienner.

Saurin, J. (1996) "Globalization, Poverty, and the Promises of Modernity," *Millennium: Journal of International Studies* 25, 3 (Winter): 657–680.

Sawyer, A. (1992) *The Emergence of Autocracy in Liberia: Tragedy and Challenge*. San Francisco: Institute of Contemporary Studies.

Sayer, A. (1995) *Radical Political Economy*. Oxford: Basil Blackwell.

Scholte, J. A. (1996a) "The Geography of Collective Identities in a Globalizing World," *Review of International Political Economy* 3 (Winter).

Scholte, J. A. (1996b) "Beyond the Buzz Word: Towards an International Theory of Globalization," in E. Kofman and G. Young (eds.) *Globalization Theory and Practice*. London: Pinter.

Scholte, J. A. (1997a) "Global Capitalism and the State," *International Affairs* 73 (July).

Scholte, J. A. (1997b) "The Globalization of World Politics," in J. Baylis and S. Smith (eds.) *The Globalization of World Politics*. Oxford: Oxford University Press.

Scholte, J. A. (1999) *Globalisation: A Critical Introduction*. Basingstoke: Macmillan.

Scott, C. (1996) *Gender and Development*. Boulder: Lynne Rienner.

Scott, J. (1997) *Corporate Business and Capitalist Classes*. Oxford: Oxford University Press.

Seabrook, J. (1996) *In the Cities of the South*. London: Verso.

Sen, A. (1981) *Poverty and Famines*. Oxford: Clarendon.

Sesay, M. A. (1993) "Interdependence and Dependency in the Political Economy of Sierra Leone." Doctoral thesis, University of Southampton.

Sesay, M. A. (1995) "State Capacity and the Politics of Economic Reform in Sierra Leone," *Journal of Contemporary African Studies* 13, 2: 165–192.

Sesay, M. A. (1996) "Bringing Peace to Liberia," *Accord: An International Review of Peace Initiatives* 1: 9–26.

Shaw, T. M. (1988) "State of Crisis," in D. Rothchild and N. Chazan (eds.) *The Precarious Balance*. Boulder: Westview.

Shaw, T. M., and Heard, K. A. (eds.) (1979) *The Politics of Africa*. Harlow: Longman.

Shaw, T. M., and Quadir, S. (1997) "Democratic Development in the South in the Next Millennium: What Prospects for Avoiding Anarchy and Authoritarianism?" in C. Thomas and P. Wilkin (eds.) *Globalisation and the South*. London: Macmillan.

Singer, M., and Wildavsky, A. (1993) *The Real World Order: Zones of Peace/Zones of Turmoil*. Chatham: Chatham House.

Sjolander, C. T., and Cox, W. (eds.) (1994) *Beyond Positivism: Critical Reflections on International Relations*. Boulder: Lynne Rienner.

Sklair, L. (1991) *A Sociology of the Global System*. Hemel Hempstead: Harvester Wheatsheaf.

Smith, D. (1997) *The State of War and Peace Atlas*. London: Penguin.

Smith, J., Wallerstein, I., and Evers, H-D. (eds.) (1974) *Households and the World Economy*. London: Sage.

Smith, R. (1997) "Creative Destruction: Capitalist Development and China's Environment," *New Left Review* (March–April): 3–43.

Speth, J. G. (1996) in *New York Times* (July 15): 55.

Stourzh, G., Lerner, R., and Harlan, H. C. (eds.) (1966) *Readings in American Democracy*. New York: Oxford University Press.

Strassoldo, R. (1992) "Globalism and Localism: Theoretical Reflections and Some Evidence," in Mlinar, Z. (ed.) *Globalization and Territorial Identities*. Aldershot: Avebury.

Swatuk, Larry A. (1995) "Review Essay: Dead-End to Development? Post–Cold War Africa in the New International Division of Labour," *African Studies Review* 38, 1 (April).

Swyngedouw, E. A. (1989) "The Heart of the Place: The Resurrection of Locality in an Age of Hyperspace," *Geografiska Annaler,* 71B.

Talbott, S. (1996) "Democracy and the National Interest" *Foreign Affairs* (Nov.–Dec.): 47–63.

Tanzer, M. (1995) "Globalizing the Economy," *Monthly Review* 47 (Sept.): 1–15.

Teunissen, J. J. (ed.) (1996) *Regionalism and the Global Economy: The Case of Africa*. The Hague: Fondad.

Thatcher, Lady (1996) "Geographical Society Presidential Dinner Address," *Independent on Sunday* (July 21): 52.

Third World Resurgence (1993) "The Struggle for the Seed," *Third World Resurgence* 39 (Nov.).

Thomas, C. (1985) *New States, Sovereignty, and Intervention*. Aldershot: Gower.

Thomas, C. (1987) *In Search of Security: The Third World in International Relations*. Brighton: Harvester Wheatsheaf; and Boulder: Lynne Rienner.

Thomas, C. (1991) "New Directions in Thinking About Security in the Third World," in K. Booth (ed.) *New Directions in Strategy and International Security*. London: HarperCollins.

Thomas, C. (1997) "Poverty, Development, and Hunger," in J. Baylis and S. Smith (eds.) *The Globalisation of World Politics*. Oxford: Oxford University Press.

Thomas, C., and Wilkin, P. (eds.) (1997) *Globalisation and the South*. London: Macmillan.

Tickner, J. A. (1992) *Gender in International Relations: Feminist Perspectives on Achieving Global Security*. New York: Columbia University Press.

Tickner, J. A. (1995) "Re-Visioning Security," in K. Booth and S. Smith (eds.) *International Relations Theory Today*. Cambridge: Polity Press.

Tilly, C. (ed.) (1975) *The Formation of National States in Western Europe*. Princeton: Princeton University Press.

Touval, S. (1994) "Why the UN Fails," *Foreign Affairs* 73, 5 (Sept.–Oct.).

Uganda Debt Network (1998) "Letter to the African Presidents Attending the Kampala Meetings." Kampala: Uganda Debt Network.

UNCLDC (1990) *Country Presentation by the Government of Rwanda*. Geneva: UNCLDC.

UNDP (1994) *Human Development Report*. Oxford: Oxford University Press.

UNDP (1995) *Human Development Report*. New York: Oxford University Press.

UNDP (1996) *Human Development Report*. Oxford: Oxford University Press.

UNDP (1997) *Human Development Report*. New York: Oxford University Press.

UNECA (1990) *The African Charter for Popular Participation in Development and Transformation*. Arusha: UNECA.

Van de Goor, L., et al. (eds.) (1996) *Between Development and Destruction: An Enquiry into the Causes of Conflict in Post-Colonial States*. Basingstoke: Macmillan.

Van der Laan, H. L. (1975) *Lebanese Traders in Sierra Leone*. The Hague: Mouton.

Viotti, P. R. and Kauppi, M. V. (1992) *International Relations Theory: Realism, Pluralism, Globalism*. London: Macmillan.

Vlachos, E., Webb, A. C., and Murphy, I. L. (eds.) (1986) *The Management of International River Basin Conflicts*. Washington, D.C.: Graduate Program in Science, Technology and Public Policy, George Washington University.

Wallerstein, I. (1991) *Unthinking Social Science*. Cambridge: Cambridge University Press.

Waltz, K. N. (1979) *Theory of International Politics*. London: Addison-Wesley.

Watkins, K. (1997) "School's Out for Children in Africa," *Guardian* (June 16).

Watts, M. K. (1991) "Entitlements or Empowerments? Famine and Starvation in Africa," *Review of African Political Economy* 51 (July): 9–26.

Waylen, G. (1996) *Gender in Third World Politics*. Boulder: Lynne Rienner.

Weeks, J. (1992) *Development Strategy and the Economy of Sierra Leone*. London: Macmillan.

Weiss, T. G., Forsythe, D. P., and Coate, R. A. (eds.) (1994) *The United Nations and Changing World Politics*. Boulder: Westview.

Wight, M. (1966) "Can There Be International Theory?" in H. Butterfield and M. Wight (eds.) *Diplomatic Investigations*. London: George Allen and Unwin.

Wilkin, P. (1997) "New Myths for the South: Globalisation and the Conflict Between Private Power and Freedom," in C. Thomas and P. Wilkin (eds.) *Globalisation and the South*. London: Macmillan.

Williams, B. (1995) "Is International Rescue a Moral Issue?" *Social Research* 62, 1 (Spring): 67–75.

Williams, W. A. (1970) "Large Corporations and American Foreign Policy," in D. Horowitz (ed.) *Corporations and the Cold War*. Boston: New England Free Press.

Wiseman, J. A. (1990) *Democracy in Black Africa: Survival and Renewal.* New York: Paragon House.

Wood, E. M. (1995) *Democracy Against Capitalism.* Cambridge: Cambridge University Press.

Woodhouse, P., and Ndiaye, I. (1991) "Structural Adjustment and Irrigated Agriculture in Senegal." *Irrigation Management Network Paper* 7, October. London: Overseas Development Institute.

World Bank (1989) *Sub-Saharan Africa: From Crisis to Sustainable Development,* 63–88. Washington, D.C.: World Bank.

World Bank (1994a) *Adjustment in Africa: Reforms, Results, and the Road Ahead.* Oxford: Oxford University Press.

World Bank (1994b) *World Debt Tables, 1993–94.* Washington, D.C.: World Bank.

World Bank (1996a) *Annual Report 1996.* Washington, D.C.: World Bank.

World Bank (1996b) *Social Dimensions of Adjustment: World Bank Experience 1980–93.* Washington, D.C.: World Bank.

World Bank (1996c) *Socio-Economic Time Series Access and Retrieval System.* Washington, D.C.: World Bank, June.

World Bank (1997) *World Development Report: The State in a Changing World.* Oxford: Oxford University Press.

Wyn Jones, R. (1995) "Message in a Bottle: Theory and Praxis in Critical Security Studies," *Contemporary Security Policy* 16, 3 (December).

"X" (1947) "Sources of Soviet Conflict," *Foreign Affairs* (July).

Young, C. (1995) "The Heritage of Colonialism," in J. W. Harbeson (ed.) *Africa in World Politics.* Boulder: Westview.

Zack-Williams, A. B. (1995) *Tributors, Supporters, and Merchant Capital: Mining and Underdevelopment in Sierra Leone.* Aldershot: Avebury.

Zartman, I. W. (1966) *International Relations in the New Africa.* Englewood Cliffs, N.J.: Prentice-Hall.

Zartman, I. W. (ed.) (1995) *Collapsed States: The Disintegration and Restoration of Legitimate Authority.* Boulder: Lynne Rienner.

About the Contributors

Michel Chossudovsky is professor of economics, Faculty of Social Sciences, University of Ottawa. He has published extensively on the impact of the global economy on inequality and poverty. His most recent book is *The Globalization of Poverty: Impacts of IMF and World Bank Reforms* (1997).

Anne Guest is on the teaching staff of the Department of Politics, Southampton University, where she completed a doctorate on critical security in the Senegal River basin. She has contributed a chapter on this topic to the collection edited by A. Linklater, *Borders in Question* (Lynne Rienner, 1995).

Ali Mazrui holds several academic positions, including a professorship at the State University of New York at Binghampton. He is a prolific author, frequently contributing to public debate on Africa in international relations.

Mohamed A. Mohamed Salih is senior lecturer at the Institute of Social Studies in The Hague, Netherlands. He has written extensively on African security issues, including *Management of the Crisis in Somalia: The Politics of Reconciliation* and *Inducing Food Insecurity: Perspectives on Food Policies in Eastern and Southern Africa* (both 1994), and contributed the chapter "Global Ecologism and Its Critics" in *Globalisation and the South*, edited by Thomas and Wilkin (1997).

Aswini Ray is professor of politics at Jawaharlal Nehru University, New Delhi. Currently heading an international project on democratization, he has contributed a view "from the periphery" over several years to key debates in international relations, security studies, and politics more generally. A recent contribution is *The Global System: A Historical View from the Periphery* (1996).

Jan Aart Scholte is senior lecturer at the Institute of Social Studies at The Hague, Netherlands. He has published extensively on globalization, including *The International Relations of Social Change* (1993).

Max Sesay lectures in politics at Staffordshire University. Building on his PhD on Sierra Leone, he researches and writes on West African security problems. Most recently he has contributed articles in the *Journal of Contemporary African Studies* and the *International Review of Peace Initiatives.*

Caroline Thomas is professor in the Department of Politics, Southampton University. She has published widely on the South in global politics and on security issues from a critical perspective. Most recently she coedited *Globalisation and the South* with Peter Wilkin (1997).

J. Ann Tickner is associate professor in the School of International Relations, University of Southern California. She has published widely on gender and security, including *Gender in International Relations: Feminist Perspectives on Achieving Global Security* (1992).

Peter Wilkin lectures in politics at Lancaster University. He is author of *Noam Chomsky: On Knowledge, Power, and Human Nature* (1996) and coeditor of *Globalisation and the South* (1997).

Index

About the Book

The globalization of world politics affects issues rarely considered in traditional security studies. This book explores the interrelationships of those issues in critical security terms, drawing on the African experience.

The authors provide a mixture of theory and case studies distinguished by thorough cross-referencing. The introduction to the book establishes the context of the security debate; it sets out the relationship between globalization and security and explores the challenges posed to the realization of security, defined holistically, by the processes of globalization. Subsequent chapters focus on class, community, gender, justice, and race—concepts central to the elaboration of the new security but too often neglected. The case studies in Part 2 empirically explore these same conceptual issues, and the final chapter presents an overview of the African experience.

Caroline Thomas is professor in politics at Southampton University. Her numerous publications include *In Search of Security: The Third World in International Relations* (Lynne Rienner). **Peter Wilkin** is lecturer in politics at Lancaster University. He is coeditor, with Caroline Thomas, of *Globalisation and the South*.